For TYLer,

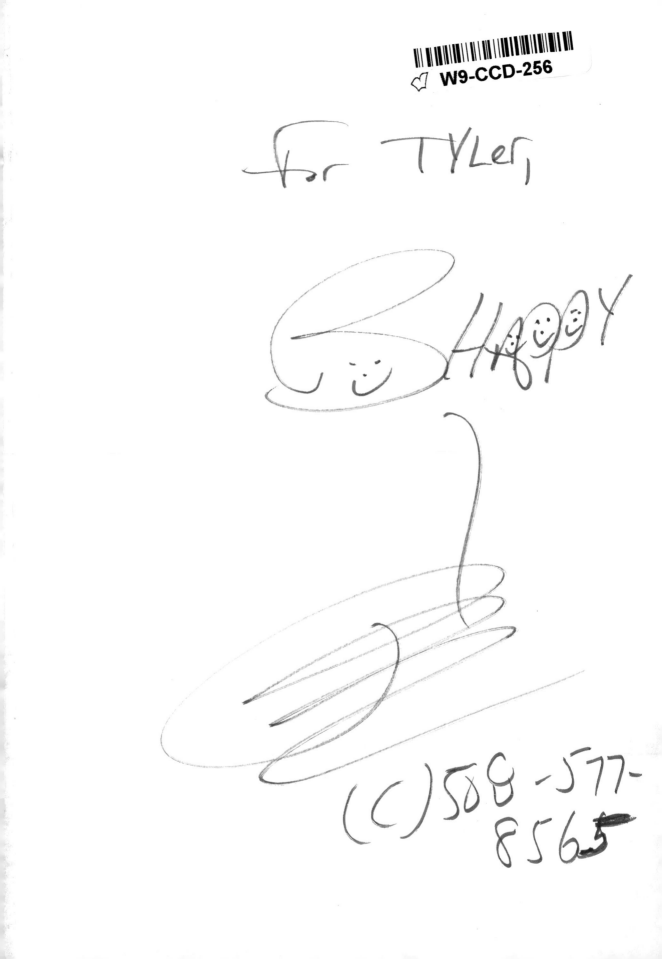

(C)508-577-
8565

"Todd is a gifted storyteller. And the powerful, uplifting stories he shares in *Finding Happiness* motivate and inspire us to strive for the stars. Juxtaposing stories about being bullied as a child with magnificent narratives about his impact on worldwide leaders, Todd provides a true-life path to follow that can take any one of us from despair to hope, from anguish to joy. Todd is the real deal; he has the credibility of life experience to guide us on a quest for happiness."

-Dr. Richard Levin
Executive Coach & Leadership Developer, Boston, MA

"Depression with high achievers is sadly too common. Todd Patkin courageously pulls back the curtain on this disorder and uses his own life experience to help us understand its perils. This is a must-read for any high achiever who struggles with depression, as Todd reveals to us through his own heartfelt story a practical prescription to a more balanced and satisfying life."

-Jeffrey S. Davis
CEO & Founder of Mage, LLC
Co-Host of MYOB The Radio Show
Adjunct Professor of Entrepreneurship, Babson College

"I am convinced that *Finding Happiness* will bring hope to many, in large part by reducing the stigma associated with depression and bipolar disorder. Todd Patkin's success in overcoming the obstacles that life and genetics have placed in his path is truly inspirational. In fact, Todd himself is a gift. He radiates positive energy and love, in person and throughout the pages of his book. There is no doubt in my mind that his story will further his lifelong goal to help others."

-Dr. Mary Ann McDonnell
CEO & Cofounder of STEP Up for Kids, Inc.
Owner of South Shore Psychiatric Services, Marshfield, MA

"This book tells one man's compelling story—but it's also a powerful call to action. It's time for us to change what we prioritize, how we live our lives, and how we measure success. We can choose to pursue our present course of being overstressed, overworked, and fundamentally dissatisfied, or we can choose to take Todd Patkin's message of healing and hope to heart. The lessons he teaches apply to people from all cultures and walks of life. And best of all, in *Finding Happiness*, Todd also gives us the tools to get started growing in a healthier, happier direction."

-Salman Ahmad
Author of Rock & Roll Jihad *(Simon and Schuster 2010)*
Founder of Pakistani Rock Band Junoon
UN Goodwill Ambassador

"Helping others—and not just yourself—is a key component of cultivating happiness. I know. I have a small optometry practice in a close-knit Massachusetts town. I like to think that my job enables me to make people's lives better—and I am continually amazed by how much joy that brings me. Quite simply, helping others *feels great.* By telling his own life story in *Finding Happiness*, Todd Patkin makes a consistent and compelling case for reaching out and giving back…for your own good."

-Dr. Fatima Garcia-Fedorowicz
Optometrist

"There are plenty of people in the world who have enjoyed financial success… but very few who have done with that success what Todd Patkin has. He has given back to the world in so many ways and with so many different causes and personal relationships. *Finding Happiness* is yet another gift to a world Todd's already done so much for. I believe that the ripple effects of this book will make the world a better, brighter place in ways that even Todd himself may not fully realize. Todd's honest account of how to finally let the sunshine in is a wonderful and educational summary of one of the most extraordinary and interesting lives I've ever had the honor to intersect with."

-Gary Marino
Executive Director of Generation Excel
Producer & Star of Million Calorie March: The Movie

"Reading this book is like having a conversation with Todd Patkin. It's frank, funny, and disarming. As one who has seen depression, I was grateful for this tour through the mind of someone who suffered from the condition and got out. *Finding Happiness* is a useful guidebook for anyone who is looking to break out of a rut as well as for those who would like to help another person through to the sunshine on the other side of sadness."

-Charity Sunshine Tillemann Dick
Soprano
Former National Spokesperson for the Pulmonary Hypertension Association

"I have known Todd Patkin for many years. When I read *Finding Happiness*, I was pleased—though not at all surprised—to see his forthright honesty on subjects that most people shy away from. He openly discusses money, religion, and politics and the role they have (and haven't) played in his happiness journey. Depression isn't an easy thing to talk about, either, yet Todd gladly does so in his desire to help others. I deeply admire him for exposing his life so that others can learn what the components of happiness truly are...and aren't."

-Brian Fox
Creative Fine Artist

"Whether you read one page or one hundred pages of Todd Patkin's book, you will find hope and inspiration in his words. He is truly courageous to reveal his personal pain and struggles, to share his experiences and insights, and then to offer practical steps that will help all of us build happier lives in today's world. As Todd reminds us, *happiness is a journey, not a destination.*"

-Renée Kwok
President, TFC Financial Management

Finding Happiness

One Man's Quest to Beat Depression and
Anxiety and—Finally—Let the Sunshine In

Todd Patkin
with Howard J. Rankin, Ph.D.

Published by:
StepWise Press
P.O. Box 4797
Hilton Head Island, SC 29938

In some instances, names and identifying details of persons mentioned in this book have been changed to protect their privacy. Any resulting resemblance to any actual person, alive or dead, is purely coincidental and unintentional. In addition, in writing this book, I have relied on my memory of events. I apologize to those concerned if I have remembered anything inaccurately.

www.toddpatkin.com

ISBN: 978-0-9658261-8-1 (cloth)

ISBN: 978-0-9658261-9-8 (paper)

Library of Congress Control Number: 2011905864

Printed in the United States of America

This book is dedicated to:

Yadira, what an amazing woman and wife you are and what a spectacular life we have built together! Thank you for all of your love, support, and for being my number one personal trainer in how to live a happier life.

Josh, there isn't a person in the world whom I marvel at as much as I do you. I so look forward to our wonderful future years together, and similarly I can't wait to see the huge mountains you surely will climb.

Mom, there is no mother on earth who has ever been more loving or wonderful to her son than you have been to me. Thank you so, so much!

Dad, thank you for all of your love and support and for doing more than anyone else on the planet to make me the man I am today.

Yadira, Josh, Mom, and Dad, I love you each so, so much. Thank you for playing the greatest roles in making my life today such a happy one.

TABLE OF CONTENTS

Foreword

BY HOWARD J. RANKIN, PH.D.

As a clinical psychologist who is very interested in clinical neuroscience, I am confronted every day by important philosophical questions about how psychology and neurology interact. For example, how much of our personal journey is determined by our psychology and how much by our biology?

What's the relationship between the brain and consciousness?

How much change is possible through conscious effort?

What really drives our everyday decisions and behavior?

How well can we manage our moods by changing our thoughts?

These are important questions that challenge neuroscientists every day in research laboratories and in academic forums. In my opinion, many of the answers regarding how we adapt and how we can keep a healthy balance between our internal and external worlds are found not in the realm of scholarship, but in real life.

To me, Todd Patkin exemplifies how one's personal journey can be influenced by biology *and* psychology. He is an amazing man, a stunningly successful entrepreneur and a passionate philanthropist who has an important story that sheds light on these fundamental questions…and he also has a crucial message to share.

I first met Todd when working on Gary Marino's *Million Calorie March* project (which you'll read about in the following pages). Like so many others, that project would have never taken its first step without Todd's incredible support. After the March's conclusion, I was happy to stay in touch with Todd. As I have gotten to know him better over the years, I have seen an immensely energetic, successful, intelligent man with massive empathy and an endless desire to help others. So when Todd was looking for an author to help him write his story, I was intrigued and, being an author in my own right, offered my services.

Initially, our project was for me to ghostwrite Todd's autobiography, but as we progressed, Todd's passion for making the world a better place inevitably changed the emphasis of the book. It grew from being primarily an autobiography with some footnotes about happiness to a book geared toward helping others told through Todd's life story. Of course, this is as it should be: Todd is never happier than when he is talking about how to be happy.

That said, what, exactly, *is* happiness? Just like love, happiness is hard to define because it is such an individual experience with so many manifestations. However, I do feel confident in saying that happiness in the sense that Todd Patkin means it isn't a fleeting mood characterized by pleasure, joy, or excitement. It's a lifestyle with contentment at its core.

As a neurobehavioral scientist, I believe that mood has two separate but related core components, biochemistry and your view of yourself and the world you live in. Of those two, biochemistry usually dominates.

Essentially, mood is a function of the way the brain responds to challenge and is largely driven by genetics and fashioned by early experience. It is almost entirely a biological system that is adaptive but difficult to modify. In fact, mood is much harder to change than people imagine, hence the low rate of success for those who try the quick-fix approach. As you will read, Todd made heroic attempts to change his habitual moods through exercise, conscious thought, cultivating positive relationships, and more. And although these efforts *did* give him some measure of control, they could not fully give him the peace he sought because they did not affect his underlying genetically programmed brain biology.

The fact is, you cannot be content under *any* circumstances if your brain chemistry is running amok and your anxiety is flying through the roof, or if your depression is sinking your emotions below the basement.

Ultimately, Todd found that his efforts to change the way he saw and experienced the world, *combined* with medications that regulated his brain biochemistry, enabled him to begin living a consistently content life. This is an important point to understand: Often, individuals *do* need medical help to manage their anxiety and depression so that they can experience the changes they seek. As Todd himself explains, this isn't a sign of weakness or failure—it's doing what's best for yourself and your future. In my professional opinion, Todd's example is admirable and will hopefully inspire you as well.

Before I move on, I would like to make one final point about happiness. I believe that contentment occurs when your actions, attitudes, and beliefs are in harmony. Contentment isn't the lack of stress or obstacles—it's a way of being. The fact is, difficulties will always be part of life, especially in today's fast-changing world. However, if you can look in the mirror and honestly see someone who is doing the best he or she can and acting according to his or her beliefs and ethics—even in the most stressful times—then, regardless of the outcome, your self-esteem will be intact and you will be content.

From here, the next obvious question is: How? How does someone gain the upper hand over anxiety and depression and work toward contentment?

Well, I could explain the nuts and bolts to you in technical terms. However, I have a reputation for making scientific concepts understandable to the nonprofessional reader, and I have found the best way of doing this is to tell the story from the perspective of the common man rather than the expert. Yes, I could easily tell you about high amplitude beta waves in the brain's right prefrontal cortex, but Todd's account of his anxiety will be so much more meaningful. If you want to really learn about neurophysiology, there are several good sources available…but if you want a story that you can relate to, this book will be both more readable and significant. And you'll learn a lot in the process.

Todd's story, and hence this book, addresses the stress of our times, the role of our culture in the creation and treatment of anxiety and depression, and the strengths and limitations of self-help psychology. Above all, it is a guide to happiness.

From start to finish, Todd's journey reflects life's fundamental truths and the issues that all of us face. This story isn't totally defined by anxiety and depression, though. We decided to include specific chapters about Todd's business life because they are an important part of Todd's story, but more importantly, because his business success is a microcosm of the rest of his world—one that illustrates the truth that if you treat people with sensitivity and compassion, you will get tremendous rewards.

As I've told you already, Todd is an extraordinary man, and it is a tribute to him and his own personal voyage that he is now dedicated to helping people in many ways. His number one goal is to help others avoid or truncate the difficulties and sometimes brutal burdens that he himself has overcome. If his goal of helping people to a happier life seems immense or even self-serving, I can assure you that his desire comes directly from an incredible empathy and sensitivity and an inexhaustible energy to help his fellow man, whoever they may be.

This is Todd's story because it is Todd's journey. I have been a co-navigator, occasionally having my hand on the tiller, sometimes suggesting course corrections and periodically offering my own views of the landscape but adamant that Todd take the helm at all times. It took me a while to learn Todd's voice and repress my own style, which led to some entertaining discussions about vocabulary and seemingly endless comma wars, but I hope that for you, the reader, the narrative flows seamlessly. Our goal was to keep this a living story, not a textbook.

That said, there are occasional footnotes to scholarly work, but that comes from our respect and recognition for those people who actually did the research as well as from a desire to provide you with an opportunity to follow up with other relevant sources if you so wish.

Throughout this book, you will also see periodic sections of text that are designated as being "An Expert's View." Those are my words that impart my professional knowledge regarding an aspect of Todd's story. It is our hope that understanding some of the science behind Todd's journey, realizations, and advice will be helpful to you.

As you will read, life-changing events are sometimes sparked by an openness to doing simple activities, like listening to self-help tapes or reading a book. Other times, change is an inspired response to brutally difficult times. For some of you, this book will be a fun-filled ride with amazing true stories and vital lessons to learn. For others, this book will literally be life changing, leading you to a much happier and more stress-free and fulfilling life.

Howard Rankin, Ph.D.
Spring 2011

Preface

My name is Todd Patkin, and I have written this book to help as many people as possible learn to live much happier lives. This is because for most of my own life I, too, felt extremely stressed-out, beat up, and, yes, often extremely depressed and unhappy. I do not anymore.

Two things I promise you right from the start. First, I have been as truthful as I know how to be throughout this book. In every instance I have been completely honest in how I believe everything to have happened, and I have also been totally forthright in how I believe I felt at each particular moment. Secondly, I was interested only in writing a book that could make a huge difference. Therefore, I chose to be totally transparent, showing my life from childhood until now, including all of its most embarrassing details. In this way you can see the effects of the training, which starts early in our childhood and continues throughout our development, that often unintentionally and unwittingly teaches many of us to live with much lower self-esteem and a lot more stress and unhappiness.

As you read about my life's journey from despair to happiness, it may seem for some of you like a distant and unattainable dream reserved only for a fortunate few. But this is not the case! The ability to find real happiness is embedded in every one of us. We just must be courageous enough to fight for it.

Your evolution as a person truly rests entirely in your own hands. You can continually pick at your old wounds as I used to do, and they will never heal. You can look at everything you could have and should have done better instead of all of the things you have done, and currently do, well. Your history doesn't have to be your jailer. Your past doesn't have to be your future. If you strive rather than settle, you can soar and honestly find happiness—trust me!!!

I hope my story inspires you to open up your mind to the idea that we are all meant to be really happy on this earth. My goal is to give you the tools you need to see the world through a new pair of glasses—ones that enable you to focus on all of the good things that are in your past and present, and that can be in your future. The problem is that we have gotten off track as a society—so many of us view our lives through lenses that focus on our shortcomings, failures, and mistakes. And no one today is teaching us how to change and live the right way—not our schools, not our places of worship, and with few exceptions, not the people who are most meant to teach us during our critical years—our often unhappy, overwhelmed, and stressed-out parents themselves. It's not their fault—they weren't shown the right path either. But you can break the chain.

By learning how to lead a happier life, you will not only find more meaning, joy, and purpose for yourself, but you'll also have the duty and privilege of showing others, including your own children, the way to greater happiness and fulfillment every day!

Acknowledgments

Roger, thank you for all you have done to support me recently and for always doing all that you could, especially during the most challenging of times. And thank you, too, Roger, for so many great childhood memories.

Kimberly, thank you for your tremendous support and guidance during my darkest hours. I will never forget how you helped me get through them. Also, thanks for being you. You are a deeply caring, warm, and fun sister.

Ann Marie, thank you for being a great friend for well over twenty years now. Without you, we could never have grown our company and then sold it for such a great price. Most importantly, Ann, thank you for growing up with me during our toughest times and our greatest.

Dzintra, for more than ten years from 1995-2006, you were my staunchest supporter and my greatest ally at work. Thank you so, so much.

Dr. Fatima Garcia, first and foremost, thanks for being such an amazing eye doctor (I can see!) and friend. And thank you for being my number one cheerleader, keeping me going during the marathon of writing this book—fully two years in the making.

Dr. Richard Levin, you have been at times my coach and confidant, and often when I needed it the very most, a wonderfully uplifting wind beneath my wings. Richard, thank you so much for all of your belief in me and specifically in this book project.

Dr. Michael Mufson, my friend, what can I say? I feel that I owe you so much. When I came to see you, I was totally broken, and within four months I felt as good as new. Dr. Mufson, I will never, ever forget that you, in my mind, literally saved my life if not just my mind.

Dr. Howard Rankin, thank you, thank you, thank you. You not only made writing this book possible (I never could have done it alone), but you also helped to make the process sensible to me, and I think that together we did write quite a good book. Also, thank you, Howard, so much and your wife, MJ, too, for putting up with all of my phone calls, changes, and revisions this past year and a half. You truly are the best, my friend.

To the amazing team at DeHart & Company Public Relations: Anna Campbell, Ashley Lamb, Heather Prestwood, Natalie Turner, Meghan Waters, and, of course, Dottie DeHart herself. Thank you very, very much for working with me so well to edit, fine-tune, and polish my manuscript into the best book it could be.

To everyone else, the hundreds and even thousands of friends, family members, associates, and acquaintances who have helped me to become who I am today, I thank you and apologize if I was unable to mention you in this book. Please know that I really appreciate you all. I am even thankful to the people who were not good to me, because in many ways you actually played the biggest role in making me the incredibly happy person I am today.

CHAPTER ONE

Ticking Bomb

"Even a happy life cannot be without a measure of darkness, and the word 'happy' would lose its meaning if it were not balanced by sadness."
—Carl Jung

Potato salad or coleslaw? The decision seemed impossible. I ran my eyes back and forth over the restaurant menu as though doing so would prompt the neurons in my frozen brain to start firing—but of course, they didn't. For all intents and purposes, my brain had short-circuited. As my silence continued, the waitress grew more and more impatient, and my father looked on with helpless despair from across the table, silently willing me to give our server an answer. Their reactions didn't make a bit of difference, though. I continued to sluggishly ponder my lunch choices with no real hope of coming to a decision.

Potato salad or coleslaw? At that point, you might as well have been asking me for the cure for cancer. Or for depression. You see, the year was 2001, and I, Todd Patkin—the driven golden-boy-in-business with the Midas touch—was in the midst of a crippling and all-encompassing breakdown. Depression had completely taken me over, and my life was more of a burden than a joy.

Although I couldn't have conceived of such a thing at the time, my breakdown changed my life irrevocably for the better. It was one of the most crucial—albeit painful—steps in a lifelong journey that has helped me to understand the true nature of joy.

My unique and at times very painful path through life has shown me firsthand many of the reasons why people are so unhappy. It has given me an understanding, for example, of how we are subtly—even unconsciously and very often unintentionally—conditioned from the very beginning of our lives to focus on the wrong things, ratcheting up our anxiety and perfectionism. My life has also given me insights into how the brain—the center of our being—develops habitual moods (for example, anxiety or unhappiness), thus leading many of us to spend our lives in quiet despair, or even worse, debilitating depression.

This book is the story of how and why I found myself at rock bottom, and of how, from the very depths of my depression, I was able to find true hope and then happiness for the first time. Moreover, it is my prayer that this book, as it chronicles the ups and downs of my own life, will serve as a guide and an inspiration to others who are facing daunting obstacles of their own.

Meet the "Old" Todd Patkin

Before I begin with the story of my breakdown, I'd like to introduce you to the Todd Patkin during the years leading up to my crash. Truth be told, in a nutshell, I was at the very top of my field. (I didn't get to that point without quite a few bumps and bruises, mind you—but I'll cover them later in this book.)

From 1989 to 2000, I was everything a young businessman dreams of being. I would arrive at the headquarters of my family's auto parts business by 7:00 a.m., and most nights, after I'd completed a great day at work and spent some time at the gym, I wouldn't step back through the door of my home until at least 7:30 p.m.

Each day, I was doing all I could to grow our family's business. Mostly, this would mean visiting our stores. First, I would pump up our people, and then I would find out what they needed to serve our customers better. Then I would come back to the Sharon, Massachusetts, headquarters and work through the necessary issues to get my people what they had just asked for.

Also, I loved being in on Saturdays. That was the day everything was quiet, and from 8:00 to noon I could catch up on anything still needing my attention. And the best part was, I relished every minute of it! I craved the feelings of pride and accomplishment that came from our record-breaking sales and a job well done, and I constantly strove to get to the next level, whatever it might be.

I was the guy whose name everybody knew and who everyone wanted to be around. I was the life of the party and the leader of the band. Although making money truly wasn't my primary goal, by 1993 we had no worries on that front either. And to put the icing on the cake, I had a wonderfully supportive wife and, by the mid-nineties, a young son who was the apple of my eye. In short, I thought, I had it all—and so did everyone else who knew me.

But that was all about to change.

My Sky Darkens

Some people look at life as a box of chocolates, others as a glass that's half-full…or even worse, always half-empty. Personally, I view life metaphorically like a landscape. You see, I believe that at any given time, everyone has a specific amount of sunshine—happiness, positivity, verve, whatever you want to call it—in their lives. Some days, the sun radiates golden warmth that leaves no room for shadows. Other days, the sun is eclipsed to some degree by clouds, leaving things colder and drearier. And sometimes, there even seems to be absolutely no sunshine at all.

Normally, I consider myself to have quite a bit of sunshine. I've always liked people. I've always enjoyed reaching out to them, getting to know them, and helping them. I'm a giver, an encourager, and a hugger. But as I've learned, even the brightest skies can go dark. As the year 2000 progressed, I had no idea that I was hurtling headlong toward the roughest sailing I'd ever encountered— although looking back, I can see that the signs were all there, forecasting my own perfect storm.

I remember the day my sunshine began to fade in very vivid detail. Ironically, that September morning dawned with nearly blinding brightness. You see, two months before in July something wonderful happened to my wife, Yadira, and me—a true blessing from God. Finally, after what seemed like an eternity of disappointment, a pregnancy test came back positive once again!

I remember the swirl of thoughts and emotions that rushed through my brain as Yadira, Joshua (five years old at the time), and I drove to the doctor's office to get our first glimpse of our soon-to-be second child. My wife was— and still is—such a blessing in my life, and I was thrilled to be able to give her the family that she so yearned for. I too wanted to be a father again.

When Josh was small, I had been so involved in growing my family's business that I didn't spend much time with him (remember those twelve-plus-hour days?), and now I was beginning to regret it. (I'm pleased to say that Josh and I today share a wonderful relationship.) Looking back, I don't think I even changed one of his diapers or gave him a single bath—not because I didn't want to, but because I either wasn't home or was in the grip of exhaustion.

Now I yearned for another chance to be part of that unsurpassed experience of watching a new life come into the world, and of acting as a navigator during that child's incredible voyage of development. And of course, I thought it would be great for Josh to have siblings to grow up with!

It was with these thoughts in mind that I ushered my wife and son into the doctor's office that September morning. After we checked in, a nurse led us to a room that housed an ultrasound machine. The lights were dimmed and all three of us waited for the grainy pictures to appear on the monitor, showing us the outline of our new family member.

Anyone who has seen an ultrasound of an early pregnancy knows that it isn't easy to make out what you are actually looking at. As I squinted at the screen, tilting my head to and fro, I *thought* I saw the outline of something familiar from Yadira's pregnancy with Josh, but I couldn't be sure. As the seconds ticked by, I looked at the screen anxiously, trying to figure out what it was I was seeing. Meanwhile, Yadira looked at the screen excitedly. Josh looked at it curiously. The nurse looked at it with concern.

After a few moments of fiddling with the machine's controls, the nurse asked to be excused and left the room. I could practically feel my blood pressure rising due to this breach of standard procedure, but I tried to remain calm. After all, I told myself, the nurse could have left for any number of reasons. Maybe the machine was malfunctioning. Maybe we were having twins!

I didn't have to wait long to find out. A short while later our doctor came into the room. He examined the ultrasound, studied Yadira, and then said, "There's no fetus. Yadira, you must have had a natural miscarriage this past week. I am very sorry."

As the words left the doctor's mouth, I felt as though my entire life force had been drained from every cell in my body. Whatever I had been expecting, it certainly wasn't this. And it was simply too much for me—the father who had been so excited at Josh's birth that I ran around the maternity ward yelling, "I did it! I did it! I did it! It's a boy!"—to handle. The sudden and unexpected loss of this pregnancy seemed like a horrendous cosmic correction, the total antithesis of that moment of ultimate joy when Josh was born.

Yadira too was in shock, but I didn't immediately notice as I nearly fainted right then and there. In fact, the doctor had to run out of the room and bring me an ice-pack and a cold compress so that I wouldn't pass out or vomit. Josh witnessed the whole thing.

Somehow, we made it home from that terrible appointment. Gloom and grief now descended on our home. I had lost a lot of my sunshine that day, and furthermore, I worried about how Yadira would cope with this loss. It goes without saying that she too was devastated, but—unlike me—she couldn't distract herself with work. I could take my mind off things during the day to some extent by diving into the pile of tasks begging for my attention, but Yadira was a stay-at-home mom. Would the relative solitude—and our home itself—be a constant crushing reminder to her of what she had just lost? And on top of it all, the unspoken question of whether we'd ever get pregnant again hovered over our lives like a heavy cloud of uncertainty and pain.

As 2000 drew to a close and a new year began, our family fell back into the rhythm of daily life—work, school, meals, chores, etc. Although there was an emptiness inside Yadira and me that hadn't been there before, we were working through our loss—both individually and as a couple. My sky was still a bit cloudy, but the sunshine was slowly beginning to return. Unfortunately, something was about to happen that would block out its warmth and light altogether.

The Storm Clouds Break Wide Open

Our lives are full of small, seemingly insignificant actions and decisions that end up changing our entire direction. *What if I'd chosen to go through another checkout line and gotten out of the grocery store faster,* you might ask yourself—*would I too have been in that big pileup on the interstate?* Or maybe, *What if I hadn't impulsively cracked a joke that had my interviewers laughing hysterically—would I still have gotten the job?* Or, in my case, *What if I hadn't been so theatrical in a routine presentation—would my breakdown have occurred, and would I now finally be a happy person and so driven by an overwhelming desire to help others struggling with unhappiness and depression?*

I don't know for certain the answer to that question, but I do know that one unlucky leap changed the entire face of my reality.

It was the second Saturday of April 2001, and my company was holding its annual spring store managers' meeting at our corporate offices and attached warehouse in Sharon, Massachusetts, so that our store managers could spend time with our corporate department managers directly after this meeting. By this point, as I've said, I was making progress in coming to terms with the previous year's loss—but my sunshine was still depleted, and although I might not have admitted it to many people, I was more fragile than "normal." Looking back, I clearly didn't realize just how fragile I was—but during that Saturday meeting, I certainly found out. A random accident pushed me over the edge of normality on which I'd been teetering, causing me to spiral downward at hyper-speed.

It was always my job to give the 8:00 a.m. kick-off motivational wake-up speech at all of our managers' meetings, because my animated, energetic speaking style fired everyone up right from the get-go. As usual, I was wearing a business suit with dress shoes to match that day, but unlike usual, this meeting was not being held in a carpeted corporate hotel meeting space—instead I was delivering my speech on the cement floor of our company's warehouse.

Regardless of how I might be feeling emotionally on any given day, throughout my career it was always easy for me to pump myself up at company meetings in order to inspire our people to set and achieve higher and higher goals. So, as usual, I was animated, urging our managers, salesmen, and supervisors on to greater and greater victories with increasing energy and unfeigned passion. In fact, I had jumped up on a chair—as I frequently did—to give greater impact to my impassioned address. And to emphasize a particularly strong point, I jumped off the chair onto the floor.

Now, I had done this type of leap many, many times before for my team with great effect—during other meetings in hotel conference rooms—but always onto carpeted floors. This time, though, my landing surface was much less forgiving, and when I hit the concrete, sharp pains shot through both of my feet. Initially, I crumpled to the hard floor. I did manage to stand back up and finish my speech. Two days later on Monday, x-rays showed that I had tiny fractures on the bottoms of both of my feet near my toes.

Unfortunately, I wasn't able to focus on recuperating or even seeking out a Boston specialist for some immediate relief, as the Saturday following my ill-fated leap, Yadira, Joshua, and I boarded a plane to Venezuela for a weeklong visit with Yadira's family. Despite my less-than-mobile condition, postponing the trip wasn't really an option in my mind as Yadira had been so looking forward to visiting her family for months.

Essentially, for me this week in Venezuela proved brutal. For one thing, because of Venezuela's warm climate, there wasn't a single carpeted room in Yadira's aunt's house, in which we were staying. Not only was I having trouble keeping up with my family, but every step I took on those hard surfaces was excruciating. And my normally gregarious nature? Well, that was nowhere to be seen.

Yes, I knew my wife was becoming a bit frustrated with my attitude, but I was incapable of stepping up to the plate for her this week because—quite frankly—I started to go a little bit insane. With every painful step I took, my anxiety over my injuries increased, and within a few days of arriving in Venezuela, I had actually totally and illogically convinced myself that I would never, *ever* be able to walk normally again!

I'm a bit of a hypochondriac to begin with, and in every fiber of my being, I simply **knew** that my pain levels were indicative of something irreparable in my feet. I envisioned a future with crutches, wheelchairs, and constant pain, and I couldn't shake the feeling that life as I knew it was over—a classic symptom, I soon found out, of anxiety. Had I been told unequivocally by a doctor before my trip that I'd be better in a matter of months, I might have been able to quell my panic—but that wasn't the case. I had absolutely no beacon of hope to cling to. And although my fears were ultimately unfounded and totally irrational, they were no less real or devastating to me at the time.

When I returned to the U.S., I did visit specialists—many, many, many of them, in fact, accompanied by my father and my wife. What saints they both were, driving a frantic and irrational hypochondriac around to appointment after appointment! The specialists gave me some symptomatic relief and told me that it would just be a matter of time before my feet would heal. "Be a good patient and be patient!" was the watchword.

Problem was, I just couldn't find it in myself to be patient. Although somewhat mollified by multiple medical assurances, I was still half-convinced that I wouldn't heal properly. Add to that the stress of pushing myself to be a high achiever in all aspects of my life almost since birth as well as living with high anxiety through so many other things that had already happened by now in my life (things you will read about later in this book), plus the lost pregnancy and the lingering physical pain in my feet…and I was a total mess. Worries, what-ifs, and worst-case scenarios zoomed constantly around my brain like mental rocket-propelled explosives…with much the same devastating effects.

An Expert View on Brain Biochemistry

Mood is influenced by your brain's biochemistry, which determines your possible *range* of emotion and is the *biological* underpinning of happiness.

Your brain's biochemistry is a function of your genetics and early childhood experiences.

Because brain biochemistry has a strong genetic component, some people are more prone to difficult emotions like depression and anxiety, for example, while many people experience none of these conditions. However, genetics aren't the only way you can end up with dysfunctional brain chemistry.

Early in life the brain is an incredible learning machine literally making the connections on which thoughts and feelings are based. If in childhood you are, for whatever reason, stressed and unhappy for long periods of time, you are literally training your brain to be anxious and depressed in the future.

So if your brain is genetically predisposed to depression or you have been trained through early experiences to be anxious and depressed, you will most likely be locked into this mode of thinking when you're older. While there are some things you can do to improve your mood, in the end, it's likely you will need psychotherapy and/or medications to help you restore a better biological balance in your brain.

Caught in a Downpour...without an Umbrella

As if my lingering disappointment over the lost pregnancy—coupled with my stress fractures—was not bad enough, the final nail in the proverbial coffin was the fact that the nature of my injury prevented me from exercising.

Since childhood, exercise had been an important coping mechanism for me, and since college I had consciously turned to it to alleviate my fears and anxiety. For years, if I had a stressful day at work or a problem to work through, I'd head straight to the gym—and even when life was smooth sailing, I'd work out or run most days.

Looking back, I believe that exercise is how I survived in my early face-to-the-fire years at work. It's also how I—an individual prone to anxiety and depression, as you'll see—made it as long as I did without cracking. The fact is, exercise is a natural anti-depressant, releasing important hormones that lift mood and increase both the quality and quantity of blood flow providing oxygen to every part of the body—but especially to the brain.

Now, I had lost this crucially important mood control mechanism. The longer I went without exercising, the worse I began to feel about myself (you do become chemically addicted to exercise the same as you do to a drug)—and on top of that, I was embarrassed by the brooding I couldn't seem to snap out of. My mental state was now completely out of my control.

In the Eye of the Storm

After returning from Venezuela, my busy life came to a screeching halt. I felt more and more useless, worthless, and detached—like an observer of rather than a participant in my own life.

Immediately, I began having trouble sleeping and eating. While my body was present in the world, my mind had checked out. I know I must have scared Yadira half to death—growing up in a close-knit family without many of the stresses inherent to the American "dream," she had never seen anything like this before.

Sad Stats

Depression affects more than 18 million people in the United States, or a little more than 5 percent of the population, each year. Nearly twice as many women as men are affected. During their lifetimes, 12-25 percent of women and 5-10 percent of men will suffer from at least one major depressive episode.

Occasionally, I went in to work to get out of the house and to give the appearance to my employees that I was still functioning. Even then, though, it took all of my strength just to sit in my office for three or four hours at a time. I'd close the door, prop my feet up on the desk, and simply try not to lose the tenuous hold I had on myself. I certainly didn't accomplish anything productive! My dad would check in on me every so often, because I was honestly afraid to be left alone for too long a period of time back then.

It was during this period that I found myself unable to make the simple choice between potato salad and coleslaw. And that incident wasn't isolated. Everyone who knew me, from family members to employees, recognized I was a sad shell of the dynamic man who had led our company for the past twelve years, motivating and driving everyone to the brink of monumental success. I could barely find it in me to care about anything, as I felt that I was just barely hanging onto my own life by my fingertips. My breakdown had caused me to completely burn out…not just at work, but in every aspect of my life.

An Expert View on Burnout

"Burnout." Popularly defined, it's that moment when, for any number of reasons, you *just don't care* anymore. You're done. Finished. Ready to walk away and never look back.

Historically, Herbert Freudenberger coined the term in 1974 and related it to several causes:

- The need to prove oneself
- Neglect of personal needs
- Dismissing friends and non-work activities
- Withdrawal and inner emptiness

Burnout is typically characterized by exhaustion, diminished interest, and cynicism. Research suggests that it usually manifests itself as emotional exhaustion and a reduced sense of personal efficacy and accomplishment. While normally referenced in the context of work, it can also happen in hobbies, in relationships, and in the home.

Stress management, finding a balance between work and play, and a fair and responsive work environment can all prevent and moderate burnout.

It's difficult—if not impossible—to describe the grinding lethargy, numbing detachment, and complete sense of worthlessness I felt to someone who hasn't experienced deep depression. Those were the darkest days of my entire life, and for the worst two months of my personal crisis, I had no hope whatsoever that I would ever return to the fun-loving, driven guy who had helped so many people with his compassion and inspiration. In fact, I couldn't even imagine that I had really ever been that person at all. I had simply lost my connection to that Todd.

I felt more and more that I was observing myself, that I was slipping into a constant state of being out of my own body. For all intents and purposes, I was a stranger to my own experience.

Almost Totally Washed Away

By the middle of May 2001, my depression had gotten so severe that I could no longer be in denial about needing professional help. Alarmingly, my nosedive into this crippling emotional state had happened in only a little over a month, and I had to admit to myself and to my family that I could not pull out of this tailspin on my own.

Also, I'm thankful that I retained the wherewithal to not only seek professional help, but to keep searching until I got the help that I needed. You see, the first psychologist I saw (who was recommended by someone in my family) was unhelpful in the extreme. During our initial sessions together, in fact, he actually told me that due to my precarious mental state, I might never be able to work again.

Not work again! My whole identity—what was left of it, anyway—was centered on my business success. Being told that I might never work again was a huge sucker punch to the gut. Granted, I was in a terrible mental state, but I still question whether or not this man did his professional best before so casually delivering this devastating piece of news.

If I hadn't been depressed before I saw this therapist, I certainly was now. Don't get me wrong—as a businessman, I certainly understand the value of being forthright, and of engaging people in reality, but I honestly do not feel that such severe discouragement was what I needed to hear at that time. What I needed most was hope—something…anything! to hold on to—not more hopelessness, no matter how accurate such a message might have been in that doctor's opinion. And, as you'll read, it wasn't an accurate message at all.

Generally, the treatment of depression consists of both "therapy" and of medication, so in accordance with standard procedure, this psychologist also sent me to a local psychiatrist friend of his so that I could be prescribed medications. Soon I found myself taking Paxil, which is not only an anti-depressant but also has powerful anxiety-reducing properties.

Modern-day pharmaceuticals are incredible, a testament to human ingenuity and to current technology. Psychoactive drugs, from antidepressants to anxiety-reducing drugs, from stimulants to sedatives, from opiates to mood stabilizers, are powerful medications with mind-altering effects. The question is, what is the appropriate use of such powerful medications? Also, often it's difficult for doctors to find the ideal medication(s) and dosage for individuals, since this varies greatly from person to person.

An Expert View on Anti-Depressants

Anti-depressants are designed to narrow a person's range of emotion. So if someone's range of emotion is spread very wide, they will experience very deep lows and very high highs, which means, at times, their emotions will likely be damaging and out of control.

The right anti-depressant, in the right dosage and properly prescribed, will narrow the extreme ends of the mood range, making breakdowns much less likely but preserving the person's ability to feel real emotions to their fullest without venturing into dangerous territory.

I found out the hard way that psychoactive drugs are not one-size-fits-all. Less than seventy-two hours into taking Paxil, I became completely paranoid, which is a potential side effect of the drug, especially if you are bipolar, which I found out later I slightly am. During my third day of taking this drug, I actually began believing for no apparent reason that my wife—my precious, loyal, wonderful wife—was thinking of leaving me! It was clear that the Paxil was not making me better. Far from it, it was pushing me closer and closer to the edge. I knew I had to stop taking it.

A Husband's Heartfelt Gratitude

It's important to me that I thank and acknowledge Yadira here. Far from thinking of abandoning me, Yadira was incredibly loving throughout this extremely tough time. Depression had not been part of her experience in Venezuela. No one in her family—in fact no one she knew—had ever experienced a breakdown, so my collapse was totally foreign to her, and that much more frightening due to her inexperience with depression. Instead of running from my problems or avoiding them, she dealt with them head-on, embraced me, did what she needed to do to keep our household functioning each day, and loved me through my depression. There's no doubt in my mind that our relationship grew immeasurably stronger because of the way Yadira stood by me in my darkest hour. Thank you so, so much, love!

For the next several weeks, I visited more and more psychologists and foot doctors and heard their opinions. And all the while, I felt that I was drifting farther and farther from reality, from health, and from myself. When people ask about that period in my life, I tell them to imagine what it would feel like to lose their business or job unexpectedly, or to be told that they had been diagnosed with a debilitating and incurable disease and not have the strength to eventually come to terms with this terrible news: an inability to comprehend reality, sickening anxiety, and nothing but a strange mixture of panic and resignation regarding the future.

That was me, every day, for six-plus weeks. I simply did not have the mental ability to rationalize my circumstances. And therein lies one of the most crippling aspects of a breakdown: I was never able to move past my initial dread and shock. I wasn't capable of formulating a plan of action. I didn't have the capacity to move forward and fight the challenges that were facing me. I remained stuck—painfully—at square one: detached, depressed, barely able to function, and my feet were still causing me incredible amounts of pain.

My lowest point came one summer day while Yadira, Joshua, and I were visiting my parents on Cape Cod. Perhaps my family hoped that a change of scenery would do me good; however, being away from my familiar surroundings only enhanced the feeling that I no longer had an anchor holding me to reality.

As Yadira took Josh for a walk down the beach one afternoon, I lay in bed and literally wished that I could just disappear.

If this is how I am going to feel for the rest of my days, I remember thinking, *I'd rather die now.* For a moment, the idea of grabbing a kitchen knife to slit my wrists flashed through my mind. I'll be truthful—at that time, I was so incredibly low and down on myself that the thought was honestly an attractive one. I would never have acted on that desire, though—because thankfully, even though the emotional pain I felt then was worse than I could ever put into words, I recognized that my wife and son were *sure* important enough to try to fight my way back for. And although I couldn't know it then, the help I needed was very close at hand.

Sunshine Returns...Along with an Epiphany

In the end, my recovery happened relatively quickly. By midsummer, with the help and support of my family, I succeeded in finally finding an amazing doctor, Dr. Michael Mufson. During my very first visit with Dr. Mufson, I could feel the first small ray of hope returning to my life—because he told me that I would of course work again—in fact, that I'd be fine! I was simply suffering from intense anxiety and depression, and he assured me that with the right medication, I would be able to return to the normal life I loved.

He was right. It took only about three weeks for the medications he prescribed to kick in. And on top of that, during our very first meeting, Dr. Mufson referred me to a fabulous foot doctor, Dr. Richard Cullen, who quickly gave me the orthotic relief I so desperately needed for my feet, too.

Back on My Feet

I'm happy to report that my stress fractures were, in the end, run of the mill as these things go—and completely capable of healing. After a visit to an insightful specialist, Dr. Cullen, I learned that in addition to my recent injury, I'd also been propelling myself through life on flat feet. With the proper orthotic to lift my arch, I've even since run the Boston Marathon—pain-free.

By September 2001 I was amazingly 100 percent the old fired-up Todd again, brain chemistry restored—with one major exception. I had a brand-new outlook on life. Remember the "Old Todd" I introduced you to at the beginning of this chapter? The successful, driven hot shot with the seemingly perfect life? Well, now I realized that my life, while exciting and full of accomplishments, was not a truly happy one. I had been proud of my successes, but I was never truly content. This is because I simply did not love myself yet and thus was always trying to feel okay with myself through achievements and "that-a-boys." And this unending need of mine to succeed had eventually caught up with me and completely broken me.

My breakdown was a turning point for me. The lessons I learned from it have enabled me to become truly fulfilled. Perhaps my breakdown was a disguised gift from God, something I had to experience in order to finally understand that while I had enjoyed success, I was driving myself too hard, and for the wrong reasons. Perhaps I needed a definitive cosmic kick in the pants to make me say, "Enough is enough! I am done destroying myself and ruining my life!" Whatever the reasons for my breakdown, though, it was the beginning of my road to recovery and true happiness. Exactly how I managed to emerge from deep despair and to embrace a happier life will unfold as you turn the pages of this book.

I'm totally convinced now that happiness is a possibility for everyone. If you're not living the life you want, however, you must learn—and I can help you to do this—how your thinking has gotten so off track and how you can change it. I'm more certain than ever that living with compassion, charity, and love for others—but **especially for yourself**—is the real secret to living a happy life.

> *Happiness is not just about feeling good on a momentary basis. Almost all the experts say that happiness is about more than a temporary feeling, that it has to do with self-esteem and purpose and a much bigger picture than just temporarily feeling good.*
>
> *The Grand essentials of happiness are: something to do, something to love, and something to hope for.*
>
> —Allan K. Chalmers

> *But what is happiness except the simple harmony between a man and the life he leads.*
>
> —Albert Camus

I'm now excited to share with you my life, its ups and downs, from the magnificent highs to the brutally difficult lows. I hope in some way that through my experiences and insights I can help each of you learn to live a much happier and more stress-free life.

Before You Go Any Further: It Really DOESN'T Buy Happiness!

You've just read about my transformative, traumatic breakdown and the circumstances surrounding it. Before you learn about me in more detail and become familiar with my life's story, though, I want to make one thing clear! Today, I am very privileged. I was born into a middle-class family. I didn't want for anything materially growing up, and then as an adult I've been incredibly successful in what many people mistakenly think is their life's purpose: making money.

I've made significant amounts of money in my lifetime, and I can categorically tell you that money is *not* the key to happiness. (In fact, my breakdown occurred during the time that my family's company was making the most…and only a short time before my dad, brother, and I were to achieve our greatest business triumph: selling our family business for a sum that we'd never dreamed was possible.)

Money allows you to suffer in comfort, true—but that's it. It's important to me to make this point right here, at the beginning, so that you won't read my story and discount it because of my success.

Let me put it bluntly: Losing a pregnancy is devastating, no matter how big your house is. Feeling as though you'd rather die than endure one more moment on this earth is no less terrifying because you've got money in the bank. Being teased as a kid isn't any easier because your parents drive nice cars, and being humiliated in the dating world as a teenager isn't any less traumatic because you can afford to take girls to nicer restaurants.

If anything, I want you to understand that if such devastating unhappiness can befall someone who seems to have it all, it's real. And I also want you to understand that if such a brutal breakdown could happen to someone with my supposed assets, maybe it's time we all revised our definition of what constitutes happiness. I have—and I hope you will, too.

The world has to learn that the actual pleasure derived from material things is of rather low quality on the whole and less even in quantity than it looks to those who have not tried it.
—Oliver Wendell Holmes

TIPS FROM TODD:
CHAPTER ONE

Happiness and depression are polar opposites—but it's essential to have a good understanding of each of them.

C'mon, Get Happy: What Held Me Back

Often, I've asked myself the following questions: What is this thing called happiness? Is it the opposite of depression? Is it a genetic trait, or can anyone experience it? And most importantly, how much conscious control do we have over it? What do we have to do to live a happier, less stressed, and more fulfilling life? How must we change as a society in order to reduce depressions, breakdowns, and even suicides, and increase happiness in America?

I'll address these questions throughout this book, but for now, here are some of the conclusions I've come to in regards to why happiness eluded me for so long:

- **I put emphasis on the wrong things.** Throughout my life, my main stressor was my need to always be number one. This is because prior to my breakdown, my level of satisfaction with myself was based solely on my achievements. First, my self-worth was based on my grades in school, later on my success at work, and most recently on how much money I could raise for politicians and charities. The problem is, this outlook caused me to become riddled with nonstop anxiety, never allowing me to rest and enjoy all of the good things in my life.

- **I drove myself too hard.** For years before my breakdown, Betty Barton, my good friend and credit manager at our company, had been telling me that if I didn't let up on my seventy- to eighty-hour work weeks and my insane way of continually pushing myself and my people to achieve higher and higher goals without a break, I would eventually break down myself. Boy, was Betty right!

   Back then, as I've said, I felt as if I had to continually drive myself to prove my self-worth. "Rest and relaxation" were synonymous with "irresponsibility and slacking" in my personal dictionary. I had failed to learn to simply love myself for who I was—a good person trying to do my best. If I wasn't going full speed ahead to new heights, I was almost unable to function day to day. The problem was, human bodies—including my own—were never designed to keep up this sort of demanding pace. Thus, I was destined to break. It was just a question of when.

- **I needed validation from others.** As you've probably guessed, I was never proud of a job well done for its own sake—I needed to hear compliments and accolades from others. The thing is, though, if you constantly need approval from others, you open yourself up to being used. Plus, if you are always working to make others happy, you may never experience that great feeling of happiness for yourself. You might not even learn how to.

Ultimately, your self-esteem must not be based on what other people think of you, but on your own view of yourself and the roles you play in the world. You must learn to accept and be happy with yourself. And let me tell you from experience, that will happen only when you can honestly say that you are doing everything possible to effectively and lovingly manage your life to the best of your ability each day. Here's what I mean: When you know on some level that you are avoiding issues, under-performing, or being childish and mean-spirited, you won't feel good about who you are, regardless of any material or ego-boosting success that might come your way. This is one reason why money is not the key to happiness.

Someone's opinion of you does not have to become your reality.
—Les Brown

- **I didn't love myself.** I believe that until you learn to truly love yourself as you are, you cannot ever really be a happy person. In fact, I believe that each person must make loving him or herself their primary goal in life. This is because first, you owe it to yourself to be happy, and second, nothing is more important for your children's own future happiness than for them to learn from you how to love themselves. Unfortunately, very few people realize the importance of self-love because it's not something we're generally taught, told, or shown when we are young.

  One way to test whether you truly love yourself is to simply consider whether you treat yourself the way you treat others whom you love (such as your spouse or your children) when you make mistakes or do something you think is really dumb or foolish. I certainly didn't before my breakdown.

  For example, if your child or loved one was fixating on something she thought she had done wrong and was beating herself up about it, I hope and believe you would show her loving compassion and try to comfort her by attempting to shift her focus to all of the other wonderful things she has done well in the past. However, if you are like most people, you do the exact opposite with yourself. Instead, when you make just one mistake in an otherwise perfect week, you probably use it as an opportunity to hammer yourself and make yourself feel just awful about it. This behavior is particularly dangerous because you are "with" yourself in your thoughts 24/7. Also, if you are prone to beating yourself up, you have at your disposal a lifetime of bad memories to draw upon with which you can reinforce just how incompetent and inadequate you really are.

It's important to understand and accept that because you are human, you are fallible, and thus you are going to make mistakes and poor decisions at various points in your life. And in fact, the more ambitious and adventurous you are in your life, the more mistakes you'll make. So if you want to live a happy life, when these inevitable follies happen, you have to learn to laugh at yourself and be willing to give yourself a break. I actually keep a Chinese fortune cookie quote that I received during dinner one night in my wallet to remind myself of the importance of cutting myself some slack. It reads: "You grow up the day you have your first laugh at yourself."

I do want to be clear—when I talk about loving yourself, I mean doing so with humility. Yes, there are many arrogant, selfish, and narcissistic people who seem to love themselves a bit too much, but that's usually a facade. Their extreme self-centeredness is often a defense against their own insecurity, not a true appreciation of who they are.

A Field Guide to Depression

I've also learned quite a bit about depression in the past decade—both from personal experience and from reading and research.

If you're not clear on the reality of depression, here are a few of the very basics:

- **The symptoms of depression are serious.** The symptoms of depression are easy to see, and they can severely impair or completely erase your ability to lead a normal life. They include: loss of appetite, poor sleep or too much sleep, social isolation, a colossal loss of energy, and a psychic blackout that robs you of the ability to think positively—or even to think at all.

- **Depression is often outside of your control.** Our moods are very often the result of genetics and early childhood experiences. Overall, long-term ingrained moods—whether positive or negative—are not choices you make consciously.

- **Often, depression is sparked by specific circumstances.** There are many situations that can cause depression, but most of them have to do with loss—uncontrollable, incomprehensible, unacceptable loss.

  In my own case, as you know, my slide into depression began with the loss of a pregnancy, and was compounded by the loss of my health, mobility, and thus my ability to exercise. As you'll read, these traumas descended on a man who from a young age had struggled with low self-esteem, anxiety, perfectionism, and worry—the perfect recipe for a breakdown.

- **Depression is not a cause for stigma.** Since depression is largely outside of your control, it is not a sign that you've done something wrong, or that you are in any way "weak." In fact, science has helped us to identify its causes and to develop treatments that can effectively combat mood disorders and even all-out breakdowns. While the social stigma that has accompanied depression is beginning to lessen, it still has not been eradicated.

  It is my greatest hope that this book will help to bring the conversation about depression and anxiety out into the open in America. I have no doubt that there exist thousands, if not tens of thousands, of people who have experienced actual breakdowns and have gone on to lead very successful and happy lives after recovering, like I have. However, one of the major problems is that so few talk about these success stories—I believe that if more people did, they could serve as a tremendous source of hope to others who currently feel hopeless.

  If you are struggling with feelings of depression, please know that you are not alone, and that you *can* have a very positive and happy future. For your own sake, as well as for that of your family and friends, please reach out and seek professional help. Don't let fears of being seen as "weak" or "sick" hold you back!

  Again, I cannot stress strongly enough that receiving treatment for depression is *not* a cause for shame or stigma. On the contrary, it is one of the healthiest things you can do, and you will be amazed by how much better you will feel once you and your doctor have found the correct combination of medication and therapy. Seeking professional help can change your life for the better—you may very well come to look at it as a turning point in your personal journey toward happiness.

The Beginning

> "God's gift to you is your life, and your gift back is how you live it."
> —Tony Robbins

It's 1965. Lyndon B. Johnson is president of the United States, and he initiates the Great Society Program. The first 3,500 Marines are sent to Vietnam. *The Sound of Music* debuts in New York, and *My Fair Lady* wins eight Oscars. *Tom and Jerry* premieres on CBS and The Beatles perform at Shea Stadium. The Pillsbury Doughboy is created. The Red Sox lose 100 games and finish ninth in the American league. The Celtics win their eighth NBA championship by beating the Lakers in five games.

And on the twenty-fourth of May, at approximately 9:30 a.m. at the Brigham and Women's Hospital in Boston, Massachusetts, I am born to Steve and Sally Patkin.

That morning I become another branch on a family tree that stretches back in living memory to Lithuania and beyond that into Judea.

The Seeds of Life as I Knew It

While I'd love to tell you all about each branch and twig of that extraordinary family tree, for now I'll stick to the shoots that will give you the foundations for understanding my story.

Let's start with my dad's father, Ruby. Without him—the founder of the Patkin family business—I'm not sure what path my life might have taken. Ruby had little formal education, but he became the quintessential self-made millionaire due in large part to his great intuitive business acumen and an incredible work ethic. In fact, it is common knowledge that Ruby would be at his office in Watertown, Massachusetts, by 4:00 a.m. and in bed by 7:00 p.m. (You know what they say about early to bed and early to rise…!) Through the years, Ruby grew his car dealership into one of the largest in the northeast.

The three great essentials to achieve anything worthwhile are,
first, hard work; second, stick-to-itiveness; third, common sense.
—Thomas Edison

My dad, his older brother, Burt, and his younger brothers, Murray and Jim, all joined Ruby in the car business in one capacity or another. As a result, I was able to get to know all three of my uncles—especially Burt and Jim—as businessmen and as colleagues. My dad's brother-in-law Ronnie also joined the car business for a time.

On the other side of the family, my mother's father, Max, was extremely hardworking too—just like Ruby. In fact, Max put himself through Dartmouth College by working two jobs in addition to attending his classes. He didn't stop there, though—he also attended Dartmouth's Tuck School of Business and afterwards rose quickly all the way to the top of the Boston shoe industry.

Max truly had a fascinating career. In fact, I could probably write a whole other book on the stories that he told me about his experiences in the shoe industry. The accomplishment Max was most proud of was being charged by the Roosevelt administration during World War II to convince the shoe manufacturers in the Northeast to switch their entire productions indefinitely to making only military boots. Max's ability to successfully convince all of these shoe manufacturers to switch their total productions over to military output—even though it cost them a lot of their profits—was an essential part of the war effort.

I can't move on without mentioning my grandmothers, either. Ruby's wife, Bertha, was the epitome of a nurturing stay-at-home wife and mother, while Max's wife, Ruth, was more spirited and colorful. (Ruth believed that she possessed extra-sensory perception, and claimed in 1958 to have turned down then-senator John F. Kennedy's overtures to her!) To say the least, my grandmothers were very different from one another, but they had one major thing in common: Each was an invaluable pillar of support to her husband. Ruby and Max would have probably done well for themselves without their wives, but I'm not convinced that either would have reached the heights they did without such love and support at home.

Looking back, I can see that Bertha and Ruth, as well as my own mother, Sally, were instrumental in shaping my own ideas of what male/female relationships—and the "ideal" marriage—should look like. As my own story unfolds in later chapters, you'll see that I was fortunate enough to find a partner—my wife, Yadira—whose personality is a wonderful combination of Bertha's nurturing nature with a hint of Ruth's interesting individuality.

That's the essential background information—in a nutshell, you might say that the ingredients for achievement and success were in my blood. I understood very early on that my family valued hard work—after all, I'd seen firsthand the hours my father put in, and I'd heard folks speak reverently about the work ethics of both of my grandfathers. As I grew older, this oft-expressed nose-to-the-grindstone attitude set me up to believe that I too had better be hardworking and successful.

He followed in his father's footsteps, but his gait was somewhat erratic.

—Nicolas Bentley

My Early Years (The Nickel Tour)

By all accounts, I was a very content and generally easy baby who could entertain himself quite happily in his crib. My parents tell me that not only was I a pleasant baby who slept well, but also that as a toddler I always seemed happy and was very sociable. I guess you could even say that I was a ham—I loved to wear a lot of different hats as a youngster, as you can see when you look at my earliest childhood photos.

Growing up, I was especially close to my mother, Sally. She was twenty-five and two days old when I was born, and she was a middle child just like me. It isn't surprising, therefore, that we were like two peas in a pod. Furthermore, my dad was busy growing the family's new auto parts company, so he simply couldn't be around very much during the days and early evenings when I was awake. As a toddler, I would be tucked into bed by my mother long before he came home from work.

Because of the way Dad's schedule worked out, my older brother, Roger, certainly saw more of him when I was a young boy. Looking back, I think that this state of affairs sparked off my feelings that my father favored Roger, whether it was true or not. On the other hand, though, it certainly seemed to me that my mother was more protective of me.

> *We've never shown any favoritism!*
> —Marie Barone, *Everybody Loves Raymond*

As I consider my childhood family dynamics with an adult's perspective, it has become clear that my mother may have worried about me—the middle child—a bit more than my brother or sister because of her own middle child experience. As a result of my mother's attention being focused on me, I think that my dad tried to compensate by spending more time with my older brother, Roger, and my younger sister, Kimberly. I'm sure that this extra love from my mother made me feel special, particularly at such a young age. I also believe, though, that this family dynamic affected all three of us kids—Roger, Kimberly, and myself—and our relationships with one another…and probably still does to this day.

The Middle Child Blues

As you've just read, I was a middle child—and I can assure you that in my case, many of the birth order stereotypes held true, and most certainly contributed to my anxiety growing up.

Middle child syndrome is typically characterized by feeling like an outsider in your own family, sandwiched as you are between the oldest (and first) child and the youngest—both of whom are likely to get special treatment from your parents. (As I've said, at least for me this wasn't the case regarding my mother, but probably was with my dad.) This problem is particularly pronounced if you are the same sex as your older sibling and a different sex from the youngest, as I am.

Middle children, therefore, often have low self-esteem and can be loners. Many drift through life without much drive or direction. On the other hand, though—as was the case with me—middle children can be just the opposite: more fired up and competitive. Personally, I developed a major sibling rivalry with my older brother, Roger, especially in terms of our school grades. This instilled in me a very strong desire to succeed, which served me well in school and later in work—but it also made me a nervous wreck.

Whether due to middle child syndrome or not, I also had major issues with low self-esteem growing up. These feelings caused me a great deal of pain for many years and needed to be overcome before I was able to find true happiness.

An Expert View on Middle Child Syndrome

While this so-called syndrome doesn't apply to every middle child, there are a constellation of symptoms that are often observed in this particular birth-order position. They include:

- A tendency not to be a leader
- A tendency to be shy
- Difficulty in forming healthy relationships
- A tendency not to work well under pressure
- Dislike of monotonous tasks

Of course, these are *tendencies*, not set-in-stone qualities. With work and focused effort, almost any personality characteristic can be overcome.

I was also way too sensitive to Roger's teenage moods growing up. I remember feeling nervous and depressed when he seemed quiet and unhappy. Roger and I did, however, share some great times together. For example, we loved to play baseball, street hockey, and ice hockey. And we would often wrestle in the house, too. (I clearly remember one cringe-worthy incident during which we broke a glass door while trying to perfect the "suplex overhead throw"—which, I might add, we were *simultaneously* watching a professional wrestler perform on TV.)

As for my sister, Kimberly, while my parents might tell you that both Roger and I were very good to our younger sister, I believe she'd tell you that I teased and wrestled with her the way Roger had done to me. That's just how things work with siblings!

> *Our siblings. They resemble us just enough to make all their differences confusing, and no matter what we choose to make of this, we are cast in relation to them our whole lives long.*
> —Susan Scarf Merrell

Don't Judge a Book by Its Cover

I have many great memories of my early childhood with my family and our friends, and I fondly remember many special occasions, including some wonderful vacations. Yes, I think that overall I was very happy, sociable, and fairly secure during my early years. And I know that my family, friends, and acquaintances would agree with that assessment. But as I moved through childhood and spent more time away from home, I began to develop some issues that would fundamentally affect my life for a very long time to come. As you'll read, I struggled with anxiety, perfectionism, and bullying, to name just a few.

To put it simply, many very stressful emotional challenges I faced when I was young colored my entire growing-up experience, as well as how I viewed myself later on in life. But here's the thing: 85 percent of the time, I was (now that I have really analyzed it) indeed a happy, popular, athletic kid with very little trouble on his plate. Nevertheless, that 15 percent of stress and anxiety was so painful to me that it has just about overshadowed everything else in my memory about myself as a young person.

In fact, when my parents, brother, and sister read the rough drafts of this book, they told me, "Todd, this is crazy! You had a great childhood! You were a happy kid. This stuff didn't bother you nearly as much as you're making it out."

Likewise, any peer who knew me in kindergarten, in third grade, in junior high school, or even in high school would probably also respond to this book with, "This isn't the Todd I knew. Todd was as happy and popular as just about anyone I can remember."

I would like to make two points here: First, there's no guarantee that anyone, even those who are closest to us, know what we're really thinking or feeling. The outward appearance you present to the world may be very different from what you're actually experiencing inside.

Secondly, our view of ourselves is often greatly distorted, especially if we experienced prolonged periods in our early years that were very negative emotionally. And there's no doubt that how we view and perceive the way we were as children (even if others didn't see it) becomes the foundation for how we view life and feel about ourselves as adults. Thus, a great deal of people, I believe, are feeling more inadequate, untalented, uninteresting, etc. than they actually are, all because of a relatively small percentage of their early childhood experiences. And because we're hanging on to these misconceptions about ourselves, we are being held back.

Throughout the following chapters, I hope you'll keep this in mind as you read my story…and I also hope that you'll take the opportunity to examine how your own childhood experiences and perceptions may be influencing your outlook and your life even now. Once you've identified these things, you'll be in a position to start actively changing how you assess yourself and your capabilities. You'll be able to start loving yourself for who you are, not beating yourself up for who you (probably incorrectly) *think* you are (or are not). It is my hope that this book will give you the tools to begin that process.

TIPS FROM TODD:
CHAPTER TWO

- **Be aware of birth order. It really *can* have an impact.** Research has shown that birth order has a direct impact on personality. We've already discussed "middle child syndrome," but middle children aren't the only ones whose position in the family can lead to problems down the road.

  Firstborns are prone to be perfectionists and overachievers, too, since they're often told that they should be "the older, more responsible one who should know better." On the other hand, lastborn children are more likely to be immature and manipulative, and to take less conventional routes to their destinations.

In most cases, I don't believe birth order determines a person's ultimate success or failure. However, it is important to recognize how your family position might have shaped your attitude and outlook. Knowing the "why" can be very helpful if you want to move forward.

- **Parents, take care not to play favorites.** In general, parental favoritism can occur due to a variety of reasons, including a child's age, gender, personality, or level of achievement. It's also not uncommon in families with stepchildren. When a child believes that he or she isn't as pleasing to one or both parents, self-esteem is impacted. Usually, that leads to the child giving up too easily or trying too hard to be "worthy," as I believe was probably the case with me as I strove for my dad's affection.

- **Don't let sibling rivalry get too dirty—no matter how old you are.** They say that a little competition is a good thing—but not an excessive amount. When a child (or an adult!) is zoom-focused on beating or out-performing a sibling, he or she is essentially living to please someone else or to prove something, rather than to achieve a fulfilling lifestyle. (Also, no matter what its nature, competition at this level is inherently stressful and unhealthy.)

- **Also, make a conscious effort to help your relationships with your siblings grow as you do.** The fact is, you probably won't outgrow the childhood dynamics you had with your siblings *unless* you make a conscious effort to do so. Without realizing it, many adults treat their brothers and sisters the same way at age fifty as they did at age ten. Instead of competing for Mom's and Dad's attention at bedtime, you're now trying to edge one another out of the spotlight at a cocktail party or family gathering. Or perhaps you're still trying to be "right"—but instead of proper backyard fort construction, you and your brother are now debating which automobile model is the most economical.

  No, things may never be totally friction-free between you and your siblings—but you'll find that if you make a conscious effort to better identify and work through your childhood hang-ups and hot-button issues, you'll have a better chance of enjoying adult relationships with your brothers and sisters that are characterized by mutual respect and much less resentment.

- **Be conscious of how your childhood has affected your outlook.** To some extent, everyone experiences childhood struggles. Periods of anxiety, low self-esteem, and insecurity are part of growing up. The problem is, many of us hang on to these negative feelings and low opinions of ourselves well into our adult years, believing that they are truly indicative of who we still are and what we are thus capable of. Even if they comprised a relatively small percentage of our childhoods, extreme negative periods have the power to greatly influence our adult-hoods. For this reason, it's important to think back through the years and determine if your memories and perceptions of yourself may be disproportionately dark and thus holding you back even today.

My Heritage

"To be a Jew is a destiny."
-Vicki Baum

"No people has ever insisted more firmly than the Jews that history has a purpose and humanity a destiny. At a very early stage in their collective existence they believed they had detected a divine scheme for the human race, of which their own society was to be a pilot. They worked out their role in immense detail. They clung to it with heroic persistence in the face of savage suffering. The Jewish vision became the prototype for many similar grand designs for humanity, both divine and man-made. The Jews, therefore, stand right at the centre of the perennial attempt to give human life the dignity of a purpose."

—Paul Johnson, *A History of the Jews*

Have you ever wondered about the men and women who came before you, whose actions and choices led to your existence? What were your ancestors like, anyway? For instance, how did your great-great-great-grandparents raise your great-great-grandparents, and how did they, in their turn, raise your great-grandparents...and so on down the line to you? What character traits did all of these individuals exhibit? What did they look like? What were they interested in, and what did they find funny?

The answers to these questions—and so many more—are, in many ways, the "key" to unlocking the hows and whys of your own personality, behaviors, preferences, and appearance.

Yes, your past deeply influences your present reality—perhaps more than most people realize. In a majority of cases, family heritage provides very important clues as to the type of person you will become and, more specifically, sheds light on the origins of many of your strengths and weaknesses. As science continues to advance, genetic links to your immediate family members—and even those extending to your more distant forebears—will become easier to explore. What's more, your connections and similarities to these relatives will also become both more specific and obvious.

Even without genetics charts and DNA tests, though, understanding your family history can be an invaluable aspect in understanding and determining who you are, what things you may be best at, and who you have the possibility of becoming. That is certainly the case for me. Looking back I can see that certain traits—both genetic and behavioral—are direct products of my individual upbringing and the larger cultural context within which I was raised. In short, I wouldn't be the Todd Patkin I am today if not for my heritage—and learning about that part of me is important in understanding my overall journey.

I was born into a Jewish family, and as my childhood advanced, both the positive and negative aspects of being a Jewish American began to become evident to me. My religion, culture, and heritage certainly shaped my growing-up years—and in fact, have continued to significantly shape my adult life. As you will read, I exhibit four major attributes that are historically common among Jews: ingenuity, emotional intelligence, worry (or anxiety), and depression. While the first two are excellent characteristics to have, the second two aren't—and in fact, it's because of them that this book was written.

A Jewish History Primer

If you aren't familiar with Jewish history and faith, the following section will give you a basic foundation that will help you to understand various elements of my story.

If I was an atheist and believed in blind eternal fate, I should still believe that fate had ordained the Jews to be the most essential instrument for civilizing the nations…They have given religion to three-quarters of the globe and have influenced the affairs of mankind more and more happily than any other nation, ancient or modern.

—John Adams, Second President of the United States

Origins

The Jewish Orthodox tradition is based on a strict adherence to the Torah, also known as the Old Testament of the Christian Bible, and on an oral tradition describing rituals that date back over three thousand years. According to this tradition, the religion of Judaism began roughly four thousand years ago when one of the religion's patriarchs, Abraham, recognized one sovereign God and acknowledged that man had a moral contract with this single Creator. Under this contract, individuals who lived good lives would be rewarded, and those who sinned would be punished. Until this time, civilizations had worshipped many gods, so the idea of a moral contract with only one deity was an incredibly radical change in human thinking—and it has affected the entire course of human history.

Around 1313 B.C.[1] at Mount Sinai in present-day Egypt, God appeared to the Jews as Moses led them to Israel on their exodus from Egypt. This was a unique event in human history because instead of appearing to one or two chosen individuals, God appeared to *all* the Jewish people!

Due to this transformative experience, a ramshackle group of escaping slaves became a nation at Mt. Sinai by pledging to live their lives according to the Torah's commandments and by following the dream that they might one day return to their longed-for homeland. At this point, the Jews became the nation of Israel. Since then, their shared history and dream have made Judaism a cultural and historical heritage as well as a religion, and the Jewish people's special relationship with God has resulted in an all-encompassing view of how to live one's life.

---

1   Because Judaism doesn't recognize Christ as the Messiah it does not base its calendar on his life and death. Instead, Judaism uses B.C.E. (before common era) in place of B.C. and A.C.E. (after common era) in place of A.D.

Exile

It should be noted that Jews have spent much of their existence not in Israel, but in exile dispersed across the world (this exile has been concentrated mainly in Europe and the Middle East). This dispersion is known as the *diaspora*, which literally means "the dispersion of a people formerly concentrated in one place."

The Orthodox Jewish tradition has always included the belief that one day the Jews would return to the Promised Land, and as a result, the Jews harbor a natural and religious connection to Israel. During the hundreds of years before the nation of Israel came into being in 1948, Jews understandably clung to Orthodoxy, because the shared traditions were a way of keeping together and of preserving their identity as they constantly settled and resettled in foreign lands.

While difficult in so many ways, this continual migration did have an upside: It forced Jews to become very adaptive as they needed to rapidly adjust to ever-changing environments. Also, it made it necessary for them to become innovative and ingenious. And because the exiled Jews were almost always faced with hostility and conflict, they collectively developed notable negotiating, people, and business skills. Today, this ability is known as emotional intelligence.

An Expert View on Emotional Intelligence

Unlike cognitive abilities, which can be accurately determined using the Intelligence Quotient (IQ) test, emotional intelligence is more difficult to define and measure. Generally, though, emotional intelligence can be understood as the capacity or ability to accurately perceive and interpret the emotions of oneself and other people, and to use them to shape, manage, and improve behaviors.

The concept of emotional intelligence was widely popularized by *New York Times* science writer Daniel Goleman, author of *Emotional Intelligence: Why It Can Matter More Than IQ* (1996). Goleman breaks emotional intelligence down into five basic competencies, which build on each other. They are:

- Being aware of your emotions and how they influence your thoughts and behaviors
- Being able to manage your emotions (not allowing them to control you)
- Using your emotions to help you succeed
- Being aware of and able to influence others' emotions
- Being able to form, build, and maintain relationships

IQ was once thought to be the primary determinant of success; however, it is increasingly clear that emotional intelligence also plays a large part in influencing the path of a person's life since it is so strongly tied to self-control, the ability to form relationships, conflict resolution, accurately interpreting one's environment, being able to feel empathy for others, and so forth.

As a result of living as outsiders in other groups' homelands, the Jewish people were frequently harassed, or even worse, used as convenient scapegoats for troubles they had nothing to do with. Not surprisingly, they developed a fine-tuned awareness to brewing trouble, which required them to be acutely conscious of potential problems and to be able to plan accordingly. It's understandable, therefore, that worry and anxiety are also a part of the Jewish heritage. Given the incredible stresses and difficulties that punctuated Jewish history, it's also no surprise that Jews (especially Jewish men) are more prone to depression than people of other ethnic and cultural groups.[2]

The Pale of Settlement

Jews across what is now Eastern Europe were frequently persecuted by the Russian czars, and beginning in the late eighteenth century were forced to live within a geographic area called the Pale of Settlement (literally, "borders of settlement"), which extended along what was then the western border of Imperial Russia. About 5 million Jews, approximately 40 percent of the world's Jewish population, lived within the Pale during the nineteenth century. (*My great-grandparents and their families were part of that number.*)

Jews in the Pale of Settlement lived under numerous restrictive laws and regulations that perpetuated poverty and difficult living conditions. As a result, they developed quite an extraordinary system of volunteerism (essentially, a very comprehensive social welfare program) designed to meet the needs of the group including struggling families, students, soldiers, orphans, the elderly, and those needing medical care.

Actually, this emphasis on social welfare was a natural extension of a Jewish heritage, which had always been marked by a concentration on community and charity. (In fact, the great twelfth-century Jewish philosopher Maimonides wrote that he didn't know of a single Jewish community that didn't have institutions in place to support the needy.)

2　　For example: Golding, J.M., R. Kohn, I. Levav, and M.M. Weissman. "Vulnerability of Jews to affective disorders." *American Journal of Psychiatry* 154 (1997): 941-7.

Reform Judaism

By the early twentieth century, as Jews became more settled in the West after leaving the Pale of Settlement—especially in America where there was religious freedom—some of the external pressures that had perpetuated strict adherence to Orthodoxy began to dwindle. In the great melting pot, many cultures mingled and eventually assimilated into what has become a uniquely American culture. So, it was no surprise that as more Jews immigrated to America—the land of religious freedom—the Jewish Reform movement gained traction.

Judaic Reform movements had begun to appear in Europe in the eighteenth century during the Enlightenment, and they flourished as Jewish emigrants found their freedom and niche, particularly in American society. In many ways, Reform Judaism reflected reform movements in other religions. It de-emphasized a literal understanding of religious observance and instead set out a more liberal agenda that allowed individuals to determine their own practices within a broad tradition.

For example, within Orthodox Judaism the mother's faith determines the child's religion, whereas in today's Reform movement a child can be Jewish if either the father or the mother is Jewish. The Reform movement also allows for services to be conducted in English (or other native tongues) rather than in Hebrew, and it also ended the gender segregation of Orthodox Judaism wherein men and women are kept separate at religious services.

A Strong Heritage

My father's parents and my mother's mother came to the United States from Lithuania in the early part of the twentieth century. Around the same time, my mother's father's family came from Ukraine. As Eastern European Jews, all of my grandparents were brought up in the Orthodox Jewish tradition that dominated the Pale of Settlement in which they had lived.

My father was raised in the Jewish Orthodox tradition; however, he struggled with many of the issues that led second-generation Americans to seek the Reform movement. My father found that the Judaism his parents practiced was too far removed from his experience. Religious services, for example, were in Hebrew, which he didn't understand. The laws governing food seemed too restrictive, and he thought they were based on considerations that didn't apply three thousand years after they were adopted. My father also found it difficult to relate to the education he received about Judaism. In short, he didn't feel comfortable with the Orthodox tradition even as he was involved in the accompanying culture and lifestyle.

My mother's parents were also first-generation Americans who each came from an Orthodox tradition. However, within a generation of arriving in America, they had both decided to follow a more Reform path. It's no surprise, therefore, that when my parents met and started a family they decided that they felt most comfortable at a Reform temple. They wanted to engage their children in the religion while making the experience as fun and meaningful as possible.

A Jewish Childhood: My First Impressions

One of my first recollections of anything Jewish was dressing up as a king in a Purim play when I was around seven years old. (Purim is a holiday that celebrates the Persian Jews' escape just prior to their extermination during the reign of King Achashverosh, who had initially decided to follow the advice of his grudge-bearing advisor Haman to kill all of the Jews, as told in the Book of Esther.) What kid wouldn't enjoy getting to dress up as a king? I also recall attending a cousin's Bar Mitzvah when I was nine or ten. While the details are fuzzy, I remember having fun, and I enjoyed the sense of family I felt.

My family also went to the High Holiday services at the Temple every year. The High Holidays mark the most sacred times of the Jewish calendar, beginning with Rosh Hashanah and building to the holiest day of all, Yom Kippur. As any ravenous teenage boy would, I still recall—vividly—making my own first twenty-five-hour fast on Yom Kippur when I was sixteen.

Jewish High Holy Days: Rosh Hashanah and Yom Kippur

Rosh Hashanah is the holy day that ushers in the Ten Days of Repentance. It is Jewish tradition that on Rosh Hashanah (which means "the beginning of the new year") God sets out each person's fate for the coming year. During the Ten Days of Repentance, a Jew seeks forgiveness for wrongs against God and against others.

Yom Kippur is the Day of Atonement, which marks the end of the Ten Days of Repentance and is the holiest day of the entire year. On Yom Kippur there are public and private confessions of guilt and prayers for forgiveness, after which Jews consider themselves absolved by God. One's fate, set out in Rosh Hashanah, is finally sealed after Yom Kippur. On this solemn day only confessions should be on a Jew's lips, and as a result there is a fast that lasts twenty-five hours.

As a child, I liked the traditions and the sense of community I felt at the temple during these holidays. Even though I was young, I could feel that I was taking part in something much larger than myself. And because many parts of the services were in English, I could follow along fairly well.

Of course, I also liked the less sacred and more celebratory holidays as well because they were spent quite pleasantly with my family—and they usually included special, tasty meals prepared by my mother. To this day, I still have a soft spot for matzo ball soup, brisket, and potato kugel. And like all kids, I especially enjoyed Passover with its *Seder* ceremony and the hunt for the afikomen. (The afikomen is a piece of matzo that is hidden during the main meal. When the meal is over, all of the younger kids go on a scavenger hunt to find it, and the winner usually gets a monetary reward.)

Passover

Passover celebrates a pivotal event in Jewish and human history. In an attempt to force the Pharaoh to permit all Jewish slaves to leave Egypt, God subjected Egypt to ten plagues, the last of which was the killing of every male firstborn in the country. Prior to this last plague, the Jews were instructed by God to mark the doorposts of their homes with lamb's blood so that the spirit of the Lord would *pass over* them, thus sparing their families from this plague.

I marvel at the resilience of the Jewish people. Their best characteristic is their desire to remember. No other people has such an obsession with memory.

—Elie Wiesel

The day that was, of course, especially monumental for me was my own Bar Mitzvah, which I remember with joy and pride. A Bar Mitzvah (or Bat Mitzvah for girls) is that special moment when, at the age of thirteen, each Jewish child crosses the boundary from childhood to adulthood. To the embarrassment of my newly teenage self, part of the Bar Mitzvah ceremony involves the celebrant singing in front of the entire congregation—and I had a lousy singing voice! (Still do today, truth be told.)

Other than having to sing solo, though, I loved every minute of the entire day, from being the center of attention while leading the prayers to being with my family and so many of my friends. Looking back, I've recognized that a big part of what made my Bar Mitzvah so memorable was seeing the joy on my parents' and grandparents' faces. As an added bonus, the day marked the end of my mandatory attendance at Hebrew school classes, which I didn't care for at all.

In addition to my own special day, I also thoroughly enjoyed my brother Roger's Bar Mitzvah and my sister Kimberly's Bat Mitzvah, because of the family pride and joy that was evident on those occasions. Oh, and the great parties that followed the ceremonies didn't hurt either!

An Expert View on the Value of Community

Primates (and possibly even lower species) are hardwired to be cooperative. What's more, parts of our brains are designed to feel empathy. Both of these facts mean that being part of a "tribe" benefits the individual and the community as a whole.

What, exactly, is a "tribe"? The term might refer to a large, faith-based community such as Judaism, Christianity, Islam, and so forth. It might mean a smaller group such as a synagogue, church, or mosque. It might even be a group dedicated to a cause such as ecology, animal rights, or world hunger.

It's clear that being part of a group—especially one that focuses on spirituality and the collective good—promotes mental and emotional well-being. Almost all theories about happiness stress the concepts of belonging and of doing good for the other members of your community.

The Downsides of Being Jewish...from a Child's Point of View, Anyway!

All of these are very happy memories that capture some of what it was like for me to grow up as a Jew in America. There were, however, some aspects of Jewish life that I didn't like.

First and foremost, until my Bar Mitzvah, I had to go to religious education classes for an hour and a half on Mondays, Wednesdays, and Sundays. Often, I was dragged very reluctantly away from a neighborhood pick-up baseball or football game, which didn't do anything to endear religious education to me. As a typical kid who'd already spent enough time behind a desk during the actual school day, I found these classes to be incredibly boring, and if I ever had the chance to get out of going to them I would.

I now know the richness and importance of learning about Israel as well as about Jewish history and its traditions, but for whatever reason—my own lack of excitement or the dry manner in which the material was presented—my current interest in my heritage was not sparked by those classes. As an adult, I now make it a point to contribute to organizations whose goals include making Jewish religious school education a more exciting and inspiring experience for our next generation.

A Scholar in the Family

Despite what my youthful disinterest in learning about most things religious might indicate, the Jews in general have a strong tradition of intellectual scholarship and study. As I have mentioned, most of my ancestors came from Lithuania, and it's part of my family's lore that we are direct descendants of that country's great Rabbi Elijah ben Shlomo Zalman, also known as the Vilna Gaon.

The Vilna Gaon was born in Vilnius, Lithuania, in 1720, and he was to eighteenth century Judaism what Einstein was to twentieth century physics. A child prodigy who studied astronomy when he was eight and could recite the entire Talmud by the age of 11, the Vilna Gaon published many works on Judaism and is widely regarded as one of the religion's greatest scholars.

It's certainly a point of pride to (probably) have such an illustrious personage in one's family tree, but beyond that, I've sometimes wondered if perhaps I might have a little bit of the Vilna Gaon in me. No, I'm not at all suggesting that I'm a noteworthy religious scholar—but the fact is, it's possible that my need to excel academically was sparked not just by a desire to out-do my brother, Roger, but also by a more deep-seated ancestral drive to learn and achieve.

I'm pleased to say that while religious education wasn't high on my list of fun things to do as a kid, I *did* enjoy spending time with my Jewish friends and schoolmates. However, I wasn't so keen on some of their parents. From the perspective of a child growing up in a country of equal opportunity, some of the adult Jews in our area seemed downright elitist and snobbish to me. Their "club" seemed to be exclusively Jewish, and actively appeared to confine non-Jews to the perimeter of its social circle.

This exclusionary behavior seemed inherently unjust to me. My way was just the opposite. I embraced friends from all religions and walks of life. At school, in fact, I specifically worked hard to build friendships with many of the African-American kids who were being bussed into our school from Boston as part of the popular new Metco program.[3] My nature has always been that of an "includer," making me one of the first students to introduce myself to these newcomers. I just didn't think it was right that they were sitting all alone off to one side at lunchtime. Plus, even then I loved learning about people with different life experiences than I had!

These three are the marks of a Jew: a tender heart, self-respect, and charity.

—Hebrew Proverb

Unlike my friends' parents, I was open to forming a wide variety of relationships as a youngster. What a child of my generation couldn't realize, however, was that many of these seemingly snobbish Jewish adults had been raised by parents who themselves had seen the most savage and evil assault on a people—my people—that had ever been perpetrated. In fact, many of these adults were merely one or two generations removed from their own parents' or grandparents' persecution during the Holocaust.

The Jews are the living embodiment of the minority, the constant reminder of what duties societies owe their minorities, whoever they might be.

—Abba Eban

---

3   The Metco program is a grant program funded by the Commonwealth of Massachusetts. It is a voluntary program intended to expand educational opportunities, increase diversity, and reduce racial isolation by permitting students in certain cities to attend public schools in other communities that have agreed to participate.

In addition, many were old enough to have witnessed the difficult birth of the State of Israel and the constant and ongoing attempts to murder it by its neighbors. In retrospect, it's hardly surprising, therefore, that a large portion of the Jewish community in the 1970s was still wary (or even a little paranoid!) of others. I believe now that this group's insistence on sticking together was almost a primitive survival instinct. Ultimately, though, I didn't understand these underlying circumstances as a child, and the insular behavior I saw helped to foster in me a strong belief that no one on the planet is better in God's eyes than anyone else due to religion, race, or any other characteristic.

This clannishness displayed by many Jewish adults post-World War II, I believe, has also helped to give Jewish people as a whole a bad rap. It has led to negative comments and sneers at the concept of a "chosen" people. However, such contempt does not take into account the *real* meaning behind the notion of being chosen. My life experiences have led me to believe that *every* individual on earth is "chosen" because each of us has some unique purpose through which he or she can enhance this world. In fact, spreading that message and encouraging everyone I encounter to embrace and develop their own unique gifts has become an important part of my life's mission. I firmly believe that when people succeed in finding their own special purposes in life, greater happiness follows.

Words Well Said

"Yes, I do believe in the chosen people concept as affirmed by Judaism in its holy writ, its prayers, and its millennial tradition. In fact, I believe that every people—and indeed, in a more limited way, every individual—is 'chosen' or destined for some distinct purpose in advancing the designs of Providence. Only, some fulfill their mission and others do not. Maybe the Greeks were chosen for their unique contributions to art and philosophy, the Romans for their pioneering services in law and government, the British for bringing parliamentary rule into the world, and the Americans for piloting democracy in a pluralistic society. The Jews were chosen by God as the pioneers of religion and morality; that was and is their national purpose."

—Rabbi Immanuel Jakobovits, former Chief Rabbi of the
United Synagogue of Great Britain

I'd also like to point out that I often feel very embarrassed and uncomfortable when non-Jewish religious people tell me that I am one of the "chosen people" after finding out that I am Jewish. To be honest, not a single other Jewish person has ever talked to me about feeling chosen or being chosen.

We All Need to Believe in Something

Regardless of your own perception of churches, temples, mosques, and formalized religion, the fact is that a belief in a Higher Power or Greater Purpose, as well as in a code of ethics and sensitivity to your fellow human beings, are often important components of happiness. If you don't believe in these things, all that remains for you to worship is your own ego—and I do not believe that you were put here on earth to solely satisfy your own selfish desires.

Targeted for Teasing

Partially due to my Jewish heritage, I am sure (see "A Jewish History Primer" found earlier in this chapter), I have always possessed an inherent sensitivity and respect for other people. Most of my Jewish relatives and friends have the same sensitivity. It was quite a shock for me, therefore, to encounter other kids at school, beginning as early as the second or third grade, who were neither very sensitive nor respectful—who were, in fact, quite nasty, and who picked on me simply because I was an easy, insecure target. (I'll tell you more about my bullying trials and tribulations in the next chapter.)

Now, I know quite well that neither I nor my other Jewish friends were angels. But the fact is, I had never encountered this level of hostility before, and it threw me for a loop. I simply didn't know how to deal with this sort of antagonism, and being on the receiving end of it made me feel weak. As you might guess, my developing inferiority complex and the feeling of being vulnerable only added to my incredibly high levels of anxiety.

Unfortunately, when I was growing up, parents either weren't as aware of the discomfort that bullied kids like me felt, or if they were, they didn't know how to teach their children to deal with it. As a parent myself, I have tried to be as vigilant and sensitive to bullying as possible. I believe that my son, Josh, is more capable than I was of handling aggression, hostility, and bullying. *For other concerned parents, Chapter 5 contains a more thorough treatment on the topic of bullying.*

Touch-and-Go with Israel

As I grew into adolescence, issues pertaining to my people's ancestral homeland—Israel—became harder for me to ignore. And believe me, at that point in my life my support of the nation was already touch-and-go at best.

> *Israel has created a new image of the Jew in the world—the image of a working and an intellectual people, of a people that can fight with heroism.*
>
> —David Ben-Gurion

I was happy, relieved, and proud, of course, that Israel always seemed to win its wars, but I honestly didn't feel much of a connection to the country. These feelings of apathy (at best) were always exacerbated when I saw my father make generous contributions to Israel during the High Holiday services each year. I didn't understand why my dad felt the need to give so generously. In fact, the whole situation made me so mad that I vowed never to raise a single dollar for Israel, a country that was winning every war and yet was still taking money from my family—who at the time (I felt) needed that money more than Israel did. As you'll read later, though, the concept of "never saying never" is quite applicable in terms of my charitable relationship with Israel!

As it turns out, my experience with Israel would not to be limited to my father's donations on religious holidays—far from it, in fact! My up-close-and-personal relationship with Israel was sparked by my brother, Roger, who was more involved in Jewish youth group activities than I was. In fact, he was a national board member of the North East Federation of Temple Youth (which was and still is today, I am sure, a very important position for a young person to hold). As a result of Roger's interest in and involvement with Jewish youth, he went to Israel when he was eighteen, and absolutely loved his experience. In fact, he came back home so pumped up about it that when I was nineteen, I followed in his footsteps.

The summer before my Israel adventure, my parents had given me a similar high school graduation gift—a trip to Europe that just so happened to be with an amazing group of young adults from all over the United States. In short, I had a blast! First, many of my fellow travelers were beautiful women with sexy Southern drawls: What eighteen-year-old guy wouldn't enjoy that sort of company? And making things even better, our Austrian tour guide let our group know from the outset that his number one goal was to make sure we all had the time of our lives. As long as we were back at London's Heathrow Airport in ten days ready to fly home as scheduled, he said, he didn't mind if any one of us decided to alter our itinerary in any fashion.

As a result, I absolutely had the time of my life that summer. For one thing, my attractive traveling companions distracted me to the point that I wasn't always sure which country (we visited twelve countries in nine days) I was actually in at any given moment! The point is, that trip to Europe ended up being the most enjoyable week and a half of my life up to that point, and I was revved up for more of the same as I prepared to go to Israel the following year.

An Unorthodox Trip

It was the summer of 1984, and my Israel pre-trip itinerary was very similar to what Roger's had been four years earlier. The first two weeks would be spent traveling and sightseeing in Israel. Next, our group would recharge its batteries by staying on a kibbutz for two weeks before resuming our tour of Israel for a final two-week stretch. Then, after a total of six weeks away, we would return to the U.S.

The first piece of bad luck occurred, unbeknownst to me, months before my departure. You see, my particular Israeli tour had been chosen to be the first of its kind ever to be led by two women. And that meant that unlike my carefree European tour guide the year before (who was my "measuring stick"), the first priority of my Israeli tour guides was to ensure that nothing went wrong. That way, women would continue to get future opportunities to be Israeli tour guides.

Looking back, I see clearly that my tour guides were exercising very sound judgment, but at nineteen, I chafed at their ultra-cautious approach. In fact, it made me feel as though my trip was a jail sentence…at least compared to my previous year's tour of Europe.

To make matters worse, while we were in the air en route to Israel, the tour organizers got an emergency call from the kibbutz at which we were to spend our second two-week period. This call changed our entire schedule. Now, instead of touring around the country during our first two weeks, we were to go straight to the kibbutz. Turns out, it wasn't a very inviting place at all because it was on the verge of bankruptcy; hence, the reason for our change in plans.

Immediately upon our arrival at the kibbutz, I was assigned to the midnight "graveyard" bread factory shift—where my job was simply to squirt butter on bread. No more, no less. I'm sure my efforts were a truly hilarious sight, bearing a marked resemblance to the famous *I Love Lucy* episode in which Lucy and Ethel take jobs in a candy factory and find the conveyor belt too fast for them to handle.[4] As for me, I was to sit on a chair while freshly baked loaves of bread continuously came down a metal chute toward me. I had to pull a lever when a light flashed so that some butter would squirt on top of each loaf. Only after I had squirted the butter would the bread then move to the next part of the process for bagging.

By itself, this task would have been manageable. However, it was complicated by the fact that I couldn't sleep during the day due to the oppressive combination of Israel's incredible heat and the absence of any air conditioning. So, while sitting on my chair at the end of the bread chute in the middle of the night, I would often doze off. As a result, the unbuttered loaves would pile up at the end of the chute and eventually fall to the floor, at which point a loud alarm bell would ring, waking me from my slumber. Frantically, I would run around now in an attempt to retrieve the burning hot loaves from where they had scattered on the floor, hastily placing them back on the chute. All the while, of course, other newly baked loaves continued to rocket towards me in order to get their squirts, too!

Let me assure you, my fellow travelers and I couldn't wait to complete those first two weeks at the kibbutz and commence the touring portion of our trip. You see, in addition to putting its American volunteers to work at mindnumbing jobs, the kibbutz was in such financial hardship that it could afford to feed us only the vegetables grown in its garden—no meat, chicken, or fish. To a group of American teenagers who were used to very comfortable lives and who were already sleep-deprived due to the heat and working ourselves to the point of exhaustion, we felt that being forced to "starve to death," as we saw it, was simply too much.

Then, just when we thought our situation couldn't get any worse, it did. Our group was told that we had to stay a third week because the kibbutz still needed our help. This was the final straw. My fellow travelers and I were up in arms. We decided to go on strike! (In fact, I believe ours was the first-ever strike

---

4   This was the famous "Job Switching" episode, which aired in September 1952.

on an Israeli kibbutz since the founding of the state in 1948.) I happened to be the oldest of the lot, so I was elected to represent the group and make an official complaint.

Much to our surprise, our unhappiness reached important ears, and a politician came down from the Knesset (the Israeli equivalent of the United States Congress) to defuse the situation. I remember sitting across from this man while my fellow protesters sat behind me. Conscious of the fact that they were relying on me to be their voice, I told the politician that we were upset about the change in plans because we had come to see the country—and so far, we hadn't seen anything but the kibbutz at which we were being held, we felt, against our wills.

The Knesset member replied to our grievances, saying that while he truly understood our frustration, this was what being a Jew meant: helping out for the greater good, even when you want to do something else. He then described events throughout history in which Jews had made great sacrifices. He talked about our common ancestry and the Holocaust, and pointed out that while his parents had come to Israel, our grandparents had chosen America. So, he concluded in a burst of inspired oratory, while his family had been fighting for the last thirty-six years to ensure that we would all have a homeland if another Holocaust occurred, we were living lives of luxury in America. Couldn't we just stay and work one more week for him and the State of Israel?

This politician sure knew what he was doing—but I wasn't buying any of it. I felt that we had all been cheated, and I wanted to leave the kibbutz in our dust right away—homeland or no homeland. I was particularly adamant because I had promised the rest of the group that as their representative I would not back down under any circumstances during this negotiation. Our parents had paid for four weeks of travel and two weeks of what we *thought* would be fun at a kibbutz—not three weeks of hell before any travel and fun.

However, what I *didn't* know, because they were seated behind me, was that my younger traveling companions had all bought into the politician's spiel hook, line, and sinker! So, as I continued to argue our case, my own group turned on me and assured this Knesset member that no matter what I said, we would all be happy to do our part for Israel. Now I stood alone with no backing, and there was nothing left to do but to give in. I felt humiliated and betrayed.

I did learn one very important lesson in negotiation that day, however: *Never underestimate your adversary.*

After the negotiation debacle, the trip continued to go downhill for me. Of course, our group stayed the one extra week at the kibbutz doing what seemed like hard labor, and I resented every minute of it. Also, my younger traveling companions with whom I had begun the trip with little in common now really disliked me—and I them. And Murphy's Law (in other words, what can go wrong, *will* go wrong) continued to manifest itself, incredibly, as my Israeli disappointments still weren't over.

Following our seemingly interminable stint in the kibbutz, our group did eventually get a chance to do some sightseeing—and, much to my delight, I met the most beautiful girl I had ever seen. She and I seemed to hit it off despite a significant language barrier, and arranged to meet two nights later at a local amusement park at which I knew our group was scheduled to be. I arrived eagerly anticipating a night of fun (and maybe even some romance) and waited for my alluring date...and waited and waited. I eventually gave up, and admitted to myself that I had been stood up.

Later, in a stroke of incredible luck, I bumped into this elusive girl at the airport just as my group prepared to leave Israel. She and I realized after a few minutes of perplexed conversation that there were actually *two* amusement parks with similar names in the city we'd been in, and she had gone to the other one! *At least*, I told myself as we entered the departure area, *I wasn't rejected outright.*

Needless to say, I couldn't wait to get on that plane and leave Israel. There was still time for one more sting in the tail, however...a bomb threat delayed our departure by two more days!!!

Flying back to the States (finally), I couldn't have felt more disillusioned with Israel. I was frustrated, angry, and firmly committed to never, ever set foot in that country again *or* donate one single cent to the Israeli cause. If you had told me then that two and a half decades later there would be a pillar on Rothschild Boulevard, the main street in Tel Aviv, honoring my contributions to the State of Israel, I would have told you that you were nuts. Yet, as you will discover later in this book, my feelings toward Israel were destined to change in a very big way as I grew and evolved.

> *Above all, this country is our own. Nobody has to get up in the morning and worry what his neighbors think of him. Being a Jew is no problem here.*
>
> —Golda Meir

TIPS FROM TODD:
CHAPTER THREE

- **It pays to know where you come from.** If possible, find out about your family history and heritage. Having a sense of belonging is a basic human need, and knowing that you are part of a larger familial or cultural tradition can be more valuable than you realize. This type of knowledge gives you pride in an ongoing legacy and sparks sincere gratitude for the sacrifices and efforts that you are benefitting from today. What's more, having some knowledge of your more immediate family history can give you important insights into traits, strengths, and weaknesses that you may well exhibit.

- **Find something to believe in.** No matter what religious tradition you identify with (or even if you consider yourself nonreligious but guided by a set of ethics and morals), believing in something larger than yourself grants you perspective, empathy, and sensitivity toward others. Much more than serving your own selfish desires, these traits will go far in bringing you a deep, fulfilling sense of happiness.

- **Worship with your kids.** If you have children, it's important to consider the potential benefits of raising them within a religious tradition, even if (like me) you only go to temple, church, or a mosque a few times a year. Believe it or not, numerous studies have shown that kids who grow up in a faith community tend to engage in fewer risky behaviors and to lead happier, longer, and healthier lives than their peers. That's because religion and spirituality (and the communities associated with them) often serve as moral guides, stress relievers, extended families, and sources of purpose, strength, and support.

- **Don't embrace faith blindly.** While there *are* many benefits to incorporating faith into your life, be sure that you're not checking your judgment, common sense, and other convictions at the worship center door. First of all, make sure that you know and agree with the basic tenets of your faith, and make adjustments if necessary (as, for example, my parents did when they moved from Orthodox to Reform Judaism).

Also, remember that although many religious traditions venerate an all-powerful and infallible Higher Power, that Higher Power's followers are still human, and hence, fallible. Be careful not to confuse personal opinion, social politics, or the bureaucracy of your faith community with that faith itself—and try not to let those things compromise your own spiritual walk.

- **Know who you're dealing with.** Never underestimate your opponent, as I did when I sat across from the much more experienced Israeli Knesset member with whom I was trying to negotiate our release from the Israeli kibbutz. If possible, find out as much as you can regarding the other person's background, experience, and tactics when entering any sort of dispute or negotiation. If you aren't able to do that, consider being as brief and conservative with your responses as possible in order to avoid inadvertently getting in over your head.

Trouble Starts at a Young Age

"It's hard to fight an enemy who has outposts in your head."
—Sally Kempton

Now that you know the basics of my heritage, let's pick my life story back up in the early years. But before we do, I'd like to offer my quick perspective on parenting.

First, let me say that I believe the vast majority of parents do their best to provide a loving, stable environment for the growth of their children. However, the truth is that children present an unending parade of challenges for their parents.

I've wished a million times that there was an instruction manual on how to be a successful parent. I suspect that if such a manual existed, though, it would be so general as to be almost useless. That's because children are individuals—complex individuals with incredible developing brains. There's no one way to raise children.

Parenting is, in many ways, an impossible job. Let's face it: Any situation involving a child can be dealt with at present in only one way—but that leaves an almost infinite range of other choices not acted upon. And in hindsight, some of those choices will seem like they would have been far better alternatives. Most parents are familiar with this type of regret, and they hope that the wrong choices they *have* made won't be too damaging to their kids.

No matter how calmly you try to referee, parenting will eventually produce bizarre behavior, and I'm not talking about the kids.

—Bill Cosby

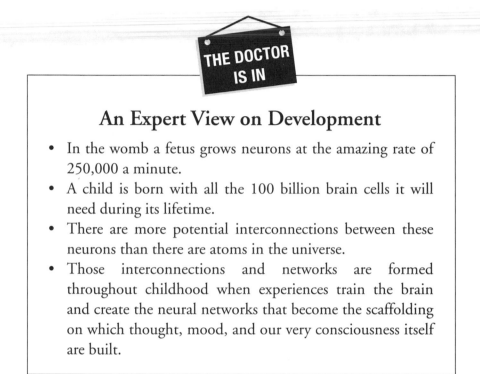

THE DOCTOR IS IN

An Expert View on Development

- In the womb a fetus grows neurons at the amazing rate of 250,000 a minute.
- A child is born with all the 100 billion brain cells it will need during its lifetime.
- There are more potential interconnections between these neurons than there are atoms in the universe.
- Those interconnections and networks are formed throughout childhood when experiences train the brain and create the neural networks that become the scaffolding on which thought, mood, and our very consciousness itself are built.

Every experience a child has—every interaction with a parent, sibling, aunt, uncle, grandparent, teacher, neighbor, friend, or stranger—helps to shape critical thought processes, as well as confidence levels, self-esteem, mood regulation, and even the child's biochemistry itself. Nope, parenting isn't brain surgery—it's way more complicated than that!

Having babies is fun, but babies grow up into people.
—Colonel Potter, *M*A*S*H*

Who are parents, really? They are typically not brain surgeons or rocket scientists, that's for sure. They're ordinary people who almost definitely have never received a single lesson on how to raise their infinitely complex children. They are individuals who are usually the products of their own dysfunctional childhoods, shaped by their own parents' often uninformed and muddled approach to the awesome task of raising a human being.

Is it any surprise, therefore, that so many parents "mess up" their children (at least to hear the children tell it)? Of course not. Is it their fault? Most of the time, I think, the answer is a definite "no." Parents can negatively influence their offspring through their own ignorance and limitations, and very often due to their *best* intentions. (Ever bought your daughter an ice cream cone she didn't need, simply because she pouted?)

If you ask me, our society needs to educate parents more. After all, how to be an effective mom or dad certainly isn't covered in high school—or even college! But we also need to accept that children are highly complex beings who, during the critical years of their development, are incredibly vulnerable to the emotions, motives (which again, are often positive), and even the neuroses of the flawed people around them—all of which can lead to unhappiness later in life.

> *The trouble with learning to parent on the job is that your child is the teacher.*
> —Robert Brault

Looking back now, I see that things could have been managed differently by my own parents. Had they been, I suppose some aspects of my childhood and adult life might have been easier for me. On the other hand, some of my difficulties—and especially my attempts to overcome them—have taught me many of my most valuable lessons, and they've contributed enormously to who I am today. So in the end, I would not change anything from my childhood because I really love who I have become.

A Shadow Appears: Separation Anxiety

I've told you about some issues that arose during my early childhood; but despite sibling rivalries and being born in the middle, I can say without hesitation that my family was close and loving, and that as a toddler and young child, I was very happy. (Remember those photos of me in funny hats?)

As I left that stage of life behind, though—and especially when I started school—I became a little less relaxed and carefree, and I started to experience emotional discomfort and tension. To make a long story short, this anxiety started around the time of first grade, appeared periodically through my elementary and middle school years, got progressively worse through high school, and ended up being positively debilitating for me by the time I finished college.

My earliest memories of anxiety go back to the Saturday nights when my parents would go out to dinner or to the movies. Saturdays were their date nights, helping to keep their relationship strong—a good thing in and of itself. When they went out, my parents would hire a babysitter, typically a local girl, to take care of Roger, Kimberly, and me. And that was the trouble.

You see, as far back as I can remember, being separated from my parents—but especially from my mother—was uncomfortable for me. Saturday nights were the first instances of my being "left behind" by my parents. Regardless of who was babysitting, I found the initial separation period to be very difficult. I'd cling to my mother, cry—sometimes to the point of feeling slightly sick—and become totally overwhelmed with fear. These feelings lasted for ten minutes or so after my parents' departure, at which point I began to calm down.

> *My mom is a neverending song in my heart of comfort, happiness, and being. I may sometimes forget the words but I always remember the tune.*
>
> —Graycie Harmon

I can't tell you why I reacted this way, exactly. I wasn't aware of any traumatic thought occurring to me, like believing that my parents wouldn't come back and that I would never see them again. Nevertheless, I felt really scared as they pulled out of the driveway. And I believe that this feeling wasn't just confined to me. I think my brother and sister also had these feelings to one degree or another—as, I suspect, do many young children.

An Expert View on Separation Anxiety in Children

Many children suffer from some degree of separation anxiety, and might have difficulty leaving their parents to attend school or camp, staying at a friend's house, or being alone. Often, they will "cling" to their parents and have trouble falling asleep.

If your child falls into this category, here are some strategies that may help to relieve some of his or her stress:

- Try not to leave abruptly for a long period of time. Instead, start with small separations and gradually increase your time apart.
- Harness the power of distraction. Try to make sure that your child is engaged in enjoyable activities that will keep him or her occupied (and not focused on your absence) while you are separated.
- Ensure that your child is equipped with coping strategies such as deep breathing to manage anxiety, as well as the possession of phone numbers to call for reassurance.
- Don't be too quick to provide an out. If you do not allow your child to deal with your absence on his or her own (within reason), you could actually be making the situation worse by preventing emotional growth.

Also, be aware that about one in every twenty-five children experiences a major separation anxiety disorder, which may be accompanied by depression, sadness, withdrawal, or fear that a family member might die. If you are worried that your child's separation anxiety is severe, talk to his or her doctor about whether professional help should be sought out.

In retrospect, I see that my mother's presence was a very calming influence for me, and was probably my first major coping strategy for handling my genetically programmed overactive brain. (Remember all of those high achievers in my immediate and extended family?) Without easy access to my mother, my naturally high levels of anxiety kicked in. And as a result, I was more panicked when she wasn't around.

If Saturday nights were bad, the week-long vacations that my parents took a couple of times a year were much worse. Again, my parents would hire a babysitter to look after us kids while they were gone. And my anxiety was present pretty much all week long regardless of who was looking after us. I would sleep poorly and worry more—and when my parents called home to check on us throughout the week, it nearly killed me! Instead of comforting me and calming me down, hearing their voices simply underscored the fact that they weren't with me, and my anxiety levels would spike through the roof once more.

There was one small reprieve from this semi-annual torture—for a year or so we had a live-in au pair from Sweden whom I really liked. She made my parents' vacations a little easier for me because I was very comfortable with her, but I still experienced anxiety while they were gone. Without a doubt, though, one of my worst experiences was with a babysitter who threatened to lock me in my room until my parents came back if I didn't behave better, which (of course!) did nothing to help my anxiety.

> *Mother—that was the bank where we deposited all our hurts and worries.*
>
> —T. DeWitt Talmage

It probably won't surprise you to learn that when school started, my difficulties with separation anxiety came along with me. Even though I enjoyed myself once I got settled into my kindergarten class at Green Acres in Waltham, Massachusetts, getting me *through* the door was a major challenge for my parents. I hated—absolutely hated!—being left at school. I cried and screamed when it was time to get out of the car, regardless of whether it was my mom or dad dropping me off.

I remember feeling very, very scared at the thought of them leaving me, although once again I couldn't tell you what exactly I was scared of. The teachers and administrators always tried to reassure me and calm me down during my meltdowns. I'm sure they advised my parents to simply drop me off and leave as quickly as possible so as not to prolong my agony or theirs. Thankfully, I settled down once I got into the classroom—but there was always a part of me that couldn't wait until my mother came back to pick me up again.

This fear of separation still remained with me when I began first grade at Angier Elementary School in Newton, Massachusetts. I wasn't kicking and screaming as much on the outside, but on the inside I felt unaccountably nervous. Again, once I settled into class, I enjoyed myself—and I especially remember being enthralled by the popular pastime of trading baseball cards.

Baseball Cards from Heaven

As an adult, I look back fondly on my memories of flipping through baseball cards at Angier Elementary School. It was something my friends and I did nearly every day. One incident in particular stands out, and as a kid, I thought it made for the best day of my life (initially, at least). You see, as a result of some dispute or prank, one student threw another boy's entire collection of baseball cards out of one of the school's highest windows, and I was one of the incredibly fortunate kids who happened to be outside at recess at the time.

The second I saw those cards floating toward the ground like some sort of magical precipitation, my competitive instinct kicked into high gear. Through determination and hustle, I ended up with a majority of my unfortunate peer's collection. For the rest of the school day, I was a rich man.

Despite having won my own personal version of the lottery, my elation didn't last long. By that evening, my natural sensitivity had asserted itself, and I couldn't stop thinking about how terrible I'd feel if I had lost all of my cards in one fell swoop. And so, the next day at school, I sought out the cards' rightful owner and returned them.

The Makings of an Overachiever

When I was seven years old, my family moved to the neighboring town: Needham, Massachusetts. As a result, I changed schools once again—this time to the Dwight Elementary School on Highland Avenue in Needham. And the next year I moved on to the Highland Elementary School in the center of town and started third grade. I'm sure all of these new schools didn't help my anxiety either.

At Highland, I remember well that two new worries arrived on the scene to accompany my separation issues: stress over grades and lack of social confidence.

As everyone knows, first grade and most of second grade are as much about getting used to the structure of the classroom and developing basic educational skills as they are about doing a lot of schoolwork. By the time you get to the third and fourth grades, however, there is very definitely a sense of being rated for your academic performance. There are quizzes and grades and report cards based on your actual abilities.

From the moment these tests became part of my life, I worried excessively about my scores on them. I don't recall my parents ever pressuring me too much about grades or telling me that they expected me to get all As. They didn't need to. I put enough pressure on myself—I was terrified that I would be less than perfect. Thus, I would study much longer than was necessary for each exam, and I would complete assignments the day they were given to me even if they didn't need to be turned in for another few weeks. If I had anything unresolved or hanging over my head, I just couldn't relax completely. I was definitely turning into a perfectionist and my own worst critic—before I was even out of the fourth grade!

The Peanut Gallery on Perfection

I am far from being the only person who has dealt with perfectionism. Here, see what others have to say about it:

Striving for excellence motivates you; striving for perfection is demoralizing.

—Harriet Braiker

The thing that is really hard, and really amazing, is giving up on being perfect and beginning the work of becoming yourself.

—Anna Quindlen

Perfectionism is slow death.

—Hugh Prather

No one is perfect... that's why pencils have erasers.

—Anonymous

Gold cannot be pure, and people cannot be perfect.

—Chinese Proverb

Once you accept the fact that you're not perfect, then you develop some confidence.

—Rosalynn Carter

The closest to perfection a person ever comes is when he fills out a job application form.

—Stanley J. Randall

Try as hard as we may for perfection, the net result of our labors is an amazing variety of imperfectness. We are surprised at our own versatility in being able to fail in so many different ways.

—Samuel McChord Crothers

An Expert View on Perfectionism

Perfectionism is a coping strategy designed to calm the brain by replacing anxiety with good feelings that come from achieving success and from pleasing people whose opinions are most greatly valued. However, perfectionism backfires in a majority of cases. Rather than alleviating anxiety, it simply increases feelings of stress, because it causes sufferers to set standards that are too high, thus paving the way for failure—and the self-deprecation that goes along with it.

If you are a parent and notice perfectionist tendencies in your children, it's important that you try to minimize these unhealthy behaviors (while not devaluing achievement and success). Here are some suggestions for getting your kids to lighten up:

- Don't overemphasize the end over the means. Many parents inadvertently feed their children's perfectionist tendencies by praising the A on the report card, for example, rather than the months of work that earned it. This particular behavior can cause a child to believe that any grade below an A is unacceptable.
- Model adaptability in your own life. Make sure your kids know that it's okay to change course if Plan A is compromised.
- Set reasonable time limits on tasks such as homework so that your kids don't spend hours overpreparing.
- Focus on the positives. Point out to your budding perfectionist all the things he or she has done well instead of focusing on what he or she hasn't.

Outside of the "In" Crowd

Being a kid who expects constant perfection from himself is bad enough, but it wasn't going to be my only obstacle during my school years. I also became anxious about my social standing at school, especially as I began to notice girls. Let's face it—kids can be mean, and at times I was the target of their teasing. Add another two items to the worry list: being bullied and being seen as weak.

Have you ever noticed that no matter how old you get, certain memories stick with you and remain as clear as the day they happened? Well, for me, one particular incident that really helped to fuel my social insecurity stands out in this manner.

Struck Down by Love…Literally!

I was seven or eight years old at the time, and I was riding home from school on the bus. I had known Betsy Brown for about a year, and we lived in the same neighborhood. Betsy was cute with long brown hair, a tanned complexion, and a very athletic build—and I wasn't blind. Truth be told, I had a big crush on her.

Little by little, I summoned up the courage to tell Betsy that I liked her. (By the way, that *never* ceases to be a big deal no matter how old the man or woman doing the declaring happens to be!) The details of my confession are a blur—I might have even tried to hold Betsy's hand. This was one of those milestone moments: my first advance to a member of the opposite sex, my first time putting it all on the line with a girl. So, how did the object of my affections respond? Did she respond with a coy smile, endearing blush, or even reach out to hold my hand? Not exactly. Once we got off the bus, she punched me very hard—several times!

I was stunned and hurt—literally. This was, of course, in complete contrast to the rest of the kids at the bus stop, who found the whole incident highly amusing and were laughing their heads off at me. I was totally humiliated, and I didn't know what to do. I knew I *couldn't* punch Betsy back, even though there was a part of me that felt I needed to. I was embarrassed and ashamed, and I just wanted to hide.

When I got home, I told my parents what happened. They comforted me and agreed that there really was nothing I could do about the situation—which didn't make me feel any better. The whole incident simply caused me to become even more self-conscious and weak. It further drove home the fact that bad things could happen to me whenever I was not at home, and it also rocked my self-confidence with girls.

Athleticism: A Brief Reprieve

The saving grace for me in this ever-increasing tide of uncertainty and anxiety was my sports ability. I played tennis, baseball, and soccer growing up, and I was good at all of them. I especially excelled at tennis when, at the tender age of six, I often wowed spectators with my skill. And in baseball, I was one of only three ten-year-olds in Needham chosen to move up and play with the eleven- and twelve-year-olds.

Strong-Arm Neighborly Relations

In at least two instances, my high degree of athleticism actually caused quite a stir! As a gesture of friendliness on the day my family moved to Needham (I was seven years old at the time), my next door neighbor Mark Abrams asked me if I would like to throw a baseball with him. I was happy to make a new friend, but there turned out to be one problem: Mark had a plastic mitt. I threw the ball with my normal strong velocity and acute degree of accuracy, and on the very first throw I broke Mark's mitt and his nose to boot!

Talk about "oops!" moments! Needless to say, it wasn't the most comfortable introduction to the neighborhood. And not so surprisingly, things were a bit tense with the Abrams family forever after that. (However, no one on the block could deny that I was a force to be reckoned with in pick-up baseball games.)

My run-ins with the Abrams weren't quite finished, though. Several years later, Mark's younger brother, Dennis, pushed my sister, Kimberly, to the ground. I responded by doing something very out of character for me: I punched Dennis as hard as I could in the stomach. Well, I had to protect my little sister, didn't I? And boy, did it feel good! (For me, anyway…Mr. Abrams was not very pleased at all!)

Even with baseball, however, my nervous, fearful nature did me in. After being hit by just one hard fastball in the back while batting in eighth grade, I quit forever the sport that I loved most.

Thankfully, I never abandoned athletics altogether. And due largely to my love of sports, my whole world changed in the summers. Hands down, the place that I enjoyed the most during my childhood was Rivers Day Camp in Weston, Massachusetts. I started attending Rivers when I was just five, and was a regular camper there for many summers—eventually even joining the ranks of the counselors. We played sports all day long, so I really felt in my element. Also, the camp was co-ed, and the counselors were great. It was the perfect spot for me; in fact, I felt like a totally different person when I was there. Once away from the pressures of school, I could be my true self again—happy, more carefree, and easy-going.

An Expert View on Exercise and the Brain

Exercise doesn't just improve your cardiovascular health and tone your muscles—it's also a very powerful medicine for your brain. Research has consistently shown that exercise elevates mood *and* alleviates the symptoms of anxiety and depression. Furthermore:

- When you consistently exercise, the reward system in your brain is activated. This means that once your brain assigns a positive value to exercise, it will modify your desires to include an increased craving for physical activity.
- Exercise increases successful neurogenesis, or the creation of new brain cells that happens throughout your lifespan.
- Exercise encourages good oxygen flow into the brain, which promotes effective information processing.

A Rivers Romance

As I got older, summers at Rivers were also accompanied by an unexpected bonus: In the sun and with less stress, my teenage acne vanished, making me more self-confident—especially with the opposite sex. Looking back, therefore, it should be no surprise that as a teenager I had my first successful romantic encounter at Rivers Day Camp, with a girl named Ally Hansen. Ally was blonde, blue-eyed, and very, very pretty. Each summer at Rivers, there were two optional overnights—and during one of these summer overnights, Ally and I snuck out to the tennis courts, held hands, and kissed. Ooh-la-la! Now I could finally begin to replace my memory of Betsy Brown's punch with a much more pleasant reminiscence.

A Summer Sleep-Away Setback

If you're like most parents, when your child shows a liking for a certain hobby or activity that you approve of, you'll probably look for related opportunities he or she can get involved in. My parents were no different. I had enjoyed my initial summers at Rivers Day Camp so much that when I was ten, my parents decided to send me to Camp Manitou, a sleep-away sports camp in Maine, for four weeks. I went with my brother, Roger, who had already been going there for several years.

Up to this point, I had successfully avoided all sleepovers except for one action-filled night each year at Rivers. And as the date of my departure to Camp Manitou drew near, I felt my apprehension about going to a sleepover camp growing—after all, I had an established track record with separation anxiety. I became very concerned about whether I'd be able to actually get any sleep there at all. To combat my fears, my family focused on the fact that Manitou was a sports camp. Considering my love of athletics, they figured, I'd soon be in my element.

Mom and Dad were right…to an extent. It was true: Once I hit the sports fields, I did get distracted and absorbed in the games. And my fellow campers did recognize and appreciate my sporting ability, so I didn't have to worry too much about being bullied. But the truth is that from the moment I got on the bus to leave for the camp, I was totally overwhelmed with homesickness. To be honest, I'm surprised I even lasted seventy-two hours in Maine.

The first night away from my own bed, I was miserable. In fact, I think I barely slept at all. By the third day, I was feeling totally panicked and sick. I sought out my brother, hoping for some comfort or commiseration, but he didn't really understand what I was going through–nor did he know how to deal with it. The panic rose rapidly. I couldn't control my anxious thoughts, and my heart was pounding so hard I thought I was going to die. It was unquestionably the worst I had ever felt emotionally thus far in my life.

Desperate, I remember thinking that I must do something dramatic enough to get me sent home. After seventy-two hours away, I was ready to face any amount of punishment and consequences if they occurred in a place where I was comfortable. After a bit of frenetic thought, I settled on trying to drink the paint in the art shop, which is where I was at the moment I "snapped."

Fortunately, one of the counselors found me in this totally desperate state of mind before I could do myself any real harm. Generally, it was the camp's approach to talk to the homesick campers and encourage them to stick it out at all costs. After my desperate attempt at self-poisoning, though, the owners of the camp decided that it was best to call my parents so that they could come and take me home. Thank God!

An Expert View on High Anxiety Levels and Panic Attacks

When anxiety or panic attacks are triggered, individuals have little to no control over their initial severity (though coping mechanisms can be learned). From a medical perspective, here is what goes on physically during incidents of high anxiety:

- Brain activity increases (this shows up on an EEG scan as increased beta wave activity), which causes the mind (in other words, your thoughts) to speed up.
- A structure called the hypothalamus (which controls fundamental mechanisms like appetite and emotion) signals to the pituitary gland, which in turn signals to the adrenal gland to secrete stress hormones, particularly cortisol, growth hormone, and the neurotransmitter norepinephrine.
- Blood is moved from the organs to the muscles as the brain prepares for fight or flight.
- Muscle tension increases.
- The mind becomes hypervigilant or superaware.
- The body experiences an increased demand for more sugar in order to keep up energy production.

Coping mechanisms for anxiety and panic attacks include deep breathing exercises, visualization techniques, and relaxation exercises, to name a few. However, since everyone is different, you should consult your doctor to determine which strategies are best for you, as well as to receive proper instruction on their use.

Obviously, the experience at Camp Manitou set me back badly. It was a stunning and disheartening example of how much anxiety I was capable of feeling, and of how helpless I was in the face of these overpowering feelings. Believe it or not, that horrifying seventy-two-hour period haunts me even to this day. At age forty-five, when I'm about to go overseas alone on an extended trip, I have to push myself through a period of anxiety, usually while packing. Back then, my ignominious retreat reinforced all of my insecurities and self-doubts.

It would be another three years before I would even attempt another sleepover outside of my house—this time, at the home of Karl Ravech, now a well-known ESPN sportscaster, and at the time my best friend. I lasted only until about 1:00 a.m., at which time Karl's mother had to drive me home. At thirteen, this too brought me no end of personal embarrassment and humiliation.

Junior High Purgatory

As I moved out of elementary school and began seventh grade at Newman Junior High School, my perfectionism and need for straight As on my report card only increased in intensity. I would sweat over the subjects I was really good at, like math and social studies, and sweat even more over the subjects that didn't come so naturally to me, like Spanish and English.

> *When you aim for perfection, you discover it's a moving target.*
>
> —George Fisher

I struggled socially as well, never really feeling at ease with the other kids and always concerned about being bullied, threatened, and embarrassed. At nights I'd often have difficulty falling asleep and would toss and turn for what seemed like hours, worrying about most everything—grades, girls, and bullies, to name a few. When I told my father about my sleep difficulties, he tried to reassure me by saying that as long as my eyes were closed that was as good as actually falling asleep. Dad might have actually believed what he was telling me, or more than likely he was just saying what he thought would help me relax. Unfortunately, his reassurances didn't have much of an effect.

An Expert View on Sleep

Despite what you may have assumed, all sleep is NOT created equal (and just closing your eyes doesn't count as "sleep" at all). In fact, there are five (normally sequential) stages of sleep that your body and brain go through when uninterrupted, with a complete cycle usually lasting 90-110 minutes. Most people experience three to five cycles a night. The stages are:

Stage 1: Light sleep. You're easily awakened, and your muscles might jerk suddenly.

Stage 2: Your brain waves begin to slow down, and you are less aware of your external environment. About 50 percent of sleep is spent in this stage for adults.

Stage 3: Deep sleep begins. It's usually difficult to wake someone in Stage 3, and the person who is awoken might feel groggy or disoriented. Night terrors, sleepwalking, and talking in one's sleep usually occur in this stage as well.

Stage 4: Deep sleep continues. Both Stage 3 and Stage 4 sleep are essential for feeling refreshed and rested after waking.

REM: Rapid Eye Movement (REM) sleep is the fifth stage, during which most of your remembered dreams occur. It typically starts 70 to 90 minutes after sleep begins. Interestingly, while your eyes move, your arm and leg muscles are temporarily paralyzed—probably to prevent you from acting out the scenarios in your dreams. The optimal time to wake up is during this stage—you will actually feel more rested after waking up in REM than in a deeper sleep—even if the overall time spent sleeping is less. Most adults spend 20-25 percent of sleep in the REM stage.

Your sleep cycle can be compromised by a number of outside factors, including a sleeping space that is too light or too warm, eating directly before bed, being woken in the night, smoking, drinking…and even having cold feet! This is important because poor-quality sleep usually leads to inadequate time spent in deep sleep (Stages 3 and 4). These stages are the most critical, healing parts of sleep for children as well as adults. Without deep sleep, you are deprived of energy and don't function anywhere near your best. Hormones and moods are also thrown out of balance without deep sleep, which contributes to feelings of stress and depression.

A Cautionary Word for Parents

They say that everything happens for a reason…and I'm inclined to believe that's true. My difficult time growing up has really sensitized me to be on the lookout for kids who are not fitting in and/or seem unhappy. I am also very sensitive to teenagers putting far too much pressure on themselves in school like I did. I try to encourage my friends and other adults I meet to keep a close eye on their own kids so that they can identify these devastating states of mind.

It is perhaps a parent's most important obligation to his or her children to ensure that the normal stresses and anxieties that are part of the growing-up years don't become too much to handle. Furthermore, parents must realize that each child is different, and that a significant number of kids—although thankfully still a minority—inherit the propensity for brutally high levels of anxiety and/or depression like I did.

An Expert View on Indentifying High Anxiety Levels in Children

It is typical for parents to question whether a child's stress levels are "normal" and manageable, or whether they are indicative of a problem that needs to be addressed by a professional. Below is a list of symptoms that, displayed consistently, may point to unhealthy, high levels of anxiety:

- Physical symptoms: Nausea, stomachache, headache
- Behaviors: Poor sleep, irritability, difficulty socializing, avoidance, withdrawal
- Psychological: Worry, rumination

In general, any negative change in a child's behavior or personality is a huge warning sign that things aren't right. If you notice such a change, see a professional immediately.

Many, many kids today face problems similar to the ones I did, including feeling uncomfortable with the opposite sex, facing bullies, anxiety over their grades, etc. And because they aren't sure how to handle these issues, they silently suffer from stress and depression. Often, they are too ashamed to admit to and/or talk about their problems, especially if they think they aren't normal—and are "screwed up"—in comparison to their peers. It's equally troubling if most of a young person's friends feel similarly to him. If that's the case, the child or teen may think just the opposite: that his brutal worries and fears—the ones keeping him up at night—and his depressive moods are normal and thus not fixable.

Childhood is the time when the foundations of thinking and feeling are set, so it is absolutely crucial that these basics be set in a constructive and healthy way. Believe me, changing them later—while possible—is so much more difficult.

You cannot protect your children from the ups and downs of life, but you can—no, you must—show them how to deal with these shifts effectively. And if you need to get a professional involved to do this, so be it. Healthy outlooks and good coping mechanisms will be the greatest gifts you can give your children. Don't let them suffer in silence. Don't let them suffer, period. And, please, please, please don't wait until their minds have been shaped by years of low self-esteem, high stress, or terrible depression. They might never recover.

Anxiety and Depression Stats

- Anxiety disorders are among the most common mental, emotional, and behavioral problems to occur during childhood and adolescence.
- About thirteen of every one hundred children and adolescents ages nine to seventeen experience some kind of anxiety disorder; girls are affected more than boys.[*]
- About half of children and adolescents with anxiety disorders have a second anxiety disorder or other mental or behavioral disorder, such as depression.
- In addition, anxiety disorders may coexist with physical health conditions requiring treatment.

* U.S. Department of Health and Human Services—Substance Abuse and Mental Health Services Administration

As I approached my high school years, I came to accept that being a perfectionist, running on adrenaline, and having difficulty sleeping due to incessant worrying were simply parts of my life that I would have to endure. I did not think that these difficulties could possibly get any worse. Boy, was I in for a surprise...

TIPS FROM TODD:
CHAPTER FOUR

Essential lessons to learn:

...for parents:

- **Strive for conscious parenting.** If you're a parent, you'll make mistakes no doubt about it. That's because there's no foolproof way to raise a "good kid." To create a best-odds scenario for yourself, though, educate yourself as much as possible. Read parenting books. Write down specifically how you do and don't want to treat your children and what values you want them to grow up with. Observe the methods and tactics of other parents you admire and ask them for help and support. And above all, make sure that unconditional love is your primary motivator!

- **Realize that not all kids can "get over" separation anxiety.** While it's somewhat distressing for all young children when their parents leave, one in twenty-five suffers from an identifiable anxiety disorder. If your child is consistently and strongly distressed at leaving you, consider asking a professional for advice.

- **Don't let low self-esteem take root.** Children begin to develop their self-images very early in life. Bullying, social exclusion, favoritism at home, and excessive criticism (for starters!) can have long-lasting impacts on how a child sees himself as he grows up, as well as on his attitude, behavior, and choices. While parents can't always control what happens outside the home, they *can* ensure that their own parenting styles are affirming and encouraging.

...for everyone:

- **Take a dose of "muscle medicine."** Aside from the obvious physical benefits of exercise, it also works wonders for your mental state! Physical activity increases self-confidence and also releases endorphins, which act as a natural mood-booster. In fact, exercise has been proven to alleviate the symptoms of depression and anxiety!

    The benefits of exercising don't stop there, though. If you exercise, your children and thus their children will probably also make exercise a lifelong habit. This is because your children are much more likely to do what you do—not what you say.

- **Aim for your best—not for perfection.** It's important to understand that there's a crucial difference between doing your best and being perfect. Namely, the first is actually an achievable goal. It's healthy *and* helpful to put forth your best efforts, as long as you are able to come to terms with the fact that you (along with everyone else on earth) are fallible, and will thus make mistakes from time to time. If you expect perfection from yourself, you'll perpetually be disappointed—and your outlook, self-esteem, and (ironically) performance will take a hit.

  And remember, as with exercise, your children are much more likely to be plagued by perfectionism if you are. By expecting too much of yourself, you'll not only be driving yourself crazy—you'll also be teaching your kids how to live a life full of stress and unhappiness as well.

The Terrible Teens

"Today is the tomorrow we worried about yesterday."
—Author unknown

High school. Some of us loved it. Some of us hated it. And all of us remember it well, whether we were jocks, bookworms, prom queens, teachers' pets, or something else entirely. Personally, I enjoyed high school. I had good friends and good teachers, and I liked quite a few of the subjects I studied. Not surprisingly, though, my anxiety level was often high enough to impact just about every aspect of my day—schoolwork, sports, and social life.

Now, I don't want to imply that I was consumed with worry or dealing with low-grade fear all day, every day—far from it. But I *was* anxious a lot of the time. Most often my anxiety seemed to be lurking right under the surface, and I knew that it could rear its ugly head at any moment…for a variety of reasons.

High School: the mouse race to prepare you for the rat race.

—Anonymous

Bigger School...Bigger Bullies

For ninth grade, I applied to Roxbury Latin, an elite all-boys Boston private school that just happened to be an Ivy League feeder. (Remember, high expectations were a cornerstone of my makeup!) Roxbury Latin boasted smaller classes, highly qualified instructors, and motivated kids.

That environment might have provided me with less to worry about socially, although I suspect the academic competition would have been fierce. However, the purported benefits of Roxbury Latin were rendered moot when I wasn't accepted, so I adjusted to the fact that I would be going to public high school.

To my teenage brain, going to Needham High School definitely had its benefits: more girls (as opposed to zero at Roxbury Latin) and less academic competition. However, it also had disadvantages: namely, more bullies. I was, therefore, understandably apprehensive when I started the tenth grade. (In Needham, junior high school included grades seven through nine, and high school was comprised of grades ten through twelve.) There were about 500 students in each grade at Needham High, and I intuitively felt that some of them were going to give me trouble. I wasn't wrong.

Adolescence is...the cruelest place on Earth. It can really be heartless.

—Tori Amos

It wasn't long before two kids, Jim Neal and Donny Wallach, were on my case. I had known these two since junior high, when our soccer rivalry had culminated in Jim felling me with a nasty slide tackle just before his cross-town team beat mine 3-2. This bad blood now continued, unfortunately for me, in tenth grade.

Jim was tall and rough while his sidekick, Donny, was short and mean—a classic bully combo. It didn't take long before they were giving me all sorts of trouble in high school. Whenever our paths crossed, they didn't waste a moment in trying to embarrass me, either by verbal taunts or physical abuse.

One of their favorite stunts was to sneak up behind me and dump my books all over the ground. And as was the case with the Betsy Brown punching incident years earlier, I simply didn't know how to respond to this public humiliation. Face flaming, I'd pick up my books and walk away embarrassed, all the while worrying that the same thing might happen again tomorrow. Fortunately, I was able to mend fences with Jim and Donny by the eleventh grade, and their bullying stopped.

An Expert View on Bullying

Yes, sticks and stones can break your bones…but words can hurt you just as much, if not more. Whether a child is experiencing physical or emotional bullying (or both), permanent damage can be done, especially as young people approach their pre-teen and teen years. Specifically, children can experience:

- Increased anxiety levels and constant worrying related to bullying. Such chronic preoccupation can cause academic performance to suffer.
- Poor self-esteem due to feeling weak or unable to cope.
- Social anxiety due to feeling like an outcast.
- Depression, possibly leading to suicidal thoughts.

Unfortunately, bullying that starts with one instigator is likely to spread as others "pile on" in an onslaught of merciless teasing. In such cases the negative effects will be magnified. Therefore, it is imperative that bullying be dealt with as soon as possible.

If your child is being tormented by peers, share the following strategies with him or her:

- If possible, avoid situations where you might run into bullies.
- Get a friend to accompany you if you feel that bullies might be waiting in a certain situation.
- Stand tall and be brave—fake this if you have to. Bullies feed off of anxiety and target individuals who don't resist them, so showing your fear will only encourage more tormenting.

> • Tell an adult about any incident that makes you feel uncomfortable—and certainly about ongoing bullying.
>
> If at any point it becomes clear that your child is not equipped to handle a bullying situation, don't be afraid to step in. As a parent, it is well within your rights to approach teachers, administrators, and other authority figures if your child's well-being or safety is at stake. And don't be afraid to be persistent, because your child will never have a better advocate than you.

My two other high school nemeses, Jeff Israel and Karen Clark, were not so easily deterred. They plagued me throughout all of my high school years, and their abuse had a much deeper impact on my psyche. Jeff and I had actually been friends when we were younger, but by the time we hit high school, I believe he saw me as his competition because we both hung out with the same Jewish crowd and fit the same academic profile. Jeff never lost an opportunity to make sarcastic comments about me. Much worse than that, though, he had become good friends with Karen, the one person whom I dreaded the most in high school.

Boys are naturally competitive and rag on each other, so I could understand (somewhat) being mocked by Jeff and bullied by Jim and Donny. But I just couldn't figure out why Karen, to whom I had done absolutely nothing, decided it was her singular mission in life to make me miserable—or so it seemed to me.

If Karen could find me at a social function, she would cheerfully call me a loser in front of as many people as possible. Sometimes, she'd even dump my drink onto the floor for good measure. Again, I simply didn't know how to respond to such viciousness—especially because it was coming from a girl, and because I had no idea why she was treating me this way.

In the end, I wasn't capable of doing much except trying to avoid Karen when I could, and when I couldn't, I tried to ignore her and act as though her comments didn't hurt—but, of course, they did hurt.

A Belated "Why"

When I decided to write this book, I called Karen Clark and asked her why she had treated me so badly back in high school. Rather than giving a concrete reason to which I'd been oblivious as a teen, she replied that she was now extremely embarrassed and ashamed of how mean she had been to me and to two other students. She apologized to me and admitted that there was no particular reason why she had chosen to focus on me or her other victims. I suppose that after noticing that we wouldn't fight back, she simply pursued her advantage.

This is an important lesson for all of us—especially our children. How people treat you is often more closely related to what is going on in their own heads at that time than it is to you or your behavior—but your behavior *can* impact whether or not that treatment continues.

Bullying: An Increasingly Dangerous Problem

Although back then I thought I was alone in the depths of my misery, I now realize that I am one of many adults and children who have experienced bullying and felt its horrible consequences.

Stats on Bullying

It is estimated that between 15 and 25 percent of children experience bullying, and that on any given day in the U.S. more than 160,000 children skip school to avoid being bullied.

Bullying is still a widespread problem in the United States, and if anything, it appears to be growing worse. At the time of this writing, a tragedy occurred in my own relative backyard: Phoebe Prince, a fifteen-year-old high schooler whose family had just moved to the Boston suburb of South Hadley from Ireland, committed suicide after being tormented by bullies. Like me, she was also a victim of hurtful name-calling and having her books knocked out of her hands...but much more seriously, her tormenters are also accused of stalking her, assaulting her, scribbling her face out of photographs, insulting her on social networking sites, and sending her threatening text messages.

THE DOCTOR IS IN

An Expert View on Depression-Related Suicide

Unfortunately, feelings of depression can sometimes prompt suicidal ideas in individuals who are suffering. That said, there is a large and pivotal difference between having the *thought* that you'd be better off dead, and actually planning how to carry out this plan and/or trying to execute it. In fact, many people question at some point in their lives whether they'd be better off dead; it's the planning of a suicidal gesture that is much more serious. However, no type of suicidal thoughts should be dismissed.

In terms of children and young people specifically, approach any instance of detachment, quiet, or loss of motivation to an uncharacteristic degree by investigating its source. Remember, suicide is typically not about sadness so much as shame, humiliation, and helplessness. If you suspect this level of depression in your child for *any* reason, you must take him or her to a psychiatrist or psychologist immediately.

Clearly, the bullying trend has escalated far beyond stealing lunch money and even dumping a peer's drink onto the ground—and thus its consequences can be far worse than any I experienced. In my youth I could at least come home at the end of the school day and escape any tormenting and bullying that might have occurred. But now, because of cell phones, the Internet, and social networking sites, there is simply no escape from nasty comments, vicious attacks, and even threats that kids might be facing. What's even worse, mean comments and young people's very social standings can now be displayed in a public forum for the whole world to see, any time of the day or night, every day of the year. Technology truly has made bullying infinitely more destructive and far-reaching, and sadly, its negative—and even deadly—effects continue to make headlines.

I can only hope that legislative bodies do take action, and that teachers, students, counselors, and parents all become more educated about the potentially destructive effects of bullying. Somehow, we must make bullying as unacceptable within teenage society as driving drunk or committing any other crime. Yes, teenagers may still torment their "weaker" peers, but these bullies must know that they will face major consequences when their actions come to light.

Also, it's easy to assume that while bullying is uncomfortable and even dangerous while it's happening, the wounds it inflicts will fade in time. But the fact is, that's simply not true. Research shows that "the bullying experience stays with many victims into young adulthood, middle age, and even retirement, shaping their decisions and hindering them in nearly every aspect of life: education and career choices; social interactions and emotional well-being; even attitudes about having children."[5]

Essentially, fear, social anxiety, shame, low self-esteem, and anger at oneself can rear their heads throughout adulthood, often at crucial moments, causing individuals who were once bullied to stick with "easy," "safe," or "defensive" choices instead of those that might prove most beneficial. Being bullied as a child or teen often irrevocably shapes one's personality and/or self-image, and these are emotional scars that do *not* fade with time. In fact, there is a definite link between childhood bullying and adult depression, because victims have been deprived of "considerable joy and satisfaction with their lives."[6]

I cannot state strongly enough the vital importance of combating bullying whenever and wherever it happens. By preventing a young person from being bullied, we may be freeing him or her from a lifetime of feeling inadequate and being haunted by horrible memories.

---

5   Russell, Jenna. "A World of Misery Left by Bullying." *The Boston Globe. Boston.com.* 28 November 2010. <http://www.boston.com/news/local/massachusetts/articles/2010/11/28/a_ world_of_misery_left_by_bullying/> (30 November 2010).
6   Russell, Jenna. "A World of Misery Left by Bullying." *The Boston Globe. Boston.com.* 28 November 2010. <http://www.boston.com/news/local/massachusetts/articles/2010/11/28/a_ world_of_misery_left_by_bullying/> (30 November 2010).

The Perfectionism Noose Tightens

The presence of people like Karen and Jeff in Needham often made me feel more comfortable conducting my social life in other towns. As I got older and more mobile, I hung out frequently in the next town over, Wellesley, Massachusetts. I was relieved to have friends and acquaintances there who accepted me and enjoyed my company, but I still felt the strain of not being comfortable in my own town. And because my goal was to avoid negative attention, I grew into an accommodating young man whose aim was simply to blend in—and as I'll discuss now and later, that desire to fit the accepted mold sometimes got me into a bit of trouble.

I remember one instance in particular of going along with the crowd. For a time, I hung out with a young man named Jason Tims. Jason was a star soccer and hockey player for Wellesley, and I hoped that some of his popularity would rub off on me. That is, until I found myself running through the woods with him as the Wellesley police chased us due to some disturbance he and his friends had created in town earlier! After that, I sought out other friends.

In addition to the shift in my social life, another result of being harassed was a ramp-up in my efforts toward being the perfect student. Because bullies like Jeff and Karen were so derogatory to me, I wanted to outperform them academically. I suppose I felt that this would make me "better" than them on some level. As a result, I became increasingly hard on myself, wanting to earn marks higher than As—if that were even possible.

It's true—the taunts and the bullying did really have this unexpected upside (at least, I saw it as that at the time). My anger at these people who were hurting me fed my desire to be a lot more successful than all of them. Looking back, I'm still proud of the fact that I did well at my studies, but I wish my conscious motivation had come from a more positive quarter.

As high school progressed, I studied increasingly long hours, and worries about my grades often consumed me. I would routinely beat myself up if I lost points on an assignment or test, and even if I was in wonderful standing in any given class, I'd convince myself that I was about to blow it all because I didn't understand the material well enough. I truly enjoyed learning, but I denied myself much of the pleasure because I focused so unhealthily on the marks I earned.

To make matters worse, I gradually quit all of the sports that had been such a positive part of my life until then. Simply put, on top of the brutal school pressure I was feeling, I couldn't handle any of the high school sports teams' demanding requirements as well. For one thing, there simply wasn't enough time in the day for me to attend practices and games into the evenings, only to return home to face hours upon hours of schoolwork and studying.

Looking back, I can only shake my head at my high school self, because I realize that I gave up one of my most important coping strategies in high school: exercise. It's no surprise that my anxiety shot through the roof after I stopped hitting the sports fields regularly. In fact, school now caused me to become so tense that simply coming home at the end of the school day was a huge relief.

> *It is exercise alone that supports the spirits, and keeps the mind in vigor.*
>
> —Marcus Tullius Cicero

Although she probably didn't realize it at the time, my mother was a life-saver. As soon as I got home, Mom would make me a snack, typically a grilled cheese sandwich, and ask me about my day. She listened and gave me support and feedback, but overall she really didn't know how much stress I was feeling because I didn't share all of the details with her. I suppose on some level I was ashamed by how much I was struggling. Just having Mom there at the end of the day, however, was incredibly reassuring and helpful to me. Thank you, Mom!

After I had my snack, my mother and I would settle down in the family room and watch an episode of *Guiding Light*, Mom's soap opera of choice. This TV show became my escape—my tranquilizer, if you will—during those years. Suitably relaxed now, I would set about doing my homework.

An Expert View on Coping Strategies for Children

As you have just read, Todd found solace from his anxiety by watching *Guiding Light* with his mother. Positive coping strategies like this can be incredibly valuable because they provide a much-needed reprieve from worries and stresses. If your child is fixating on his or her anxiety, introduce one or more of the following coping strategies:

- Physical activity. Its mental, emotional, and physical benefits are well documented. You might consider fun activities like karate, gymnastics, or any team sport that isn't too intense.
- Other fun, absorbing activities. Reading books, drawing, or watching a favorite movie can capture a worried child's attention.
- Positive interaction with peers or mentors. Encourage your child to invite friends over or enroll him or her in an enriching, confidence-building activity like Boy or Girl Scouts, for example.

Two caveats: First, all effective coping strategies place their emphasis mainly on fun, not on achievement. Competitive sports or playing an instrument can be mixed blessings, because budding perfectionists will carry their high self-expectations to these activities, too, making them counter-productive.

Secondly, guard against letting any coping mechanism become your child's primary method of managing anxiety, because it will become compulsive and potentially destructive in its own right.

If I could share with my mom some of the details of my school life, I certainly did not want to share them with my dad. First, he was working very hard at the time building the family auto parts business, so I didn't want to burden him with my own issues. Secondly, I was just too ashamed to tell him about my tormentors, my inability to deal with them, and the helplessness—and anger—they induced within me.

I do want to point out that while I never gave my dad the opportunity to help me deal with the bullying I experienced, he was very supportive of me in other ways. He always encouraged me, often even assisting me with my studies, and eagerly followed my progress. He and my mother would shuttle me to and from my sporting events (while they lasted), as well as cheer me on while I was playing. Occasionally, my dad and I would also go to the movies or go bowling. I don't think I ever talked to him much about girls, though—and that, perhaps, was another error, since the female half of the population caused me quite a bit of worry as well!

Navigating the Strange and Scary World of Dating

Girls were, in fact, another reason for me to feel insecure and inadequate. If Karen and Company's taunts were unique to me, Nature's trick on adolescents—especially boys—wasn't. And what exactly was that trick? Well, while Nature provides boys with a surge of testosterone that would power a decent-sized bull, it provides absolutely no mechanism for dealing with the fallout.

Essentially, this means that as teenage boys are discovering powerful sexual feelings, they have virtually no experience and even less skill in dealing with the opposite sex. Of course, there are always a few guys who seem to have been born with the natural confidence and ability to successfully court the young ladies, but for the rest of us the learning process is about as pleasurable as a trip to the dentist—sans Novocain. Simply put, adolescence is uncomfortable, anxiety-provoking, and potentially humiliating—especially for someone with low self-esteem.

It probably doesn't come as a shock to hear that I was awful with girls at this age; in fact, I saw myself as a complete and utter failure in the romance department. In retrospect, I realize now that I was probably no worse off than your average teenage perfectionist with low self-esteem and major anxiety (of which there are, I am sure, quite a few). I wanted to date girls, of course, but I never knew what to say or how to act around them. And even when God threw me a bone, my instincts for handling the situation weren't exactly up to par, as the following story illustrates.

Cotillion Crash and Burn

We've all had experiences that feel like they should have happened on a sitcom. Years down the road, we can see the humor in them…but as they were happening, we'd have given our life savings to just disappear. For me, one such moment occurred—not surprisingly—in the dating arena.

When I was in tenth grade, an absolutely gorgeous girl, Jill Kaplan, asked me to escort her to her junior-year cotillion in Framingham. Jill and I had met through our local Jewish youth groups. I was thrilled, and frankly very surprised, that Jill thought enough of me to ask me to be her date for her cotillion.

Jill, who by this point had her driver's license, came to pick me up. At first she seemed pleased to see me; however, as she looked me up and down I could tell from her changing expression that something was wrong. I believe she liked the "up" part: my freshly laundered shirt, tie, and suit. It was the "down" part that prompted Jill's gasp of unpleasant surprise: I was wearing my work boots!

To this day, I still do not understand why my parents didn't tell me to wear a pair of my father's dress shoes instead of my brown work boots for this big event. After Jill almost passed out from well-bred horror, I did hurriedly change into more suitable (although I'm sure still not ideal) footwear—but the damage had already been done. Off we went to the cotillion, Jill mortified and me very ill at ease.

I was now intent on making the evening up to Jill after my initial faux pas. So when we arrived at our dinner table, which included all of Jill's friends, I pulled back her chair, as any fine date would do so that she could more easily and elegantly take her place at the table. Unfortunately, I didn't push the chair back fast enough to meet Jill's derriere. To my absolute horror, she landed inelegantly on the floor. Luckily, Jill wasn't hurt—although that wasn't much comfort to either of us at the moment. Strike two!

I never did get another chance to impress this beautiful girl, since my first two blunders totally destroyed any opportunity of our developing a relationship.

Like I said, it's funny *now*. I hope Jill looks back on it this way too!

Was It Really Work Boots?

The memory of me oh-so-embarrassingly dressing in work boots for a formal dance has on some level, I know, made me feel worse about myself through the years. And here's the kicker: I now believe, after writing this book, that my footwear faux pas may not have even happened in the way I've remembered. My parents certainly don't recall my work boots making an appearance, and after recently seeing my sixteen-year-old son go to his first semi-formal, I'm inclined to agree that they would not have let me greet my date dressed this way. Most likely, I was just wearing ugly old dress shoes that didn't work with my outfit.

The important thing is, though, that *in my mind* I convinced myself that it was so much worse, and—right or wrong—*that's* the memory that has influenced my self-image and development. Again, as I first pointed out in Chapter 2, how we remember our worst and most embarrassing moments can impact our self-esteem and sense of worth for years to come—so it's important to guard against letting inflated negative memories make us feel bad about ourselves today. (But boy…do I wish I could go back and see for myself what I was *really* wearing on my feet that night!)

A New—and Unwise—Coping Mechanism

Considering all of the incredible stress I felt over grades, girls, and bullies, it is no surprise that by tenth grade I was drinking alcohol with my friends. And by the twelfth grade, we had begun to experiment with marijuana as well. Our weekends were now usually spent playing pickup basketball or football games during the day. And then, once night fell, we'd often drink some alcohol, maybe smoke a little marijuana, and head into Boston's Chinatown district for a late-night meal around 11:00 p.m.

Marijuana and alcohol naturally made me feel much more at ease socially (after all, that's what they're meant to do!), especially when going to Needham parties where I might run into one or both of my twin tormentors, Jeff and Karen. While feeling uninhibited and relaxed was (I thought at the time) a nice change from the ball of stress that usually sat in my stomach on such occasions, it also set the stage for some reckless behavior.

> *Alcohol is necessary for a man so that he can have a good opinion of himself, undisturbed by the facts.*
> —Finley Peter Dunne

Clearly, I was already aware on some level that I wanted to experience increased happiness—but obviously, I went about capturing it in an unwise and dangerous manner. I'm ashamed to admit it now—especially as a parent of a teenager—but we did do some drinking and driving in those days. Boy, were we stupid and irresponsible, and boy, are we lucky to still be alive today!

I realize now that as a teenager who suffered from considerable anxiety, it wasn't surprising in the least that I gravitated to alcohol and marijuana in order to calm down my worried brain. People use and abuse these substances for a reason—they ease both physical and emotional discomfort. And therein lies another reason why children who suffer from anxiety and depression must get help as soon as possible: If anxiety and depression aren't treated, young people (and adults!) are at risk of medicating themselves with alcohol and other drugs—sometimes to a disastrous degree. Even more frightening, for adolescents this experimentation is happening just as they are getting used to driving cars as well.

Substance Abuse Stats

- In a 2009 survey, alcohol use in the past year was reported by 30 percent of eighth graders, 53 percent of tenth graders, and 66 percent of twelfth graders.
- Marijuana use in the previous twelve months was reported by 11.8 percent of eighth graders, 26.7 percent of tenth graders, and 32.8 percent of twelfth graders.
- Past-year nonmedical use of Vicodin and OxyContin increased during the last five years among tenth graders and remained unchanged among eighth and twelfth graders.
- Nearly one in ten high school seniors reported nonmedical use of Vicodin; one in twenty reported abuse of OxyContin.

—National Institute on Drug Abuse, 2010

An Expert View on the Allure of Alcohol and Drugs

It's common knowledge that drugs and alcohol are used by individuals the world over to relax, de-stress, escape, and have fun. Here's why: Overall, these substances influence the brain's neurotransmitters, or the chemicals that allow neurons in the brain to communicate with each other.

Some drugs, like morphine and other opiates, have a very specific and desirable effect. For example, morphine stimulates endorphins, the brain's natural painkillers.

Alcohol, on the other hand, has a very generalized effect on the brain because it affects several neurotransmitters. Specifically, it:

- Increases dopamine, which is responsible for feelings of well-being, excitement, stimulation
- Enhances GABA (gamma-aminobutyric acid), which is associated with a feeling of calm and relaxation
- Inhibits glutamate, which creates muscular relaxation and, at higher levels, lack of coordination and slurring of speech
- Raises endorphins, creating a feeling of "high"

All of the above effects can lead to some amount of temporary relaxation and a sense of well-being, which is understandably tempting—especially to people who are suffering from anxiety and depression. For this reason, such individuals are more at risk of developing an addiction.

A New Challenge Looms

As my high school career was winding down, I, of course, began getting really stressed out over my future. (No surprise there, huh?) I'm fairly sure that the process of visiting and applying to colleges can unsettle even the most even-keeled young men and women, so you can only imagine its effects on my already-frantic brain.

My father and most of my uncles had attended Tufts University in Medford, Massachusetts (just outside of Boston proper), and my brother was already in his junior year there. Tufts is a great school and is considered just one notch below Ivy League. So naturally, due to my sibling rivalry with Roger, I approached my college selection process with the view that anything less than an acceptance letter from an Ivy League school would be a huge failure for me.

After doing some research, I decided that my first-choice school was the University of Pennsylvania, and that it would be to my mental benefit to apply early decision. That way, at least, I'd know sooner rather than later what my fate was. Of course, along with this proactive application strategy came the terrible fear that I might not be accepted.

After compiling and submitting my application packet, I spent several nerve-wracking months waiting to hear whether or not I had been accepted to this prestigious school. Also in the back of my mind—well, actually not too far from the front—was the nagging worry that regardless of which college I attended, I might not be able to live away from home for an extended period of time due to my separation anxiety. These two worries—not getting into UPenn and not being able to live away from home—built as my senior year was coming to a close and I waited to learn of my college fate.

TIPS FROM TODD:
CHAPTER FIVE

Essential lessons to learn:

...for parents:

- **Realize that bullying doesn't always stop after the playground has been left behind.** Many teenagers live in fear of being picked on, teased, or otherwise singled out in a negative way at school and in social situations. Bullying in high school can take the form of physical, verbal, or online abuse, and can have a serious impact on a young person's self-esteem, anxiety levels, and social comfort. Beyond that, though, it's important to realize that bullying can become intense enough to prompt reactions as strong as suicide in its victims.

- **Watch for signs that something isn't right.** Especially as kids grow older, they might be reluctant to share that they're being ostracized, teased, or tormented. Likewise, even if bullying isn't an issue, they might keep feelings of anxiety and depression to themselves. If you notice a change in your child's behavior, approach him or her in a sensitive, nonthreatening way.

An Expert View on Approaching a Troubled Child or Teen

If you sense that something is consistently bothering your child, or if his or her behavior has noticeably changed in a negative manner, don't immediately contact a therapist or complain to school administrators. Always try to talk directly to him or her before pursuing such avenues. Remember, it is crucial to provide a positive environment of trust and respect; otherwise, your child will be reluctant to open up to you and may not receive the care he or she needs. Following are several things to keep in mind:

- Try to enter your child's world. To begin, just listen to what he has to say. Don't badger or press for more details at this stage.
- Refrain from making judgmental comments that might cause your child to shut down or hold back.
- Don't be too quick to offer advice. While the time for guidance may come later, it's important that your child initially know that you aren't trying to "control" her.
- Don't minimize your child's concerns. While you may realize that a particular worry or fear is unfounded or unimportant, this doesn't make it any less monumental to a young person.
- If possible, relate your child's concerns to incidents in your own childhood. If your child can see that you were able to overcome bullying or that you found viable ways to handle academic stress, he will probably feel much more hopeful...and your bond with him will have been strengthened.
- After listening fully to what your child has to say, discuss possible solutions with her—but don't impose them. In order for your child to positively grow as a result of her struggles, she needs to have agency in overcoming them.

If your child still is struggling despite your best efforts, seek professional help.

- **Don't let your children focus *too* strongly on academic achievement.** This piece of advice might seem counterintuitive at first glance—after all, what parent doesn't want his or her kids to do well in school? However, many teens—especially those who are anxiety-prone—become so obsessed with high performance that grade-related worries, along with excessive studying, can become an unhealthy obsession.

- **Don't underestimate the value of parental support.** Even if your kids don't specifically solicit your advice and aid, don't assume they don't need or want it. Especially if a teen is having a tough time academically or socially, a nurturing, supportive home environment can be a lifesaver. If your child is receptive to discussing his or her experiences and struggles, listen without judgment and offer constructive advice. If your child *isn't* open to talking, simply spend other types of quality time together—whether it's watching a TV show, going bowling, or cooking together.

- **Be upfront about drinking and driving.** Whether you want to admit it or not, the fact is that teenagers are apt to drink alcohol they've illegally obtained. However, we must make absolutely certain that our teens know the dangers of mixing alcohol with driving. Also, make sure that your teenager knows that getting in the car with another person who's been drinking is just as dangerous as getting behind the wheel oneself while intoxicated.

...for everyone:
- **Be on the lookout for substance abuse as a coping mechanism.** The power of drugs and alcohol to temporarily alter one's mood and experience of reality is well known. It can be especially seductive to individuals who are struggling with anxiety or depression, regardless of age, sex, or situation in life.

Inner War: The College Years

It is often through the most difficult labor that the greatest gifts are born.
—Todd Patkin

My high school career finished with a bang. I have wonderful memories of my senior year—lots of fun and adventures with friends, academic success, and, of course, the joy and pride on my parents' faces on graduation day itself. I was now ready to move on in the world and step up to a new age of independence and responsibility—or so I thought.

My first months out of high school turned out to be growth-prompting and empowering. As I've already mentioned, I thrived in the summers without the burden of school—and never more so than after my high school graduation. Much to my delight, I was able to go on a tour of Europe (which I've told you about previously). As I was having an absolute ball exploring a new continent, I had no way of knowing that I was about to go through the most brutal four and a half years of my life.

My college years were the first time I was forced to come to terms with my own limitations and make decisions based on how I *actually* functioned at that time, rather than on how I wished things were. Yes, while my journey toward a degree, as you will see, was indeed punctuated by several extremely severe bouts of anxiety and depression, those years also forced me to dig deep within myself in order to successfully reach this important goal. In fact, still to this day I consider this pivotal time of my life to be my second-greatest period of growth and my very greatest personal triumph!

Back to My Story

While my European experience the summer before college temporarily boosted my confidence level and self-esteem, as the first week of college approached, some of that all-too-familiar anxiety returned. For starters, I was worried about my ability to manage college course work and the social aspects of being semi-independent for the first time. Would I feel intimidated by the academic competition? Would I be homesick? Would I be able to quickly make new friends?

As it turned out, I had been waitlisted by the University of Pennsylvania. This admissions decision was a huge disappointment to me after all of the effort I had put into my studies and all of the stress I had suffered in my attempt to get into an Ivy League school. Still, I wasn't without options. I had prudently applied to several other schools in addition to UPenn. With the knowledge that I could possibly stay in limbo on UPenn's waitlist into the summer, I took a little time to lick my wounds, and then settled down to anxiously wait on my other universities. After all, I tried to reassure myself, I was a resilient young man, and regardless of where I ended up I was determined to prove myself to everyone as a competent college student.

In the end, I was ultimately rejected by UPenn. Denied the opportunity to attend my first-choice college, I decided to continue the family tradition begun by my father, uncles, and brother, and I enrolled at Tufts University as well. On the bright side, I told myself, I wouldn't be too far from home since Tufts was a mere forty-minute drive from my house. Separation anxiety, at least, shouldn't be a major issue—or so I thought.

So, at the end of the summer I packed up my belongings, bought the necessary dorm room furnishings, and moved into a room on campus. Almost from minute one, my insecurity reared its ugly head. The very first day of class, I found the coursework to be distressingly intense. Don't get me wrong; I loved the classes and the challenges they presented. On the other hand, though, staying on top of my studies took much more time and energy than my high school homework had—and, of course, I was worried that I wouldn't get straight As.

Socially, things didn't get off to a great start, either. I had hoped that I'd be able to turn over a new dating leaf and put my awkward, embarrassing high school romantic forays behind me. However, I found many of the girls at the university to be arrogant and distant, and after the great summer I had just spent touring Europe with women who were friendly and relaxed, I was very disappointed that I couldn't seem to connect with my fellow students.

To make social matters worse, I had inadvertently hobbled myself when I filled out my freshman housing application. You see, as I checked boxes and set forth my roommate preferences, I stressed the importance of good studying conditions and cleanliness, and downplayed socializing. This was a good idea, I figured, because it would give the Tufts administration a good impression of a serious student, and my stringent preferences would also help me to avoid having a raucous and inconsiderate roommate (which really was important to me).

Well, the Tufts housing department gave me a roommate who wasn't rambunctious or distracting, all right. I was paired with a Hasidic (Orthodox) Jew whose social aspirations were quite minimal, unlike mine. While performing well academically *was* a priority, like most college students I was serious about having a good time, too! Compounded with my academic worries, my less-than-stellar social start at Tufts caused me to panic, and I therefore didn't give my first roommate the chance he deserved. After just a week I switched dormitories and found myself rooming with Jim from Maine. Big mistake! Jim's hygiene left a lot to be desired, and to make matters worse, he hung out with a physically imposing guy who (like Karen and Jeff in high school) seemed to sense my vulnerability and enjoyed picking on me.

I felt as though someone had taken my stress level and ratcheted it up several notches in no time at all. Before long, the discomfort I felt in my dorm room had resurrected my homesickness. And even worse, as the first semester workload continued to intensify, so did my anxiety. With no social support network at college, I soon returned to my tried-and-true coping mechanism for anxiety: being at home. Before that initial semester was even half over, I was driving home and spending most of my nights in my old bedroom. Typically, my class schedule would allow me to be home at least two out of four weeknights, and it was a foregone conclusion that I would spend all of my weekends—Friday afternoons through Monday mornings—at home.

> *The University brings out all abilities, including incapability.*
> —Anton Chekhov

Understandably, my parents were worried about my inability to stay on campus and connect with my fellow students, but of course they always welcomed me home and did what they could to raise my spirits. I also continued to utilize my high school coping mechanism of relaxing with my mom by watching television—afternoon soap operas were now replaced by nightly sit-coms like *The Cosby Show* and *Happy Days*.

The sitcoms I watched at home, at least, were harmless. Unfortunately, that wasn't the case for my other primary coping behaviors, which I now carried over from high school too. When I spent nights on campus, I would sometimes smoke marijuana and/or drink alcohol to help me relax. To a certain extent, these behaviors helped me to feel more comfortable with everyone—especially the opposite sex—but mostly, they simply enabled me to literally survive until the following day. Honestly, at this time in my life my anxiety levels were so high that without these temporary reprieves from the stress I was feeling, I don't believe I could have continued with my studies.

An Expert View for Parents on the College Transition

The process of giving children independence begins early in life. It centers on teaching appropriate skills so that young people will have the confidence to operate on their own in age-appropriate situations. Taking that into account, then, preparing your child for college is essentially preparing him or her for independence—and it's a process that actually takes place throughout childhood and adolescence. As high school graduation approaches, though, there are a few more specific things you can do to make sure your student is prepared for this new stage of life:

- If possible, encourage your child to spend time on the campus of his choice, ideally overnight, without parents present. Many colleges offer this opportunity, which gives students a chance to authentically sample campus life, prior to actual enrollment. "Walking through" a typical day on campus will help your child to accurately understand the challenges and responsibilities facing him, and will give him a much clearer idea of whether he is a "fit" with any given school.

- Whether in person or online, encourage your child to talk with current attendees of the college she's looking at. They will give her a more accurate idea of what to expect than a booklet or website.
- During your child's first year of college, pre-arrange specific times to talk with your child via telephone or Skype (the latter is especially helpful—seeing loved ones is much more comforting than just hearing their voices). Unless he is experiencing difficulties, aim for twice-weekly conversations. This will give your child enough space to grow and make decisions on his own without causing him (or you!) to feel abandoned.

Warning signs that your child is not adjusting well to college include a lack of energy, despondency, an apparent lack of friends, and difficulty with the demands of schoolwork. Remember, college should be challenging, but also fun. Any indication that this is *not* the case with your child should be cause for concern, and should prompt you to delicately make more inquiries.

Despite my constant travels between Tufts and my home, I actually did very well academically my freshman year. Surprise, surprise—I got almost all As. That, at least, was an accomplishment I could be proud of…but its sweetness was tainted by the knowledge that my success was mostly due to my complete lack of a college social life. After all, what else did I have to do *besides* focus on my studies?

Going Greek

After a first college summer spent looking back at my less-than-happy freshman year, I returned to Tufts in the fall determined to build the social life I wanted. And what better way to do that, I reasoned, than to join a fraternity? I'd be provided with a group of friends—"brothers," even—as well as with a calendar full of parties, social events, and more. So, it was with high hopes that I became a brand-new member of the Sigma Nu fraternity.

Fortunately, the Sigma Nu initiation did not resemble Hollywood's depictions of similar events—there were no animals or sacrificial altars, and I was allowed to keep my clothing on and (for the most part) my dignity. I couldn't have been happier that the initiation was less than memorable. One aspect of that evening does stand out, however: clams. Yes, clams!

Ever the competitor and lover of anything involving shellfish, I managed to break the fraternity record for eating the most steamed clams and drinking the most beer in an hour. Of course, I threw up within a matter of minutes after finishing, but that didn't matter. What *did* matter was my fervent hope that I had taken my first step in creating a social identity that would attract friends and make me feel at home in my new fraternity.

From time to time, I got my wish—I *did* feel that I was succeeding in carving out a niche for myself as a Sigma Nu brother. As it had all throughout my childhood, my sporting prowess did quite a bit to give me social standing within my fraternity: Most notably, I became one of the two quarterbacks on my fraternity's intramural football team. And I can't deny that I became fast friends with several of my fraternity brothers with whom I had quite a bit in common.

In the end, however, achieving my goal of gaining social recognition and inclusion within this fraternity just wasn't enough. The mounting academic pressures, combined with the homesickness that had never entirely gone away, simply became too overwhelming for me. I had to admit that the dark shadows of insomnia, worry, and my overall sense of anxiety that had dogged me my whole life overwhelmed the bright patches of sunshine that I had found within my classes and the social circle at Sigma Nu. In fact, I felt so stressed and panicked about my ability to balance everything during this third semester of college that I went to the student health center. From there, I was referred to a psychologist.

Although I had under my belt a long history of anxiousness with a bit of depression, this was the first time in my life that I had actually talked to a mental health professional about my issues. I was apprehensive about attending my initial appointment, and I didn't relax much while it was going on. Perhaps for that reason, many of the details are a blur, except for one. I distinctly remember the psychologist asking me if I thought my father loved my brother more than me. To my utter shock, this question triggered within me an uncontrollable crying spell as I answered, "Yes, yes, yes, I do!"

An Expert View on Seeking Professional Help for Anxiety

We all experience times of worry or heightened stress. So how do you know if your symptoms are beyond the norm…or if it's time to seek professional help? If the following symptoms are ongoing, or if they compromise your quality of life or sense of well-being, see a professional:

- **Physical symptoms** such as sweating, increased heart rate, awareness of breathing, shakiness
- **Psychological signs** such as racing thoughts, worry, obsessing about problems, intrusive thoughts, poor sleep, avoidance of situations

There are different types of anxiety, including general anxiety, specific phobias, obsessive-compulsive disorders, and post-traumatic stress disorder. Often, anxiety is accompanied by depression. The best treatment for a majority of anxiety disorders is a combination of psychotherapy and medication, the latter being prescribed by a doctor (typically a psychiatrist).

It's less important whether you initially approach a therapist or a psychiatrist—or even your regular physician—because all of these individuals should be familiar with the local mental health professional community and can refer you to appropriate specialists. The important thing is that you start *somewhere* so that you will receive a proper diagnosis and course of treatment.

That said, making sure that the professional whom you approach is licensed and has experience in dealing with depression is not the final step. Therapy is very personal, and therefore the "right" therapist must be someone whom the client can trust and relate to. Great qualifications don't necessarily ensure a good fit for you or for your child.

For this reason, do not continue to stay with your initial therapist if you feel uncomfortable with him or her or if you feel that you do not have a good rapport. Continue to ask for more referrals and explore other options, and remember that an effective therapist will outline the diagnosis *and* treatment plan at a fairly early stage in the process.

This meltdown in the psychologist's office was the final warning bell for me—my unexpectedly powerful reaction was frightening. I knew that something had to change, and fast. And so, after three unhappy semesters at Tufts, I decided it was definitely best for me to take some time off from college. I now came home to regroup, feeling that somehow I'd failed. I never went back to that psychologist after that first visit (in large part because my anxiety was basically nil once I returned home and had no classes). If I had returned for a second visit, perhaps I might have realized sooner that my hurtful assumptions regarding my father's love weren't true—instead they were, in fact, merely a young child's distorted perception of family dynamics.

Also, what I didn't know at that time is that—without a doubt—many of my college friends were also struggling with mental health problems as well.

Mental Health in College: A Serious Matter

I am fortunate to have grown up relatively close to my college, because, as I've said, being able to go home so frequently proved to be an invaluable coping mechanism for me. Without that familiar "safe" place to return to and the outlet for my anxieties that it provided, my story might have turned out tragically differently.

Believe it or not, recent studies conducted at several different universities show that as many as 11 percent of college freshmen have actually had suicidal thoughts.[7] And sadly, some of those thoughts are acted upon. In the 2010 calendar year, for example, three students at the College of William & Mary in Virginia alone committed suicide. Perhaps not surprisingly, this school, like so many others, is said to be "filled with more than its share of high achievers, some of whom have difficulty admitting they might need help coping."[8]

Unfortunately, while more than half of all college students suffer from at least one mental health problem during their freshman years,[9] 85 percent of students with depression or suicidal thoughts do not get treatment. In some cases, this is because students do not want to appear weak or "less than" because they are having these difficulties coping on their own; in others, it's because students fear being deemed "too ill" to even be allowed to remain enrolled.

I am glad to say that in recent years, many colleges are attempting to raise awareness regarding mental health issues by including information in orientation sessions for both parents and students and by advising professors and residence hall staff on how to recognize the signs of depression.[10] Students who are struggling with mental health problems cannot be expected to cope or to seek out help on their own—they must constantly be told that there are supportive, nonjudgmental people just waiting to help them.

---

7   Garlow, S.J., A.P. Haas, H. Hendin, B. Koestner, J.D. Moore, C.B. Nemeroff, and J. Rosenberg. "Depression, desperation and suicidal ideation in college students: results from the American Foundation for Suicide Prevention College Screening Project at Emory University." *Depression and Anxiety* 25 (2008): 482-88.

8   Johnson, Jenna. "Third Suicide at William and Mary Illustrates Challenge of Prevention." *The Washington Post. Boston.com.* 26 November 2010. <http://www.boston.com/news/health/articles/2010/11/26/third_suicide_at_william_and_mary_illustrates_challenge_of_prevention/> (30 November 2010).

9   Eisenberg, D., E. Golberstein, S.E. Gollust, and K. Zivin. "Persistence of mental health problems and needs in a college student population." *Journal of Affective Disorders* 117 (2009): 180-85.

10   Johnson, Jenna. "Third Suicide at William and Mary Illustrates Challenge of Prevention." *The Washington Post. Boston.com.* 26 November 2010. <http://www.boston.com/news/health/articles/2010/11/26/third_suicide_at_william_and_mary_illustrates_challenge_of_prevention/> (30 November 2010).

Higher-Ed Hiatus

Once home, I quickly found a full-time job. However, after just one week at Bel Canto, an Italian restaurant in Wellesley, Massachusetts, I realized I really was not cut out for the restaurant business.

Table-waiting Woes

You know the type of restaurant server who is guilelessly friendly and who always seems to be genuinely pleased that you have graced the restaurant with your presence—and then proceeds to advise, describe, serve, and refill with ease and skill? Well, that wasn't me during my table-waiting days.

I quite clearly recall, for example, my first day making the coffee. I had not yet become an aficionado of the beverage myself, so I had no idea that the coffee machine needed a filter—and (no doubt assuming this to be common knowledge) my colleagues obviously didn't think it necessary to instruct me in the intricacies of coffee-brewing. The result? Several customers had to pick coffee grounds out of their teeth that morning.

The coffee incident was embarrassing, but it pales in comparison to what is, without a doubt, the coup de grace of my serving gaffes. While absorbed in the task of recording the drink orders for a table of young people, I thoughtlessly said, "Diet, right?" after an overweight young lady told me which soda she wanted. Immediately after the injudicious question left my mouth, I could feel the heat of my customer's glare—and I could tell that my offhand assumption had been, if not wrong, at least very hurtful. Of course this young woman would not want to be treated any differently from the rest of her friends. Needless to say, I felt horrible about that mistake.

While it was clear that I would never have a future as a restaurateur, I did start one new behavior during my college hiatus that has proven to be of immeasurable value for me ever since: I started going to the gym and exercising with my father. Since then, and to this day, I have made a habit, almost without exception, of exercising at least every other or every third day. In fact, I credit much of my success at work to my routine of exercise.

THE DOCTOR IS IN

An Expert View on Exercise

As has been previously stated, exercise is the single most important activity you can do for your overall mental and physical health. Partially review and partially new, here are some reasons why:

- Exercise helps preserve brain cells.
- Exercise creates a flow of positive chemicals in your brain.
- Exercise helps boost metabolism.
- Exercise releases endorphins, or the brain's natural painkillers, which give you a sense of well-being and drive.
- Exercise keeps a good supply of oxygen and glucose in the brain, both of which are essential for effective brain function.
- Exercise keeps a steady supply of blood flowing to the brain. Most people think of the heart as the "main" organ when it comes to blood supply because it acts as the blood's pump; however, the brain is actually the most important. Although it weighs just 2 percent of your body weight, it uses 20 percent of your blood supply.

While I knew that something just wasn't right for me at Tufts, I never questioned my overall plan to attend college. Therefore, after some discussion, my parents and I concluded that a different university environment would suit me better. I applied as a transfer student to two schools: the University of Pennsylvania (once again) and McGill University in Montreal, Canada. Much to my delight and gratification, I was accepted to both!

To be honest, my initial inclination was to pack my bags and decamp to UPenn posthaste—after all, attending this school had been my dream for years! However, something held me back. I just couldn't shake the unsettling feeling that as tempting as it was to be associated with UPenn's Ivy League status, immersing myself once again into such an intensely competitive environment—especially five-plus hours by car from my home—might have very horrific and possibly even life-threatening consequences for me. And so, I made what was probably my most adult decision to-date. I chose the better school for me: McGill.

It helped quite a bit that my good friend David Adelman was already attending McGill. While I was at Tufts, and especially as I was navigating the transfer process, I had visited David there a number of times. From the beginning I liked what I had seen: the students at McGill were friendly and appeared to enjoy a healthier balance between their social lives and their studies, which was exactly what I clearly needed.

Choosing a College: My Suggested Checklist

Deciding which college to attend is, obviously, a huge decision—and all prospective university students should consider much more than just a school's academic or athletic reputation before sending in a deposit check. Whether you are prone to anxiety or not, here are some things to take into account:

Location. Where is the school located? Is it close to your home? (This is especially important to consider if you are prone to homesickness.) Furthermore, what is the school's physical environment like? Is it urban or wooded? Spread out or centrally located? What are the climate and weather like? Make sure you take into account your own preferences for each of the above school characteristics.

Size. Is the school big or small? What percentage of students are undergraduate versus graduate students? What is the student-teacher ratio? It's important to consider whether you can thrive in larger crowds or if you prefer a more personal, one-on-one environment.

Atmosphere. Just like cities, college campuses have atmospheres for which they're known. Some are fairly laid-back. Some are known for their social events, while others exude pressure to excel academically to the max. Also, all colleges are different in terms of their progressivism, diversity, etc. Make sure the school you're considering is a fit for your priorities, preferences, and personality.

Academics. Yes, take a look at a school's academic ratings, but don't let this be your sole guide. Look into majors and courses offered, academic support programs such as tutoring, and the flexibility students have to study multiple topics or change their course of study mid-stream.

Extracurricular Activities. Students attend college primarily to increase their knowledge base, but few spend every waking hour buried in the books. Research whether or not each college offers extracurricular activities (such as intramural sports, interest-based clubs, volunteering opportunities, campus ministries, etc.) that match your current interests. Being involved in various activities is an excellent way to regulate stress.

If possible, look into these things firsthand when choosing a college. Try to visit each campus, talk to students and professors, and gauge your potential to be happy there in person.

In closing, here are two final critically important suggestions on this topic:

- If you are prone to perfectionism, try to address this issue as fully as possible before beginning college. In an unfamiliar environment, the compulsion to excel can become dangerously stressful, and can pull your attention away from the social components that are necessary to a balanced life.
- If it becomes clear that your college is not a good fit for you, don't view your decision to attend as a life sentence. Enlist the help of advisors, mentors, and family members, and begin looking into the transfer process instead of staying where you're unhappy.

God's delays are not God's denials.

—Tony Robbins

I decided now upon enrolling at McGill that I would focus the majority of my efforts on building and nurturing a fulfilling and fun social life. My academically oriented attitude had resulted only in increasing stress at Tufts, I reasoned, so I tried to convince myself that from here on out, a B in a class would be a perfectly acceptable grade, so long as I was becoming a happier person.

O, Canada!: College North of the Border

On my very first day in Montreal, I therefore entered the dorm with my "Fun, First and Foremost" attitude very much on my mind. After all, this was my chance to turn over a completely new leaf (maple-shaped, this time) and live the college experience I'd long desired.

As I made my way to my room, I passed a number of students lounging about and talking with the floor resident advisor. Recognizing opportunity when I saw it, I stepped into their midst in order to introduce myself and boldly pronounce my new mission and request.

"Hello, I am Todd Patkin from Boston. And I have a favor to ask of each of you. If any of you ever find me studying this semester, please immediately remind me to stop, close my books, and to go out for a drink instead!" I exclaimed, finishing my speech with a flourish.

One of the students there that day was a French immersion freshman named Paulie. He asked for a translation of what I had just said, and when one of the others translated my announcement to him, shock and horror were evident in his expression. Whenever our paths crossed thereafter, he'd always hurry past me with a very worried expression on his face! Later, near the end of the year when Paulie's English had improved, we became friends. I learned that Paulie was just like me when I'd first started school back at Tufts: a tightly wound perfectionist, desperate for all As on his report card. Paulie admitted that frankly, my initial all-about-fun persona had scared the heck out of him. (Actually, with my cavalier attitude, I'd have scared my first-day-of-college self as well.) By the end of the school year, I had worked through my academic burnout and found a much healthier balance—while Paulie had, in his own right, relaxed a bit as well. We often joked later about that first horrifying impression I had made on him!

What can I say? I meant every word that I said to my hallmates, and for awhile, I stuck quite seriously to my newly chosen agenda. With David and some new friends as my guides, I discovered Montreal's bars, entertainment venues, and nightlife. With Montreal being the second-largest city in Canada, there was quite a lot to experience. And, to my overwhelming delight, within a few days I had achieved an important "first": I succeeded in picking up a girl in a French discothèque!

At first, I could barely believe my good fortune. Me, the guy who'd crashed and burned on so many teenage romantic forays, had captured the attention of an attractive cosmopolitan young lady—and she didn't ditch me at the discothèque. In fact, after we had finished dancing, she came back to my dorm room at McGill, where she ended up sleeping over. Wow! Bienvenue à Montreal! After this initial evening (which was the stuff my dreams were made of), Theresa and I quickly developed a deeper relationship.

And therefore education at the University mostly worked by the age-old method of putting a lot of young people in the vicinity of a lot of books and hoping that something would pass from one to the other, while the actual young people put themselves in the vicinity of inns and taverns for exactly the same reason.
— Terry Pratchett

With steadily increasing self-confidence, less academic pressure, regular work-outs at the gym, and a full social life, I finally began to truly relax and enjoy myself instead of constantly worrying about the future. After about six weeks of fun, though, I decided that perhaps I shouldn't abandon academics altogether—after all, I *was* at college to learn, and my mind has never been content without some sort of stimulation. For the first time in my life, I was thus able to find the healthy balance between books and fun that I had been desperately seeking for so long.

Looking back, it's evident to me that the main reason for my newfound academic-social balance was probably that, unlike at Tufts, almost all of my fellow McGill students seemed to rate their own happiness as being just as important as earning good grades—and their examples rubbed off on me. *Always remember, you will gradually become more and more like the people you spend the most time with!*

Also, having completed a good deal of my standard required classes by this point, I discovered that I had a natural aptitude for management, and excelled at my courses in the world-renowned McGill School of Management with a minimum of stress.

Sometimes More Is Just…More.

"More isn't always better" is one of those sayings that often has to be experienced in order to be truly understood. That was definitely the case for me in the realm of academics! Prior to my transfer to McGill, I had always studied much more than was necessary. For example, at Tufts it was common for me to study twenty hours for a single test, even though I knew all the material after just ten hours of work. Irrationally, I was always worried that I might have missed *something*, and that if I didn't go that extra mile "just to be sure," I might forget or overlook a piece of information and not earn the perfect A I so desperately had to have.

At McGill, I realized for the first time that I didn't need to overdo it. I remember being mildly shocked after receiving my first batch of test grades, because in spite of my thriving social life, the grades I'd received weren't abysmal—in fact, they were ones I could be proud of! Because of this experience, I came to realize that it was actually unproductive to force myself to continue studying once I was confident I knew the material. Finally, I got comfortable with the idea that if ten hours of study was sufficient to cover everything, twenty hours wouldn't make things much better.

As I've suggested before, I think it's incredibly important for parents to actively combat the perfectionism impulse in their children, especially *before* those children enter college. Because while I was burning out and almost breaking down at college, at least my family was close at hand. So, I was able to work myself away from the need to earn all As—but this might not be the case for all young people. While your child is still in high school, explicitly communicate the fact that receiving a grade other than an A is all right if a sincere effort has been made. Also, consider seeing a psychiatrist or other professional to learn how you can help your child if necessary. Make your initial visit alone, though, and bring your child in later only if the professional recommends it.

For the first time in my life, being away from home was a blast. Although I could barely believe it, I was experiencing no homesickness whatsoever! In addition to dating Theresa, I had great new friends, and I was solidly involved in university life.

Ever the athlete, I even became the star player of my dormitory's intramural street hockey team. This led to a very comical situation, however, when my Canadian friends (who each had practically been born on skates) begged me to also join their ultra-competitive intramural ice hockey team. Game to give it a shot for them, I donned all of the requisite pads and gear—but after skating just one full lap around the ice, I had lost all of my wind. There was no way around it—I had to admit that I had exerted myself to the point that I couldn't breathe. And so ended my illustrious Canadian ice hockey career. Needless to say, my mainly Franco-Canadian friends all had a great laugh at the American street hockey star who couldn't skate at all!

My Sunshine Fades

Unfortunately, my newfound happiness lasted only through my first year at McGill. From the outset of my second year in Montreal, my old feelings of loneliness and homesickness began to creep back into my life. Mostly to blame for this setback, I am sure, was the fact that Theresa and I had broken up at the end of the previous school year. Plus, this year I had moved out of the dormitory and into a quiet apartment with my good friend Alex Zivic. Too late, I found that the constant social bustle of dorm life was a balm to my overactive and worry-prone brain. With very little to distract me, I was much more apt to latch onto the stresses of being so far from home and of college life itself.

La Vie en Rose No Longer

There is no doubt that my relationship with Theresa had been an important tool for me in managing my anxiety, relaxing, and finding the right balance that first year at McGill. In fact, it has been proven that being "in love"—especially the infatuation that comes in the early stages of a relationship—actually changes one's brain chemistry.

Yes, love is a great coping strategy. It makes you feel good, it distracts you from other worries, it provides you with another person to offer you support, and it will heal almost any ill—for a time. However, as anyone who has ever suffered from a broken heart knows, the crash that comes after that time of elation can inflict even greater wounds on one's emotions, mind, and self-esteem. And if a relationship has served as a primary coping mechanism for another problem (stress and homesickness, for example, in my case), that problem will miraculously reappear almost immediately after the breakup—and it might even have grown worse.

In my case, nothing really *could* change and get better over the long run until I learned to accept and love myself just as I am. That is why, whenever I lost a coping mechanism, whether it was my relationship with Theresa, or in later years my ability to exercise, I fell apart. Under the illusion that these things provided, I was still very vulnerable and susceptible to unhappiness, and thus I had no defense against my insecure and unhappy feelings when these coping strategies went away.

An Expert View on the Mood-Boosting Power of Love

There are many terms for it: "lovestruck," "smitten," "head over heels," and "infatuated," to name a few. There's no doubt about it—being in love with another person makes us feel different in a very, very good way. While some prefer to think of the "symptoms" of love as magical, though, there's actually a solid scientific explanation behind them.

- The initial stages of falling for someone (getting to know them, impressing them favorably, and so forth) activates your stress response. This increases the levels of adrenaline and cortisol in your blood, which results in high levels of brain activation and mental overactivity.

- Once you begin to feel more comfortable with your partner, things begin to change. Studies have shown that lovestruck couples have high levels of the neurotransmitter dopamine. Dopamine is related to feelings of reward and pleasure, so it's hardly surprising that we love to be in love! Increased dopamine also leads to more energy and a general sense of well-being.

- There tends to be an inverse relationship between dopamine and serotonin. When one is high, the other is low. This relates to love because low levels of serotonin can lead to more obsessive, ruminative thinking—making you "obsess" about your partner, unable to think about anything or anyone else!

Because "love" (especially in the early infatuation phase) is a wonderful feeling that typically increases self-esteem and mood, it can act as an antidote to depression. However, depressed individuals typically find it more difficult to get to this point (falling in love) because they are not psychologically capable of making that sort of connection with another individual.

The magic of first love is our ignorance that it can ever end.
—Benjamin Disraeli

Before my second year at McGill had progressed very far, I had once again begun to drive home on the weekends. However, instead of a relatively short forty-minute trip, these journeys took six hours one way in what were often snowy, dangerous conditions. Here I was, almost twenty-one years old, and still crippled by my separation anxiety. If anything—to my despair—I felt worse than ever about myself after my brief period of happiness.

There isn't a child who hasn't gone out into the brave new world who eventually doesn't return to the old homestead carrying a bundle of dirty clothes.
—Art Buchwald

In the end, my demons again were just too much for me. And so, after completing just three semesters at McGill, I transferred back to Tufts for my final two semesters of college. I simply gave up the battle of trying to lead a normal college life and began living with my parents once again. I now solely focused on finishing my studies and getting my degree. I would have had no social life to speak of during that final year of college except for my good friend Karl Kreshpane.

Karl was a life-saver. He attended Boston College and often invited me to join him on campus there so that I could also enjoy that amazing institution's nightlife. I'll never know how much farther I might have slid into unhappiness and depression if not for Karl's selfless friendship. And of course, it didn't hurt that in addition to being a great person, Karl was one of the very popular stars of the Boston College football team! Thanks so much, Karl!

A Hard-Won Fight

I cannot possibly explain to you how often and how desperately I wanted to quit college during my darkest times throughout those four and a half years. In fact, of all the things I have done in my life, I'm still the proudest of sticking it out in college despite the many challenges I faced. And, believe it or not, this accomplishment helps me even today to push boldly forward when I am faced with obstacles that seem insurmountable.

Throughout my college years, I remember there being one thing that kept me moving forward on the many occasions when all I wanted to do was quit. My father wasn't one for giving big speeches, delivering high-handed lessons, or harping on his expectations. However, the one thing that he was very adamant about—the one thing he said was a must for each of his children above all else—was that we must all earn college degrees. I could never have let my father down—and now, of course, I'm grateful that I persevered for my own sake, too.

Short of fighting my way out of the black hole of my breakdown, getting my college degree was definitely the hardest thing I have ever done. (And I even ended up with a fabulous GPA!) But after receiving my diploma, my worry now was how I would ever be able to lead a normal, independent, happy adult life if I could not rid myself of my debilitating feelings of homesickness, anxiety, and low self-esteem.

TIPS FROM TODD:
CHAPTER SIX

- **Don't underestimate the importance of finding a college that's a good fit.** Whether you are an aspiring college student, in the midst of your studies, or the parent of a child who is currently at this stage of life, be sure that you feel comfortable with your selected college. While it's tempting to prioritize a school's rankings and prestige above all else, remember that those things won't necessarily foster success there or afterwards.

   When considering potential colleges to attend or transfer to, take into account the expected workload, size, location, atmosphere, academic support, extracurricular offerings, housing, etc. Don't rely solely on brochures or websites, either—make every effort to visit the school and talk to current students and professors in person so that you'll truly get a feel for it. Knowing what to expect *before* your classes actually begin will make the transition much easier—and will help you weed out poor fits before committing to them.

- **Realize that homesickness can be serious at any age.** It's common to assume that separation anxiety and homesickness fade as one transitions into adulthood—or at least to assume that one should be better equipped to deal with these things. That's not always the case, though. Parents and family members of young people, as well as young people themselves, should be on the lookout for signs of increased dependence, a change in motivation or behavior, and depression after leaving home. If support and encouragement do not seem to make a difference, seek out professional help.

- **Don't give up easily when seeking professional help.** No matter what the circumstances are, it's always intimidating to find and initially consult with a mental health professional—not to mention nerve-wracking to discuss deeply personal issues with a near-stranger. Don't go it alone—find a family member or friend to accompany you to and from your first few appointments, and ask this person to help you stay the course. You must realize that first visits to psychiatrists are usually very uncomfortable. It might be a relief (at least initially) to "quit" your psychologist or psychiatrist, but the help these professionals often provide is, in the long term, invaluable.

- **Know when to quit—or at least change.** Human nature, the fear of failure, and stubborn pride all push us to keep going down various paths long after we should have turned aside. Even if an endeavor isn't inherently bad (such as attending college or pursuing a certain career), it might still have a multitude of negative effects on your life. While it isn't always possible to stop in your tracks, take a break, and plot a new course, be careful of pushing yourself past your limits—and be vigilant for healthier alternatives and opportunities such as a different school or workplace that better suits you. Again, stop being too hard on yourself!

- **Identify and prioritize sustainable coping strategies.** No matter the severity of your stress, worry, or anxiety, it is important to have an established coping strategy that is not dependent on time or circumstance. For instance, exercising and reading stimulating books are two coping strategies that can feasibly be relied upon throughout a lifetime. However, relying on a budding romantic relationship, for instance, to deal with setbacks is potentially dangerous. If a coping strategy ceases to become a viable option, the loss can have far-reaching consequences.

- **Continually strive for balance.** Whether you are a student, an employee, a business owner, or a retiree, balance is essential in order to have a happy life. While "balance" looks different for everyone, remember that contentment is as important as achievement. The latter often isn't worth much if it comes at the long-term expense of the former. If you are consistently unhappy, recognize that you should re-examine your priorities.

CHAPTER SEVEN

Time to Grow Up and Face the Music

"When the student is ready the teacher will come."
—Tony Robbins

Whether you loved it or hated it, whether it came immediately after high school, undergrad, or even grad school, and regardless of whether it lasted one week or ten years, you never forget your first "real" job. More than reaching a certain birthday milestone or receiving some sort of diploma, the day you begin to work full-time marks a concrete transition into the world of adulthood. After all, working full-time generally comes with the responsibility of providing for yourself...and the knowledge that the buck now stops with *you*. Not with Mom, Dad, university officials, or friends...you!

Due to these facts, stepping into the "real world" as a fledgling member of the American workforce is, even to the most enthusiastic young person, daunting—especially if, like me, said young person has been prone to worry and bouts of anxiety!

Fortunately, I wasn't deposited unceremoniously into the working world and left to sink or swim. During my senior year of college, my dad asked me to join the family business—Foreign Autopart—once I graduated. He told me that the company was beginning to struggle and that he could really use my support. I was very happy, for while I had known throughout college that I could take my place in the family business if I wanted to, this was the first time my father had said that he actually needed my help, and it felt great.

Also, frankly, I had been under so much stress in college that this explicit invitation was the answer to a prayer. I hadn't been looking forward to job hunting and carving out yet another brand-new niche for myself, and so I was very grateful for this particular advantage of being a member of the Patkin family. Thus, in January of 1988, fresh off of my bumpy, pothole-filled college journey, I began my business career.

I'd already gotten my feet wet, so to speak, in the business world: During two of my college summers I had worked for my father and for my uncle Jim in their auto parts business as a delivery driver at their Somerville, Massachusetts, store. In addition, I had worked in a NAPA auto parts store throughout another summer that I spent on Cape Cod in order to gain more knowledge of the business. (And, of course, I can't forget my less-than-stellar stint as a waiter during my break from college or my graveyard shift bread factory debacle in Israel!)

I was, as I have said, very pleased my dad thought so much of me that he gave me this opportunity. Also I knew, however, that I wouldn't be allowed to continue in my family's hard-earned business if my relatives began to think I'd hurt instead of help things. And thus, just as during my student days, I became determined not to disappoint!

To make a long story short, my first year on the job turned out to be very stressful—sound familiar? Events both at home and at work conspired to keep my anxiety on an upward trajectory. While I didn't experience an outright breakdown, I believe that this year in particular contributed a great deal to the one I would eventually suffer. If you look at my ability to cope as a bank account that slowly dwindled to nothing by the time I hit rock bottom in 2001, 1988 was a huge withdrawal year. I was able to keep moving forward back then (mostly, I believe, thanks to the gym), but because I hadn't yet learned to love myself, my mental well-being was never replenished after years like this one.

A Terrifying—and Transformative—Mistake

Like many college graduates, I continued to live at home for about a year after receiving my college diploma, and during that period I lived through one particular night that I'd sooner forget—but never will.

First, let me set the stage. Not long before the night in question I had been prescribed eyeglasses for the first time. I hated my glasses, because they were big and ugly, and they made me even more self-conscious around women. I disliked wearing them, and convinced myself that they were a huge—possibly even insurmountable—"pick-up handicap" when my friend Adam Rosen and I went out to the local bars.

After a little discussion and experimentation, Adam and I solved my problem equitably: We took turns being the designated driver. So, every other weekend I was able to not only leave those awful spectacles at home, but I could also have a few drinks while going out to the Boston bars—always hoping, of course, that I'd meet someone special.

One evening, Adam and I headed off to Copperfield's, a popular nightclub about a twenty-minute drive from our homes. It was Adam's turn to be the designated driver, so—much to my delight—I was able to drink that night *and* to leave my glasses at home. Total freedom! …Or so I initially thought.

Once established at Copperfield's, I was thoroughly enjoying myself and everything was going according to plan—until Adam met a young lady with whom he had previously had a relationship. Intoxicated by the prospect of some fun with his female friend, Adam forgot his obligation to me and proceeded to get very, very drunk. By the time we decided to head home, he was in no state to drive. Of course, as that night's "designated drinker," I'd had two or three drinks myself—but I figured I was in better shape to drive than Adam. And to make matters worse, I wasn't wearing my glasses.

I'd like to point out that now, as a much more mature adult *and* as the parent of a teenage son, I am horrified when I consider all of the tragic consequences my decision to drive that night could have had. The bottom line is, I should never have been behind the wheel, regardless of the fact that I saw myself as the "better" choice, and really not that intoxicated.

In the Copperfield's parking lot, I somehow managed to stuff an oblivious Adam into the passenger seat of his car before climbing in myself. Thus situated, I turned the key in the ignition and began to head towards our hometown of Needham, driving—I thought—as cautiously as I could. We were just a few miles from our homes when I saw lights flashing behind me. Obediently, I pulled over and waited, heart pounding, for the policemen to approach my window.

There is no safe blood alcohol level, and for that reason responsible drinking means no drinking and driving.
—Former MADD president Katherine Prescott

As I had feared, the officers told me I had been swerving while driving, and then followed standard procedure by asking me to step out of the car. They could tell I had been drinking, but unlike my passenger, I wasn't hopelessly intoxicated. Absolutely terrified, I channeled every ounce of concentration I possessed into walking a straight line and reciting the alphabet correctly at the officers' request. While I was basically successful in both endeavors, I was nevertheless consumed by visions of doom. The very last thing I needed—or wanted—was to lose my license, especially after having just started my new job.

As I anxiously considered the various ways in which my life could fall apart as a result of my poor decision to drive home that night, the officers stepped aside and deliberated my fate. After what seemed like hours to me, the officers told me because I was a local Needham kid they had decided to let me off with a stern warning and that they would drive me and Adam home. I would, however, have to leave the car behind and pick it up the following morning.

I could have hugged them! Barely able to believe my good fortune, I thanked each policeman as sincerely as I knew how and assured them I would never, ever make this terrible mistake again.

Yes, the apparent ending of this encounter seemed too good to be true—and turns out, it was. No sooner had these kind policemen finished telling me that they were going to treat me with leniency when Adam recovered semiconsciousness. Seeing the cops talking to me out of his rear view mirror and horribly misunderstanding the situation, Adam fumbled the door open and attempted to launch himself out of the car. Not even close to being in control of his movements, though, he landed headfirst in the street. From this undignified position, he started yelling obscenities at the top of his lungs, insulting the policemen and ordering them to "Leave my friend alone!"

Horrified, I didn't want to believe my eyes or ears. *Shut up!* I silently begged Adam. *We're almost out of this mess! Don't make more trouble!* Unfortunately, my fears were well-founded. Adam's offensive behavior changed the mood of the two law enforcement officers. They now rather angrily asked me to recite the alphabet backwards, which I couldn't do stone cold sober—let alone in this emotionally charged situation. Upon my failure to make it much farther than the letter "W," I was read my rights, handcuffed, and literally thrown into the rear seat of the police cruiser. Adam sloppily followed soon afterwards.

When I got to the police station, I was breathalysed and my demographic details were processed. It was fairly late at this point, and—Needham being a relatively safe town—there were no other people around. The cops who had arrested me were obviously still upset by the awful insults that Adam had hurled at them. Their demeanor was still markedly rough as they now pushed and manhandled me into a cell. On the verge of panic, I pleaded with the officers not to leave me in there because I was feeling claustrophobic, but my fears didn't matter to them now. Into the cell I went. The policemen did, however, give me an opportunity to make a phone call.

I made a Herculean effort to get my nerves under control and, hoping that I sounded coherent, anxiously called my good friend Julie Weiner. God bless her! Julie, who was probably sleeping at that crazy hour of the evening, said she'd come as soon as she could in order to bail me out. By this time, Adam had long since been released, because while his behavior had been worse than obnoxious, he had technically done nothing illegal.

I, on the other hand, was still trapped in a tiny cell at the police station, having to use all of my mental powers not to succumb to the meltdown that threatened to overcome my nerves, which were strained to the breaking point. For about an hour that seemed more like ten to me, I sat confined within three concrete walls and one solid fiberglass door that had only three inches of clearance at its top and bottom. I've experienced quite a bit of mental anguish in my life, but I believe that this time in jail was absolutely the most terrified I have ever been.

As fate would have it, my parents were vacationing on Cape Cod when this incident occurred. Although I would have preferred that they never found out about my escapade, I knew I had to explain what had just happened. With great trepidation, I called them after I made it safely home from the police station and recounted what I had done. Julie, thank you, thank you, thank you for driving me home that night!!!

Both my mother and father, to my surprise and relief, were amazing. In fact, they didn't get very angry at all. No doubt they realized, as parents often do, that I had already been frightened to death by the experience itself, and was already thoroughly berating myself. In stark contrast, though, my sister, Kimberly, was furious at what she saw as our parents' permissive approach. Clearly, she thought I was getting preferential treatment and lobbied for my public flogging, at the very least. Fortunately, her pleas fell on deaf ears.

For the next six months, I now had to wait with mounting trepidation for my court appearance on DUI charges. This alone would have been enough to keep my anxiety levels sky-high, especially because I had no clue whatsoever what my fate might be. You see, my breathalyser test had proven inconclusive because my blood alcohol level reading fell right on the line that separated "legal" from "illegal." My fate thus rested squarely in the judge's hands—I could only hope that he or she would be having a good day when I made my appearance in court!

If you must drink and drive, drink Pepsi.
—Author unknown, as seen on a bumper sticker

A DUI's Lasting Impact

Looking back at my alcohol-related brush with the law, I believe that this incident pushed me a significant distance in the direction of being "grown up." Yes, I had graduated from college, was working a full-time job, and (in theory) had control of my decisions and direction, but in many ways I was still a kid. Like many recent college graduates, I didn't fully understand just how weighty a bad decision in the "real world" could be. I needed to learn that everything you do has consequences, good or bad.

That night changed a lot of my behaviors and beliefs. Afterward, I was markedly more careful, and was much less apt to assume that everything would "be okay" if I took a risk. I considered the possible ramifications of all of my actions in much greater detail, because I now knew that they could become reality.

That said, I think it is worth noting that even an anxiety-prone young man like me was not immune from engaging in reckless behavior. Our society tends to paint the rebels, the rambunctious, and the rowdy as those much more likely to get into trouble. We are always shocked when a clean-cut, successful, authority-heeding person (like I was) makes a mistake. I'm here to tell you, we *shouldn't* be shocked. *Everyone* slips up from time to time, and nothing—not upbringing, and not even innate anxiety—can prevent it. If anything, we should expect the young people who are bringing home straight As and who push themselves to be superstars to make bad decisions too. After all, these individuals are likely feeling the greatest academic stress, and therefore are probably also prone to self-medicate in order to relieve the tension.

I am grateful to my parents for handling this situation with poise and understanding, and for not making my fragile emotional state at that time worse by berating or blaming me. After ensuring that I was truly repentant and that I had learned a valuable lesson, they set about supporting me. Their constructive reaction has influenced the way I parent my own son. I, too, realize that even the best kids (and adults!) will make bad decisions from time to time. It is always my goal to help struggling individuals (whether it be my son, a friend, a coworker, or someone I've just met) take what value they can from a regrettable situation, and then move forward in a more positive direction.

Driving and Alcohol: A Warning

I cannot stress enough that driving after even one drink is dangerous and can lead to legal ramifications—*even if your blood alcohol content (BAC) is under the legal limit.* Just a slight buzz can impair your judgment and reaction time, which can lead to recklessness, accident, injury, and even death.

In fact, most states consider a person with a blood alcohol content of 0.05 percent to 0.08 percent to be impaired, even though the legal limit in all states is 0.08 percent. And here's an especially sobering fact: If you injure someone while driving under the influence (which doesn't necessarily mean that your BAC is *over* the legal limit), you might be subjected to a mandatory multi-year jail sentence in many states.

So please—just don't risk it.

Of course in addition to all of my anxiety from the consequences of this crazy evening—I was already under a great deal of stress starting my new career, learning the ropes, and assuming new responsibilities. I thus thought I was under just about as much pressure as I could take without blowing my lid when Murphy's Law held true once again.

Learning the Ropes

During my first three months at Foreign Autopart, my father had me spend three weeks in each department in order to learn the business from the inside out. After all, how could I grow into an effective leader if I didn't understand every aspect of how our company worked?

Throughout the first week in any given department, the employees would typically be suspicious of and cynical toward me, assuming that I was there simply due to nepotism rather than talent, and perhaps even worse, thinking that I was a spy. By the second week, however, I had generally won my coworkers over because they realized that I was hardworking and genuine. And then, just as we were beginning to build good working relationships and were becoming friends, I'd be moved along to another department to begin the whole uncomfortable process all over again. Thanks, Dad! (Just kidding!)

These experiences, though anxiety-provoking at the time (there's that word again…anxiety!), would pay huge dividends for me in later years on the job due to the many friendships I gained and the respect I earned.

After completing this hands-on "tour" of the company's various departments, I went to work in our National Sales Department for the rest of 1988. This job required me to call auto parts stores and warehouses throughout the country and convince them to place more of their parts orders with us. Of my entire eighteen-year career at Foreign Autopart and Autopart International,[11] I experienced my greatest personal highs in this department.

Find a job you like and you add five days to every week.
—H. Jackson Brown, Jr.

For the most part, I spent my workdays in National Sales at my desk making outgoing sales call after outgoing sales call. I found that I had a real knack for engaging potential customers over the phone, and as I honed my skills, the satisfaction I felt continued to grow because I knew I was adding valuable accounts to our company. Later in my career it was my job to make it easier for others to score goals. In 1988, however, I myself was the goal-scorer in sales—and it felt great!

---

11   In 1998, four years after we had begun selling parts for domestic cars as well, we changed our company name from Foreign Autopart to Autopart International.

An Expert View on the Workplace

Many of us would like to think that what we do at work doesn't define us, but the truth is that your sense of self-worth is measured and developed to a large extent in the workplace. Taking that into account, your job should ideally challenge you to:

- Extend yourself in your various areas of strength
- Develop new skills
- Learn new information
- Improve communication and relationship skills

As long as most of the above challenges are present in your work in healthy proportions, you'll most likely find it fulfilling.

However, any time your work is boring, less than stimulating, or overly stressful, your energy level is likely to drop. This will cause your engagement to be far less than is ideal, potentially resulting in cynicism, anger, and depression. If you notice that your job is cultivating these negative qualities in you, consider looking for a new position. Staying at a workplace that changes you in harmful ways won't just make you loathe the 9-to-5 grind…its impact on your outlook and attitude will reach into your personal life as well.

A Rivalry Gets Personal

During October of 1988, my father also asked me to accompany Rick King, our purchasing manager at the time, to Automechanika, a huge auto parts show that is held every other year in Frankfurt, Germany.

To be honest, I was a bit uneasy with the thought of going to Germany. While I hadn't personally experienced the horrors of the Holocaust, as a Jew, I still didn't exactly consider Germany to be at the top of my travel wish list.

This general unease, combined with the residual separation anxiety with which I still struggle a bit to this day, meant that I was not completely comfortable when Rick and I were invited to a special dinner while in Germany. It was being hosted by a large Swedish exhaust manufacturer of ours.

To my surprise, of all the invited guests that evening, I was seated right next to the top brass from the Swedish company. I was extremely conscious of the honor; however, what I *didn't* realize was that it would trigger a very unpleasant set of events involving a competitor of ours from New Jersey, Jim Clark.

About ten years my dad's junior, Clark had a big reputation and an even bigger ego. Because I was new to the business, I had no idea of the extremely competitive feelings he harbored towards my father. Looking back, though, it doesn't surprise me in the least that Clark was rankled by the fact that I, Steve Patkin's wet-behind-the-ears son, had gotten a prime spot at the dining table while he was relegated to the far end, away from what he doubtless saw as the "important" discussion. (I found out later that I had been assigned my prime seat because Foreign Autopart paid its bills on time while Clark's company did not.)

Thus provoked, Clark proceeded to get drunk—but he didn't stop there. From his seat about four chairs from my own, he began to verbally abuse me. He was going to set up a huge warehouse close to our Foreign Autopart stores in the Boston area, he said, implying that he was going to try to seriously dent my family's business. Much worse than that, though, he also began calling me a "kike" (the word that the German SS soldiers used when pushing Jews into the ovens to their deaths during the Holocaust) just loud enough for me to hear him.

Not surprisingly, I found this attack to be incredibly distressing, especially since it was occurring in Germany, the country most associated with the Holocaust! It was of course also very upsetting to the other dinner guests sitting between us, but the general consensus was that there really wasn't much to be said to someone who was so drunk. And so, I spent the rest of the meal in extreme discomfort.

Later that night I called my dad from my hotel room, where I was still shaking—and frankly in total shock and dismay. My father said that I should try to let what had just happened go in order to enjoy the rest of the show, but he assured me that we would discuss how to handle Clark as soon as I got back home.

Small Businesses Can Be Very Upsetting at Times!

I came home anticipating a very sympathetic reception from our leadership team due to all that Jim Clark had put me through, and I also expected that as a group we would come up with a game plan for getting even with this terribly anti-Semitic competitor. To my total and complete surprise, what I got instead from one of our top managers was the assumption that I must have been to blame for instigating the whole incident in some way because he had never personally seen Clark act in such a poor manner before.

Outraged at this suggestion, especially after all I had just been through and feeling that my own character had been impugned, I turned to my dad for support. Ever the diplomat, though, he remained fairly passive. I was furious! Fueled by hurt and anger, I went on to tell my accuser exactly what I thought of him in extremely impassioned tones. I doubt that my dad or anyone else in the room that day had ever heard so many four-letter words in their lives!

I learned two lessons concerning the politics of close-knit teams that day, whether in a work setting or not. First, often within a group, members will prioritize maintaining harmony over doing what is right. Second, we must realize that *our* rules and others' rules for how people should behave in different situations may vary. For example, I am all about standing by my friends and family. In fact, I like to think no one could have a better friend in the world than me. Thus, according to my personal rules, *of course* all of my teammates at Foreign Autopart should have backed me against Clark—but some of the others' rules in terms of how to react to this situation were quite different at that point in their careers. It was understandable that I was upset; however, I hope today I would be more understanding of our different philosophies regarding how to handle someone like Jim Clark.

More Lessons in the School of Hard Knocks

Clark was as good as his drunken word—he did open up a Boston operation, but it had little impact on our company. Later, he did apologize through a mutual business associate for his behavior that night in Germany, saying that he was drunk and didn't, of course, mean what he had said. Eventually, Clark's company was bought out and he left the auto parts business. Unfortunately, though, the conflict he had started with me in Germany caused me to soon make a different, very costly mistake and thus learn another critical business lesson:

Be careful not to let your emotions due to one bad situation or encounter cloud your judgment for the next.

When the news that Clark's company was coming to Boston began to circulate—and probably when word of our German encounter also got around—I received a phone call from the owner of Foreign Autopart's number one Boston-area competitor. Mike James owned about five stores in the Boston area at the time. He was a smooth operator and knew exactly what he was doing when he called me out of the blue to suggest that we get together in order to form a joint strategy to minimize the impact of Clark's arrival in Boston.

I was, of course, still very young and learning the business, and I didn't have a true understanding of James or his reputation. My father, however, did, and so he tried to warn me that this meeting was a bad idea. But I was naïve, still angry at Clark (and thus quite open to making his Boston debut difficult), and frankly very flattered by James's invitation. (Isn't it amazing that my dad let me learn the business for myself—my way—even when he knew that a meeting like this could potentially cost his company in the short term?) James and I met at his favorite Newton, Massachusetts, restaurant for dinner, whereupon he got me quite drunk and grilled me about many things, including who our best Foreign Autopart store managers were.

Within three months, James hired our top three money-making store managers away from us! To say the very least, this was a significant blow to me personally and to our company. At the time, I couldn't believe that anyone could be so calculating and ruthless. I was terrified that I had totally destroyed my father and uncles' business because the three stores that these managers ran at that time accounted for over 90 percent of our entire eighteen-store chain's net profits.

As always, my dad was the best boss and father in the world. He simply reassured me that we would be fine without these three traitors. He told me not to worry about it too much. In my case, as you know though, that was easier said than done, as I now brutally beat myself up for that awful rookie mistake for months and even years to come.

Mistakes are painful when they happen, but years later a collection of mistakes is what is called experience.
—Denis Waitley

Father Knows Best

Experience has since taught me that my father was indeed correct in his reactions to my gaffe with Mike James. First, in business *and* in private life, those who can be bought, bribed, or wooed away from you will not offer you the long-term support you need—even if they remain a part of your team due to a lack of better options.

Secondly, I had to learn the hard way that it's prudent to be wary of a competitor's warm overtures. Yes, certainly listen to others' propositions and ideas, but don't give them your implicit trust as unwarily as I did. If I'd listened to my father on this subject, I could have saved myself a good deal of grief—though perhaps I would have misstepped similarly elsewhere in the future.

Don't argue for other people's weaknesses. Don't argue for your own. When you make a mistake, admit it, correct it, and learn from it—immediately.

—Stephen Covey

Ultimately, all three of these setbacks in 1988 and 1989 turned out to be incredibly important, positive lessons for me. And, by the grace of God, they all did end up well. First, in terms of my court appearance, the older judge who handled my case found me innocent, saying that in his mind I had certainly been through enough already. And, as I've said, because of that six months of hell waiting to find out my fate, I have never again made the stupid mistake of driving drunk!

As for Jim Clark and Mike James, my negative experiences with these industry "colleagues" really lit a fire under me to perform. I cannot tell you how many days I worked more than twelve hours at a time because I wanted to inflict severe pain on these two competitors. And I certainly accomplished my goal, bloodthirsty though it was! My company outperformed theirs by a mile for the next seventeen years, and Autopart International is still doing so to this day!

The difference between a job and a career is the difference between forty and sixty hours a week.

—Robert Frost

TIPS FROM TODD:
CHAPTER SEVEN

- **Realize that passion is a better motivator than money.** Ostensibly, you put in hours at work because you're paid to do so…but what many people fail to realize until they've burned out is that money keeps you going for only so long. Make every effort to find a job that you enjoy for its own sake, where completing a project, achieving a quota, or making a sale feels like a win for you personally—as well as for your company. When you find fulfillment as a "goal-scorer" at work, you will continue to have the energy, inspiration, and drive that you need.

- **Move forward positively after making a mistake.** No one is immune from making mistakes. Sometimes our slip-ups are barely noticed, and other times they seem to stop our lives on a dime. Always keep in mind, though, that no one is perfect and realize that you cannot change what is already past. The most constructive thing you can do when things go awry is to first quickly do all you can to make things right. Next, identify where you went wrong, and finally, figure out how you can prevent similar occurrences in the future.

- **Don't make a bad situation worse by overreacting.** Steering clear of overreactions goes hand in hand with moving positively forward after a mistake. Whether you're beating yourself up for doing something you shouldn't have or jumping headfirst like I did into another mistake, realize that excessive anger, accusations, re-hashing, berating, and over-reactions do not accomplish anything constructive. Instead, they cause you emotional harm and often even cause you to make costly future decisions.

- **Remember that each of us—and our "rules" for life—may be different.** Everyone has a set of personal "rules" by which he or she lives his or her life. And the fact is, your set of rules is never going to coincide completely with someone else's. Before letting a difference in opinion, reaction, behavior, etc. ruin a relationship or friendship, remind yourself of all of the things you value about that person/group of people. Unless you are facing a fundamental difference in values, don't lose your friends over differences in your respective sets of "rules"!

CHAPTER EIGHT

Into the Fire

"The difference between a successful person and the others is not a lack of strength or knowledge but rather a lack of will."
—Vince Lombardi

Like many young people in the process of launching their careers, I had gotten off to a fairly rocky start, and like millions before me, had learned some important lessons the hard way. But as a result, I was finally beginning to feel more comfortable in my own abilities, and I was in the process of carving out a career I could be proud of.

By 1989 I had a year's worth of experience at my family's business under my belt, and I had begun to get a firm handle on how its various departments were run. Just as importantly, I also was beginning to get a sense of the strengths and weaknesses of our company and its people.

In this chapter, I'd like to share with you several anecdotes from my first few years on the job that really stand out—and I'd also like to pass along the lessons they taught me. While none of these instances is by itself a "mile marker" on my happiness journey, I believe that in every life—not just mine—it's experiences like these that combine to give us the hang-ups that lead to our lows... and also develop within us the coping skills that enable us to move through those rough spots and back to the sunshine.

So, please join me as I relive another part of my education in the school of hard knocks!

Experience is not what happens to a man. It is what a man does with what happens to him.

—Aldous Leonard Huxley

A Surly Supervisor

Even to my novice eye, one area of Foreign Autopart that seemed problematic was our National Sales Department. As I have explained, I loved working in this department where it was my goal to convince warehouses and stores across the country to buy their foreign auto parts from us. My experience in National Sales, however, was still characterized by the sorts of trials and difficulties that ultimately gave me the real-world education I needed concerning business in general and management in particular.

Mario Magro, my immediate supervisor in the National Sales Department, was very helpful and supportive. That was where the affirming leadership stopped, though. The manager of the sales department—the "head honcho," if you will—was himself a much more rigid and often-critical man named Brian Jones. A devotee of the traditional command and control leadership model, Jones's use of his power often intimidated the people underneath him. Also, the longer I worked in the department, the more thoroughly I discovered just how much Jones did not get along with my father, often openly disagreeing with his decisions when talking to the salespeople. I even found out that Jones stretched the truth on occasion when telling the salespeople about the decisions he and my father made concerning the department.

People ask the difference between a leader and a boss. The leader leads, and the boss drives.

—Theodore Roosevelt

The net result of this autocratic behavior was the creation of an unproductive "us" (employees) vs. "them" (owners) culture. Quite frankly, I—a twenty-three-year-old kid at this time—was often scared of Jones. But I must say, from a professional standpoint Jones certainly knew his stuff, and when he was in a good mood, boy was he fun to be around. Overall, though, he taught me that no matter how much you know about your business, what matters the most in achieving success is how you treat people all of the time—not just some of the time.

Contentious Clients

In terms of learning the rough and tumble, very competitive auto parts business, two other incidents from my early baptism in the sales department stand out in my mind. On one occasion, I thought I had secured a large $10,000-plus order from a warehouse in Florida. To say that I was excited is a vast understatement. I could barely contain myself, because I just *knew* that I was going to be an absolute hero when this order came in. My entire sales target to reach at that point was just $30,000 per month, and most of my orders stayed in the $500 to $1,000 range. This $10,000 to $12,000 single order was thus a *really* big deal to me!

Well, the purchasing agent in Florida with whom I had been speaking told me to call back on a certain day and at a specific time to finalize the deal. Of course, I was on the phone and chomping at the bit at that precise moment. But when my contact answered, my spirits quickly faded as he told me in pungent and offensive four-letter words to leave him "the blank" alone! I was a mess. For one thing, no one had ever so offensively sworn at me before and especially in a work setting, *and* I had just lost the order of a lifetime—for such a young salesman, anyway. And I had no idea why!

Greatly disturbed and unable to rid myself of the worries and questions this encounter had sparked, I finally summoned up the courage to call this purchasing agent again about a week later. In response to my question as to what I'd done wrong, my erstwhile contact told me that if I was going to last in this business I had a lot to learn, and that I *definitely* needed to develop a thicker skin. He explained that I had simply caught him in a bad mood on the day I'd reached him, and because I had not called back during the following forty-eight hours, he had been forced to give that amazing order to my competition.

On another occasion, I called a company in Missouri to pitch our very popular direct fit original equipment exhaust for foreign vehicles. I had barely finished speaking when the buyer told me point blank, "To us, foreign parts are like foreign people—we don't like either of them in Missouri!" And then I heard a click—he had hung up on me.

Clearly, I was going to have to learn how to deal with other people's strange and often incomprehensible ways of working…and I was definitely going to have to be careful not to fall into my past habit of assuming that other people's negative actions were the result of my mistakes.

An Expert View on Developing a Thicker Skin

Logically, you know that sometimes people have legitimate complaints about you, and sometimes they don't. Sometimes those complaints are expressed diplomatically, and sometimes they aren't. But that knowledge doesn't stop many of us from taking every single piece of criticism to heart. And that's unhealthy—it leads to low self-esteem, decreased confidence, elevated stress and anxiety, and so forth.

The fact is, no one is perfect. We all have our faults—you *and* the people around you. So before you allow another's comment or reaction to deeply impact your life, it's helpful to perform a "reality check" on that person's opinion or response. Ask yourself the following questions:

- Does this person treat others the same way he or she treats me?
- Is there any other evidence supporting this person's complaints and comments? For example, have other people complained about the same thing?
- What are other people's views on comments made about me?
- To my knowledge, is this person preoccupied with or upset about anything else that doesn't have to do with me?

In many cases, honest answers to these questions will put a complaint into better perspective and help to lessen its sting. If, however, you find evidence that a piece of criticism is well founded, take the necessary steps to correct or improve that area of your life!

A (Big!) Change in the Lineup

Despite the fact that I could never predict what any given day would be like in the National Sales Department, I was nevertheless very sad to leave in January of 1989 after ten months of working there. My departure was prompted by a positive reason, though: My father now wanted me to learn more about our most critical profit-generating division: our eighteen-store chain.

I spent the next two months learning from the department's number one man himself, Bob Wicks—ostensibly an honor. As fate would have it, though, in March of 1989, Wicks had a severe heart attack—and we mutually decided that it would be best for him to leave so he could focus more on his health. And we did, of course, give Wicks a very generous severance package.

Wicks's position as head of our store chain was an extremely important one, and his heart attack thus created a huge need that had to be filled within our company. No position was more important to the profits, and therefore the health, of our company than the person who led our stores. Obviously, it was crucial to plug this void with a capable, trustworthy leader who knew the business, and I wondered who we'd find to fit these criteria.

Thus, I could not have been more surprised when my father, with my uncle's approval, asked me to run the store chain. To this day, the memory of that offer makes me thank God for the incredible dad I have! At the time, I was honored and (of course!) also quite nervous, but mostly I remember being excited. I'm sure youthful pride played a large part in my optimism. However, I honestly already believed I could do a much better job than Wicks…even though I knew relatively little about the auto parts business back then.

Hello, Authority!

So, two short weeks after Bob Wicks's heart attack, my dad and I met with Wicks's top seven store supervisors to inform them of my promotion. Six of the seven men were incredibly upset that we had decided to retire Wicks and weren't shy about giving my dad and me a very hard time in this meeting.

Their objections weren't unreasonable. After all, most of them had worked under Wicks for over fifteen years, during which time, I was acutely aware, Wicks had been the good guy. In these men's eyes, their friend and protector had been abruptly replaced with the owner's own son! They were much more upset, I think, about losing Wicks than about my taking over.

Only one of the seven men, Andy Cuneo, had the courage to go against the opinions of his colleagues. He alone had faith in my father's decision, and staunchly supported my promotion. Thank you, Andy!

Of course, the reality was that each of these men *had* to accept me as their boss—or find alternative employment. And to be honest, it didn't take very long for me to gain their confidence and to revise their opinions of the decision that my dad had made.

Leadership Lessons

I have always believed that you reap what you sow with your employees. If you treat your people well, you will get more loyalty and production. If you treat your employees like gold, you will get unbelievable commitment, performance, and results.

The worst mistake a boss can make is not to say "well done."
—John Ashcroft

Operating under this belief, it didn't take me very long to improve my initially strained relations with my store supervisors and with all of the people working underneath them in our stores. From day one, I rewarded all employees well for good work…and I rewarded them even better for great work. I took every opportunity to hug and praise everyone. In return for my sincerity, generosity, and love—yes, love!—I got terrific effort and great results from our people.

A good manager is a man who isn't worried about his own career but rather the careers of those who work for him.
—H. S. M. Burns

In a way, those six store supervisors were right to doubt me at first. When I initially assumed Bob Wicks's position, I was young and very inexperienced. The simple truth was that I didn't know a whole heck of a lot about car parts. But deep down I just knew that in management, knowledge of the product is secondary to how you treat your people. It's true: You can be relatively inexperienced and lack a great deal of knowledge about your industry, but if you are a great motivator and builder of people, you'll almost always finish first in the end.

I also believe that to get loyalty and production from a team, the team's leader must work harder and longer than anyone else. As you know, I was no stranger to hard work, so being the first to the office and the last to leave was consistent with my work ethic. It didn't take long for all of my store supervisors to appreciate how much harder I worked—not just for them, but for the rest of the people in the store chain, too.

By working faithfully eight hours a day, you may eventually get to be a boss and work twelve hours a day.
—Robert Frost

Continuing Controversy

From time to time, in my new position I was required to visit each of Foreign Autopart's eighteen stores. One of them was located in Albany, New York, a four-hour drive from my home. Whenever I needed to be at that particular store, or at any other store location for that matter, I made sure to be the first one there—often arriving as early as 7:00 in the morning—regardless of the length of my commute. Believe me, everyone in the eighteen-store chain heard about it when Todd Patkin beat the Albany, New York, store manager to work, even though he had to get up at 3:00 in the morning to do so!

Nonetheless, despite all of my attempts to win over the employees in our store chain, there were still a few people who didn't like the idea of someone so new, so young, so inexperienced, or frankly, so motivated being their boss. I remember driving to the aforementioned Albany store to meet for the first time with its manager, Beth.

The initial meetings with the store managers were stressful for me because I knew that I might find myself the target of bad feelings and negative attitudes from the people whose allegiance to Bob Wicks had been strong. On my way to this particular Albany meeting, I was especially apprehensive because I *knew* that Beth had been a big fan of Wicks's.

I mastered my nerves and was on the road by 3:00 in the morning so that I could be at that store by 7:30 for sure. Somewhat to my surprise, I left the meeting feeling that my talk with Beth had gone fairly well. But I got more of a shock (this one decidedly less pleasant) upon my return to headquarters where

I found Beth meeting with my father in his office. I had stopped for lunch on the way back, and Beth obviously had not. Turns out she was handing in her notice!

After hearing what had happened, I felt that Beth was being very impulsive—but she was determined to quit. She said she felt that I was simply too motivated to have huge sales increases in all of our stores as soon as possible. Thus I, she was sure, would be too demanding a boss for her.

Years later, Beth did contact me and ask to return to her old job. (At the time she made this request, however, that position would have required her to work three Saturdays a month, which she was not interested in doing.) Beth's request was not unusual: Almost everyone who ever left our company over the years eventually called, asking to come back. And if possible, I always gave these individuals second chances unless they had stolen from our company.

Clearly, we were beginning to create a work and reward environment that was hard to replicate anywhere else!

The Most Important Resource

Another lesson I learned during my first years on the job was the importance of recognizing, attracting, and retaining the very best talent. When your team has extraordinary people on its roster, it's crucial to make sure they are very well compensated and that they feel incredibly appreciated and happy. When those things happen, you'll get their loyalty and best work. And believe me, there is simply no substitute for outstanding people who are in the "zone" (functioning at their peak levels)!

I was fortunate enough to recognize and retain two such star employees during 1989. The first, Mario Magro, my immediate supervisor when I had worked in the National Sales Department, possessed tremendous personality, leadership skills, and ability as a salesman. However, his experiences with Brian Jones had prompted him to accept a position with another company.

I realized that there was no way I could let Mario go. Fortunately, I was able to convince him to stay with me, transfer to the store division, and be in charge of opening our new Foreign Autopart stores. (You see, Foreign Autopart had not opened a single new store since 1979, and I figured it was time for us to roar and show our teeth once again!)

Likewise, I recognized great potential in Foster Ball, a.k.a. "Buster." I had worked for Buster during my last summer of college, at which point he was the manager of our Somerville, Massachusetts, store. Through the years, though,

Buster had fallen out of favor with Bob Wicks and was even on the verge of being fired before Wicks's heart attack occurred.

Through my advocacy, Buster was now temporarily demoted instead of fired—I promised Buster that although he'd be forced to swallow his pride, he'd be rewarded in the future if he stayed on and produced to the best of his abilities. Neither Buster nor I could have known that it would only be a matter of three weeks before I could keep my promise, as I was now the brand-new head of our store chain!

Keeping Mario and Buster are the two best personnel decisions I ever made. By 1998, these two men were in fact helping me to run our entire, by then, thirty-two-store chain as co-branch store managers. And today, they each are key leaders within Autopart International's now over two-hundred-plus-store chain.

No doubt about it, my first two years on the job were jam-packed with learning experiences. You know what they say: You learn something new every day! And it's true. As I gained traction in my career, I was also on the verge of gaining quite a bit of new self-knowledge that would change the course of my life forever.

Life can only be understood backward, but it must be lived forward.

—Soren Kierkegaard

TIPS FROM TODD:
CHAPTER EIGHT

These tips are drawn from my business experience, but remember that they are all applicable to any situation involving leadership or teamwork: families, classes, groups of friends, worship communities, etc.! I hope that you will be able to apply them to your life regardless of what roles you fill.

- **Create a positive environment that's not run on fear.** It's often tempting to use the threat of punishment as a way to get what you want—but that approach only breeds fear, resentment, and unhappiness. Rather than primarily causing others to live in fear of making a mistake, motivate them to succeed and achieve instead. When people buy into a shared mission and set of goals, they will scrupulously avoid mistakes of their own accord…and they will want to exceed instead of just meet expectations.

- **Reward well and often.** In a vast majority of situations, the carrot is more effective than the stick. Think about it: Wouldn't you rather work to gain a reward than to avoid punishment? Rewards—whether in the form of a sincere compliment, departmental award, or salary bonus—serve as excellent motivators. They also create a very positive atmosphere.

- **Keep everyone on the same team.** Likewise, it's also tempting to shore up your own authority by undermining that of others. (Plus, it feels good to be the big dog!) This accusatory, finger-pointing strategy might be easy, but again, it doesn't have long-term staying power. After all, a house divided cannot stand! It is essential that all individuals within an organization, team, group, or family be of one accord about fundamentals and leadership. If not, valuable effort will be wasted working against each other instead of toward progress.

- **Don't let the negative attitudes of others affect your own productivity.** It's easier said than done, but try not to let others' negativity, unwarranted criticism, rudeness, or pessimism affect your own attitude. Think about it: An ill-considered snide comment from someone else who is having a bad day, like the buyer in Florida with the huge order I was expecting, might occupy five seconds of his day—but dwelling on it can completely ruin yours. Also, as much as possible, avoid spending time with individuals who are likely to adversely affect your emotional well-being.

- **Lead by example.** Quite frankly, "Do as I say, not as I do" is a horrible leadership example for everyone from parents to pastors to principals! You should be willing to do what you ask those who are under your authority to do, and you should put forth more than the amount of effort you expect from them. This will inspire respect and loyalty and will do wonders for your credibility!

CHAPTER NINE

Epiphany

"Man is made or unmade by himself. In the armory
of thought he forges the weapons by which he
destroys himself. He also fashions the tools with
which he builds for himself heavenly mansions
of joy, strength, and peace."
—James Allen

We are all influenced by others. Our opinions, our behaviors, our choices, our mannerisms, our attitudes, and much more are shaped by the people we encounter and spend time around. And of this group of influencers, there are always a few people who stand out positively and who make you say, "Wow! My life is noticeably different and better because this person was in it. I would never have ended up here by myself."

You don't have to be a "person of influence" to be influential.
In fact, the most influential people in my life are probably not even
aware of the things they've taught me.
                                                                              —Scott Adams

These outstanding influencers might be teachers, parents, friends, coworkers, or religious leaders, for example—or in today's world of technology and connectivity, they might even include authors, speakers, or other figures whom you've never even met in person. The point is that through their advice, guidance, or example, positive influencers expand your horizons and help you to grow in maturity. They literally change your life for the better.

Without hesitation, I can point to the well-known self-help expert Tony Robbins as being one of the most profoundly positive influencers to come into my life. And I have to give the credit for his introduction to Tom Quirk. I hired Tom in 1990 to be Foreign Autopart's very first branch store road salesman, and within a short span of time he became our branch store road sales manager. Prior to Tom, it was the norm in the New England auto parts industry to find a good location on Main Street in a city, fill it with the right assortment of auto parts and good counter people, and then just wait for the phones to ring.

Well, from day one, Tom's aggressive salesmanship turned our entire industry on its head. Wherever he went, our sales spiked significantly. Tom visited face-to-face hundreds (and later thousands) of garages, convincing them to buy more of their auto parts from us. In subsequent years, he and the team of salesmen he developed grew into one of the industry's most ferocious and respected divisions.

Twenty years after our first meeting, however, it's very clear to me that the greatest gift God brought to me through Tom was neither the millions of extra dollars he and his sales teams made for our company through the years nor the clients that they wrested away from the competition. It was something much more significant than that.

Good Things Come in Small Packages

As I began to work closely with Tom, I noticed that something was "different" about him. It didn't take me too long to figure out that that "something" was his outlook. Privately, I marveled at how unruffled he always seemed to be, regardless of the circumstances. Events that would ratchet up my anxiety and cause me to worry for days on end seemed to have little effect on Tom. He didn't stress over life's difficulties; instead, he embraced them, viewed them as challenges, and always seemed to manage them and the rest of his life very effectively.

Tom was optimistic, relaxed, and purposeful. In contrast, in 1990 I was intense, harried, and worried. Emotionally, we couldn't have been farther apart. Not surprisingly, I desperately wanted more of what he had and less of what made me so anxious and jumpy.

One day while we were working together, I asked Tom how he was able to maintain such a positive attitude.

"Being positive is a choice, Todd," he said to me. "You have too much negativity in your head. You need to clear all of that out and start to look at things differently."

"Well, that's easy to say. But how can I *do* it?" I asked, feeling somewhat skeptical.

Tom didn't reply immediately. After a slight pause, he walked over to his truck, reached into the back seat, and pulled out what appeared to be a box. As Tom returned to where I stood, the cynical gears in my brain were already revving up, tempting me to dismiss the notion that a plastic box was going to transform my personality.

"Ever heard of this guy?" asked Tom, holding out the box. "Tony Robbins. This is his Personal Power tape set."

I reached out and took the box, sweeping a cursory eye over its label. *Personal Power: The Driving Force! 30 Day Program for Unlimited Success.* I barely suppressed an eye roll. *Yeah, right*, I thought to myself. *What a bunch of mumbo-jumbo. I'm old enough not to believe in fairy tales any more.*

After all, with an adolescence punctuated by bullying and academic pressures, a hellish college roller-coaster ride, and a responsibility-filled first year on the job, the last decade of my life had been absolutely brutal. And Tom honestly thought that this tape set was going to change all of that in just thirty days? Fat chance. If this Tony Robbins program had worked for Tom, clearly he wasn't having to deal with the multitude of anxieties and pressures that plagued me.

At the back of my mind, though, there was another—albeit faint—voice. It was whispering to me that if Tom Quirk thought that this Robbins guy had something useful to say to me, maybe, just maybe, these tapes might help me a bit in some way. Even if the amount of relief they could offer me was minute, I should still take notice. And so, heeding that tiny voice, I thanked Tom and put the box of cassette tapes into the backseat of my own car. *Maybe I'll listen to these one day*, I thought as I turned back to the business at hand.

The greatest gift is to give people your enlightenment, to share it.

—Buddha

Hope Begins to Dawn

The next day began like any other. After completing my morning rituals—showering, shaving, brushing my teeth—I set out on my usual commute, a tour of many of the Foreign Autopart stores in and around Boston. I had driven only a few miles when a sudden brainwave inspired by the previous day's conversation with Tom Quirk occurred to me. I was going to be in my car for a while, I knew, so I figured I might as well use the time to give Tom's Tony Robbins tapes a fair chance. That way, if their impact on me was as negligible as I suspected it would be, I'd be able to return them to Tom sooner rather than later.

Thus motivated, I groped behind me and hauled the tape set forward from the backseat. Further one-handed fumbling got the box open and the first tape into the cassette slot. As the player's mechanisms clicked into gear, I settled back into the driver's seat, anticipating what I was about to hear with a rather jaundiced attitude. At that moment, I was twenty-five years old and struggling with tremendous anxiety and low self-esteem. I didn't know it then, but putting this first tape into my car's cassette player was to be my initial step on the road to my complete psychological transformation.

> *Nobody can go back and start a new beginning, but anyone can start today and make a new ending.*
> —Maria Robinson

Almost immediately, I was captured by the words coming out of my car's speakers. "Your future is not your past," I heard Tony Robbins say. That sentence cut through my skepticism and struck a chord deep within me.

I really hope my future is not going to be like my past, I thought to myself as I continued to listen. *If it is, then I'm always going to be a nervous wreck with self-esteem way below sea level. I really, really, really don't want that! Please show me a way to change, Tony, so that I can feel better about myself for the rest of my life.*

I now had a thin cable of hope to hang on to…but how was I going to transform and leave the past—the intense, pressured, anxiety-ridden past—behind? In hopes of finding an answer, I continued to listen to the borrowed tapes, and on the second day, my answer came through loud and clear. Essentially, it was this:

Staying the same or changing is 100 percent up to me. It's my choice!

My choice. The idea that I had the choice to direct my own life by choosing what was going on in my head was mind-blowing. The concept of directing and controlling my thoughts was strange to me then, but now I have honestly come to believe that we can all—in fact, we _must_—learn to control our minds, or they can literally destroy us! Let me repeat that: _You must learn to control your own mind; otherwise, it can literally destroy your life!_

> _You will be as happy as you make up your mind to be._
> —Abraham Lincoln

In my twenty-five years of life, no one had ever told me that—and I, in turn, had wrongly assumed that essentially I _was_ my thoughts, and that I couldn't change them. I had always believed—and had certainly never challenged—the idea that whatever was passing through my mind at any given moment was simply _there_, an indelible part of my existence. I had thought—incorrectly—that there was absolutely no way to alter this stream-of-consciousness progression. I will be forever grateful for the discovery that my assumption was wrong.

An Expert View on Controlling Your Thoughts

Most people assume that the stream-of-consciousness thoughts that dominate our minds are like rivers: constantly flowing, always changing, and largely beyond human control. However, that's not entirely true! Just as a river can be dammed and diverted, you can decide where you do and don't want your thought paths to go. In fact, doing so can literally change the way you experience your life!

You see, just because something is going through your mind doesn't make it right, true, or worth acting on. You can gradually learn to block most of your mind's negative thoughts, which will increase your self-confidence and self-control. This will also prevent you from expending worry and stress where they'll do no good.

First, develop awareness of your consciousness. Regularly ask yourself: What is going through my head? Does it have any validity, or is it just an old habit or an impulse? Do my actual circumstances warrant this reaction? Chances are, you'll find that you're wasting a lot of "thought-space" on things that have little bearing on reality. When this happens, consciously direct your attention elsewhere.

That said, controlling your thoughts is much easier said than done. Meditation is actually a wonderful way to ease into differentiating yourself and your reality from your thoughts. If you're a complete novice, try this simple technique to begin:

- Close your eyes.
- Listen to all the sounds you can hear.
- Don't try to remember or analyze them; just experience them as they occur.

Practicing this simple meditation will help you to become more objective about what is passing through your mind at any one time, and it will also give your brain a much-needed break from—admit it—all of those would'ves, could'ves, should'ves, and what ifs that typically plague it. When you can learn to banish ruminations about the past and worries about the future, your constructive thoughts will shoot through the roof.

A New Mentor

Within a couple of days, I was hooked on Tony Robbins, and I looked forward to my commutes as I never had before. I was ecstatic because I could see, for the first time ever, a future beyond stress and worry. I could also see a way of turning my potential into real success that could be *truly* fulfilling. Tony's messages were inspiring and entertaining; he was showing me viable ways to become the person I wanted to be. And to my delight, new revelations just kept on coming.

In that first week of listening to the tapes to and from work, Tony Robbins taught me another lesson that would pay incredible dividends, both for me and for those within my company:

It's the final 5 percent of the effort that often makes all the difference.

At one live seminar I later attended, Tony used a large graph to make this point extremely clear. The graph showed the relationship between performance and pay. Tony pointed out that if you do poor work in America you don't get just poor pay—you actually get fired. For average work you get paid poorly, for good work you get average pay, and for great work you get good pay. However, if you do the very best work and go just an extra 5 percent above "great," you'll get huge pay!

> *Do a little more each day than you think you possibly can.*
> —Lowell Thomas

That, my friends, is the truth. Many people work hard and enjoy some success. There are others who work a bit harder and experience a bit more success and money as a result. But those who put in more effort than everyone else—the people who put in the extra 5 percent and work more than anyone has a right to expect of them—those guys and gals are the ones who get all of the gold and all of the glory.

As you know, at no point in my life have I been afraid of working hard. In fact, I've always been one of the hardest workers in just about every environment I've been in. But never before had I appreciated the idea that there wasn't *that* much difference—just 5 percent—between doing "really good" and doing the very best. Just 5 percent! Though I didn't yet realize it, my (and my team's) use of this principle would prove to be extraordinarily beneficial for our company. From 1990 to 1997, I worked six days a week, Monday through Friday from 7:00 a.m. to 6:00 p.m., and on Saturdays from 8:00 a.m. to noon, and most of my top people did so as well. I know that this extra effort enabled us to be much more prepared, and thus successful.

> *Luck is what happens when preparation meets opportunity.*
> —Seneca

And this 5 percent rule works, of course, in all aspects of life, not just in business. For example, exercising consistently, including on the days when you'd prefer to stay at home on the couch because it is cold and rainy, makes a huge difference in terms of your physical and mental health. Likewise, sending love notes and flowers to your spouse for no particular reason keeps the love strong. These things are also what giving an extra 5 percent looks like!

Another Voice of Wisdom

After my introduction to Tony Robbins, I continued to seek out other motivational experts from whom I could learn. One of my other favorite teachers, Brian Tracy, showed me how faith and persistence play into the 5 percent rule—and I'd like to share that connection with you.

In his lectures, Brian uses many examples of people who lost faith and quit just before reaching the point at which they would have gotten "all the gold." One example involves an oil prospector who isn't quite patient enough to wait until the oil does finally come bubbling up from the ground. Another tells of the rookie farmer whose first crop is just a little bit late to grow. Due to his inexperience, the farmer assumes that all is lost and stops watering his fields—thus losing out on the great harvest that the rest of his more experienced neighbors enjoy just a few days after. So often, it is those people who stay in the game just a little longer—just 5 percent longer—who get all the spoils.

In my own life, I cannot remember a great success that didn't take significantly longer and require much more effort to reach than I had originally expected it would. Much like a marathon runner who hits the proverbial wall, we're all tempted to quit and cut our losses at some point on the road to reaching our greatest goals. Because of learning Brian Tracy's principle, though, I've always tried to keep my faith, and I have promised myself that I will never give up until I reach my goal. More often than not, I have reaped fabulous rewards as a result of my persistence.

The Stuff of Dreams

The further into Tony's tapes I got, the more I learned about what I was doing right and what I was doing wrong. Fortunately for me, it turns out, I had been viewing the world and doing almost everything all wrong up until that point. Now, before you assume that I have misspoken—or that the cheese has fallen off my cracker—let me explain that statement.

I say that I was fortunate to have been so wrong, because, to a large extent, this meant that there was a correctable diagnosis for my unhappiness (which, as you know, I had assumed was simply part of who I was). To be so far off base from the type of life Tony Robbins (and as I later learned, other masters) advocated meant that I could realize a dramatic difference between the life I had been living and the life that could be mine if I followed their advice.

As I continued to commute between the Foreign Autopart stores across New England, Tony's lessons didn't stop. Another one that now stood out to me was this:

To have great success, you have to dream big.

As you probably recall, in my teens I responded to bullying and teasing by imagining myself achieving great things that would allow me to "show up" my tormentors. In a way, this coping strategy *was* dreaming big—but in an unfocused, vengeful way. In listening to the Tony Robbins tapes, though, I learned how to *really* dream big.

Believing in yourself is the first step. After all, if you can't *see* yourself being successful, you're never going to be. Furthermore, you need dreams that are so exciting and inspiring that they energize you to the point that you can't wait to pursue them each and every day.

> *You gotta be careful if you don't know where you're going; otherwise you might not get there.*
>
> —Yogi Berra

And Tony continued…If I had a goal and decided to commit 100 percent to its attainment, nothing could hold me back from reaching it. Tony explained that the word "de-cide" is derived from Latin and literally means "to break from the past," which is what one needs to do if she has a new important dream or goal. In essence, we must refuse to accept anything short of the attainment of this new goal.

A Mountain Top Experience

This lesson of accepting nothing less than the attainment of your goal is exemplified by the true story of three mountain climbers who were preparing to scale Mount Everest. Two were from Switzerland, and were professional climbers who had summited Everest before. The third was an American amateur.

On the morning this trio was to set out, they were interviewed by the press. When the Swiss climbers were asked, "Will you successfully summit the mountain on this day?" the answer was, "We are going to do our best. Some days you succeed and some you don't, but we're going to do everything we can to get to the top!"

When the same question was asked of the American, his response was quite different: "I'll do it or die! This is my one chance. I've saved up all my money to be here, and I'll never have another opportunity to make this climb. Yes, I will succeed."

At the end of the venture, only one climber reached the summit. Which do you think it was?

Likewise, there are times in life when you've got to symbolically jump from one cliff's scary edge to the next. It's very easy to say, "I'm not going to risk it." But if it is a very important goal for you to reach, then like the amateur American climber, you must settle for nothing less than the summit. You've got to dig in, grit your teeth, and keep on climbing until you reach the top.

Next, Tony explained that your dreams need to be *specific*, not just vague fantasies. In order to move forward with purpose, you have to decide—in detail—exactly what you want to achieve and identify exactly why it is so important to you. And then once you have your "master plan," so to speak, in place, you must set smaller, more specific, shorter-term goals that you can work on weekly and even daily in order to turn your big dream into a great successful reality.

And don't trust everything to memory, either—write down all of your big dreams as well as the smaller step-by-step goals that you can reach each day to help you achieve them. Then, keep these written lists somewhere you'll see them very often (perhaps on the bathroom mirror or beside your computer monitor) so that you'll be reminded to work on them every day. This is the real key.

An Expert View on Chunking

You may not have heard the term before…but "chunking" is the name for what most of us call "baby steps," or breaking a task down into smaller, doable pieces. This technique is useful when you're tackling bigger, potentially overwhelming tasks, because you can see the progress you're making but you won't feel overwhelmed. Furthermore, if you tend to get distracted easily, chunking can help you to stay on task, because each distinct step will take a smaller amount of time to complete.

Beyond project management, though, chunking is also good for the brain. Many of us brag that we're masters of multi-tasking, but the fact is that at any given instant the brain can actually handle only one thing. (That said, it takes the brain about 0.3 seconds to switch its attention from one thing to another, which is not consciously noticeable but happens nonetheless.) Deciding ahead of time to focus on only one aspect of your project is most efficient for your brain, because it prevents you from thinking about one thing, then another, then another, and getting relatively little done in the process.

Soon after hearing and digesting this dream-big approach, I began to apply it in my business. Turns out, I wasn't the only one! I was dreaming big in good company. Years after I first listened to Tony Robbins' *Personal Power* tapes, I learned about Walt Disney's approach to setting goals. He was known for setting incredibly aggressive goals for his leadership team, assuming that they might just figure out a way to realize them (like, for example, turning a Florida swamp into the world's greatest theme park). Even if Disney's initial goal wasn't fully realized, he knew that the results were still likely to surpass the fruits of "average," "everyday" goals. By creating these challenges, Walt kept his whole team thinking very creatively and functioning at the highest level.

Likewise, I once heard Jack Welch say that one of his keys to success at GE was setting supposedly unreasonable goals and quotas. He explained that the only way his people could ever hope to reach these impossible goals was to completely reconsider how they were doing their jobs. His high goals, just like Walt Disney's, were forcing his employees to totally think outside of the box in order to create the newest and most innovative approaches. This helped GE to consistently stay miles ahead of the competition.

If you were to ask anyone who worked for me in the 1990s, I'm certain that he or she would tell you that I definitely challenged both Walt Disney and Jack Welch in setting staggeringly high goals for my store teams! And like both Walt and Jack, my teams and I were also handsomely rewarded for this practice.

> *Aim for the moon. If you miss, you may hit a star.*
> —W. Clement Stone

An Expert View on High Goal-Setting

Some people find that outrageous goals fire them up and motivate them; others become discouraged and overwhelmed if something doesn't seem readily achievable. It's those reactions (excited or daunted) that reverberate in the brain—*not* the actual goal per se. Essentially, that means you need to identify which category you fall into and set your goals accordingly.

- If outrageous goals cause you to feel inspired and enthused, the reward pathway in your brain will be activated, making you feel good and even fired up. So, aim for the stars!

- If outrageous goals cause you to feel overwhelmed or stressed, your brain's reward pathway is likely to become inhibited, exacerbating your discouragement. If this is you, you'll probably be better off setting a series of goals that become progressively more expansive, but that you know you'll nevertheless be able to achieve.

It really is that simple!

Think About It

All of the lessons I've shared so far were eye-opening, and all have changed me. But one lesson in particular had the biggest impact on how I approach my life today, and thus on my increased happiness.

What you think about you become.

On the surface, it sounds simple...but the concept is actually one of the most profound I have ever encountered. Your thoughts are not an unimportant running commentary on life that exist just in your head. More so than anything external, your thoughts influence what your focus is, what your attitude is, and what values and virtues you live by. Your thoughts also impact your confidence levels and thus the scope of the goals you set for yourself. In short, everything you do—or choose not to do—is preceded and influenced by a thought. If you were a car on the road of life, your thoughts would be the steering wheel.

Your life is what your thoughts make it.
—Marcus Aurelius

Suffice it to say, for the first two and a half decades of my life, I had been swerving quite a bit—when I wasn't going in the wrong direction entirely. My head was so often filled with unhappy thoughts, and I assumed that was the way it was always going to be. Worry, envy, and low self-esteem—but mainly worry—occupied my brain. I was often so focused on how things could go wrong that I wouldn't have been able to see how they might go right even if an explicit explanation had been handed right to me.

In retrospect, it's clear to me now that a vast majority of my anxiety resulted from my anticipating the myriad of bad things that might happen. It just makes sense: If your head is full of negative energy and images of disaster, you become trapped by the anxiety that those images generate.

The Voice of Experience

I once saw a TV show in which a one-hundred-year-old woman was asked what one lesson from her life she would most like to pass on to future generations. She said that the most important lesson she had learned from looking back on her life was that she spent a large portion of it worrying about things that never actually happened. She regretted the time she had wasted in anxious thought, and advised others not to fall into the same trap.

Amen! For a large portion of my life, this woman's "ailment" also affected me. But no more! In life I have come to realize that there truly is nothing to fear but fear itself.

Along the same lines as being conscious of your thoughts, I also learned something fundamentally true (but not obvious to most people) about our use of words in those early days of listening to the tapes:

Our words affect our emotions.

Let me explain. If I'm having a fairly bad day and I say to myself or to someone else, "Today could have been better," the effect my words have on me will be very different than if I say, "Today was just awful," or even worse, "Today totally destroyed me." The first example acknowledges that I haven't had the best day ever, and does so using positive terminology. The second two examples, on the other hand, use negative language that underscores my bad experiences—and therefore increases the likelihood of my becoming mired in a depressive thought cycle.

The words we use thus have an effect on how we feel. It is vital to realize that using more positive words and fewer negative ones to describe your experiences will bolster the quality and direction of your life.

An Expert View on Our Tendency Toward Negativity

If you've ever observed while in a cynical mood that we live in a negative world, you're actually quite right. According to research done at Penn State, people know twice as many negative words than positive ones. And on top of that, it is estimated that there are twice as many negative than positive words in the English dictionary.

Why the imbalance? Well, negative words typically convey information necessary for survival. They prohibit you from certain actions and warn you away from potential dangers. And since the brain is geared for survival, it's programmed to pay much more attention to danger and warning signs than to pleasantries that have little survival value. That means that we humans are programmed to think about danger, and guess what? An adaptive mechanism is to plan for danger. In the modern world, this planning often manifests itself as *stress*.

Now, let's make something clear: There's a difference between a contingency plan (which is healthy to have) and excessive worry or even rumination. People who have very active brains (as shown, for example, on an EEG scan) tend to be more anxious, presumably because they are more aware of "danger" and obsess about it. The following methods can be used to combat the negative effects of high brain activity:

- Medications can reduce mental overactivity, reduce anxiety levels, and even alleviate its physical manifestations.
- Therapy can help people modify the thought processes that lead to anxiety.
- Brain training techniques, such as those that use neurofeedback, directly target areas of the brain that are overactive and reprogram them to be less so, resulting in decreased anxiety.

I began to realize within the first two weeks of actively listening to the Tony Robbins tapes that I had the power to control how I was feeling each day. For me, this was as huge a leap as the first landing on the moon was for NASA. I realized that if I could stop the negativity, insecurity, and anxiety that had been a constant in my head throughout my adolescence, I would be shifting my thought processes, which could then actually lead to my own happiness and success.

Boy, that was powerful! For the first time, I could see a future in which happiness could replace depression, peace of mind could replace anxiety, confidence could replace self-doubt, and so much more. Being more positive and happy would also be much healthier, so these new ways of thinking would probably help me live longer, too!

> *The inner speech, your thoughts, can cause you to be rich or poor, loved or unloved, happy or unhappy, attractive or unattractive, powerful or weak.*
>
> —Ralph Charell

As I began to consciously observe more and more, I could see that Tony Robbins, Brian Tracy, and the other experts I was listening to were right. Most people in America *do* focus on what's going wrong in their lives rather than what is going right. Through conversations and consideration of the world around me, I actually found that many of my own employees were beating themselves up over the one or two things *not* going right in their lives while completely overlooking the many more things that were going well—just as I had done for years.

Looking back at the way I had relentlessly picked at my own faults, I now realized that I had been making my own unhappiness inevitable. We human beings are imperfect and therefore fallible, so I could always find at least one thing that was not going right in my life! And since it had become my way to dwell only on the bad stuff in my life, I had become an expert at making myself miserable!

From Theoretical Understanding to Practical Application

As I absorbed the tapes that had quickly become a staple of my commute, eagerly listening and re-listening to the messages of change and empowerment, I started to put these incredible ideas into action. After all, Tony also taught me that a great idea isn't worth anything if it isn't turned into great action.

When I initially began the process of taking over the store chain in 1989 and 1990, I struggled tremendously with stress, especially when things unexpectedly went wrong. At this point I had met Yadira (more about that story in the next chapter!), but she still lived in Venezuela, so aside from the occasional weekend party I had no distractions from work whatsoever. Not surprisingly, my career quickly became too important and too all-encompassing in my life.

In fact, around this time my dad actually had to sit me down and talk to me about how concerned he was for my health. He told me that even though he saw a lot of potential in me, he doubted that he'd be able to let me continue running the store chain unless I was able to get my anxiety under control. Truth be told, at this time my dad was right: I was completely overwhelmed and a nervous wreck due to my job. (Any businessperson will tell you that stressing obsessively when things go wrong or differently than you expected them to is not a good trait to have, since change is really the only constant in business.)

There were three recurring work situations that I found especially brutal in terms of my anxiety levels during those early years. The first involved my store managers. Occasionally, a manager would show up unexpectedly at my office—usually on a Monday morning—give me the keys to his or her store, and quit with no notice. This opened up a stressful can of worms for me because at the time I didn't yet have enough quality supervisors whom I could rely on to quickly go and cover stores for what could potentially be several months. Thus I had to frantically switch people around just to keep that store up and running.

The second situation that really drove me crazy involved store break-ins. Along with each store manager (who was responsible only for his or her own store), I was on *all* of our twenty store alarm lists at this time. So, whenever a store within one hour of my home was broken into, it was my responsibility to immediately go to that store after receiving the call from the alarm company. I would then meet the store manager and the police, assess the damage, and call a company to come out and board up the broken window or storefront. Often, our stores were in dangerous neighborhoods and the police never waited around with the manager and me for the security company to arrive. These situations, which usually occurred in the middle of the night, would have been nerve-wracking even for someone who didn't already suffer from high anxiety.

The third situation that sent my blood pressure through the roof involved employees (usually the store managers themselves) who were caught stealing from our stores. When this happened, I always felt betrayed. I knew this was not an uncommon problem in the retail world, yet I simply could not help taking it personally. I also, of course, had to fire the employee in question, and again scramble to find a replacement to cover that store.

With my father's necessary ultimatum about replacing me if I couldn't learn to relax a bit echoing in my head and all of the new information and guidance from Tony's tapes at my fingertips, I finally resolved to do something about these three specific work situations that were a risk to my health—and hence to my job.

I vividly remember sitting at my kitchen table one night and—incredibly—solving the entire problem right then and there in just one sitting. The secret to my transformation was recognizing that each of these three scenarios was unpleasant and that I couldn't do much about them. *However, what I could do was control my reaction to them!*

Specifically, by taking into account past company statistics and balancing them against my salary, I figured that it was reasonable during one calendar year for me to be expected to deal with three managers who quit without notice, three break-ins that I would have to handle and manage in person, and three employee thefts. Handling up to three of each of these situations each year was now simply part of my self-imposed job description. I concluded in my mind that these unenviable situations were why I earned what I did.

Forewarned, forearmed; to be prepared is half the victory.
—Miguel de Cervantes Saavedra

However, I told myself that if more than three instances of any one of these problems occurred in any twelve-month period, then I would be justified in feeling aggravated and upset, and I could totally freak out. Reframing how I thought about these problems (and others in the future) certainly allowed me to manage situations more calmly—and realizing that for the first time I had taken control of my life by managing my brain was a huge self-esteem boost.

And in case you're wondering, there were never more than three instances of any one of these three crises in any one-year time frame after I made up my mind to manage them this way! Thus, from that one amazing night at my kitchen table on, I honestly was able to handle these situations almost flawlessly and with so, so much less stress!

An Expert View on Contingency Planning

If you're an anxious person and/or prone to rumination, now's the time to start employing contingency planning as a weapon against worry and stress. When you don't take an analytical view of planning, your thoughts grow into full-fledged anxieties that rattle around the unedited privacy of the mind, growing disproportionately and tumbling out of control. To combat this exponential increase of stress, try the following when you're making any type of major plan:

- Write down outcomes—positive and negative—that could occur.
- Identify which of these is your "worst-case" scenario.
- Decide how you might best respond to each of these possibilities.
- Identify potential roadblocks and obstacles to your preferred outcome.
- Discuss your thoughts and plans with others to get third-party feedback.

Knowing beforehand that you're prepared for likely eventualities will help your mind to get off the constant-worry track so that it can move on to more productive tasks.

Subsequent Lessons and Realizations

Ever since that first introduction to Tony Robbins, I have spent hundreds of hours listening to Tony's wisdom, as well as that of many other incredible masters. This list includes Tony's late friend and mentor, Jim Rohn, as well as Joel Osteen, Brian Tracy, and the late Napoleon Hill—to name just a few. These experts have so much to teach all of us, starting with how to reframe your perceptions—a skill that enables you to view life in the most positive and wonderful of ways. I owe so much to all of these amazing teachers—and I'd like to share a few final lessons I've learned from them before continuing with my own story!

As you've read, I first applied the wisdom of these masters to my professional life, but many things I learned from the tapes greatly improved my life outside of work, too. For example, Tony Robbins explained that having rigid (or inflexible) expectations concerning your interpersonal interactions and relationships leads to trouble, as does assuming you know why someone has acted toward you in a certain way.

As a result of assumptions we make about others, our interpretations of their behaviors are often dead wrong. Let me give you another one of Tony Robbins' examples to illustrate this concept of projection:

A businessman had arranged for his wife to pick him up at his office at 6:00 p.m. because his own car was in the shop being repaired. Six o'clock came and went, and his wife still hadn't shown up. Unfortunately, it was a snowy, cold evening, and the man was forced to wait outside because his office building had been locked up. After about ten minutes, he called his wife but got no reply. After another ten minutes, he began to get frustrated. He started to imagine that his wife had taken a detour to the mall and had been distracted by her favorite activity, shopping. Five minutes later, smoke was coming out of his ears as he planned how he would yell at her and make her "pay" for this indiscretion!

Also, because he was angry, he began to run through a mental litany of all of the things that irritated him about his wife. She could be inconsiderate and unappreciative. She procrastinated, and wasn't the best timekeeper or housekeeper, either. Just then, the man got a call from the hospital informing him that his wife had been in a fairly serious car accident. You can imagine how guilty he felt for his uncharitable assumptions and thoughts! Here's the lesson we can all take away from this story:

Learning to recognize and then manage your own projections will make a huge difference in your life, and it will help to transform your ability to manage your relationships and your stress level, too.

THE DOCTOR IS IN

An Expert View on Projection

"Projection" is a psychological defense mechanism whereby one creates stories about other people's moods, motives, and actions that are based on one's own fears and defenses, and not on reality. In other words, if you're projecting, you're transferring your own hang-ups to another person.

For example, let's say your spouse arrives home after work in a less-than-pleasant mood. Truth be told, he is downright grumpy and unfriendly, snapping at you and slamming his briefcase onto the kitchen table. Naturally, you assume that your spouse is mad at you, and you start racking your brain in order to figure out what you've done to warrant this anger. However, you can't identify a single thing that might be the culprit—so *you* start to get mad in turn because you think that your spouse is upset with you for no reason.

At this point, you're at a crossroads. You can choose to unleash your own newly sparked anger on your spouse…which will probably degenerate into a nasty argument. On the other hand, you can choose to ask your spouse what the matter is… and find out that he's actually had a horrendous day at work. Clearly, projecting your own fears onto your spouse in this situation would be inaccurate and unproductive!

Projection is one of the biggest problems in all relationships because it influences so much of our communication. Here are some steps you can take to identify and begin the process of repairing your own projections:

- Identify the negative relationships in your life.
- Ask yourself why, exactly, you dislike the other party. Is it the way he or she acts, or a personal quality that he or she possesses?

- Now, identify how this action or quality manifests in your own life, and whether or not it's currently present. (It's important to face up to truths that may be unpleasant or harsh.)

Once you are consciously aware of your own driving thoughts, opinions, and motivations, make every effort to deal with and come to terms with them in your own life. When you begin to solve longstanding issues in your own life, you'll be less likely to assume that others are motivated by the same things—and you'll be able to interpret their behaviors much more objectively.

This story has really stuck with me and helped me to view many situations—both past and present—through a more logical, less emotionally charged lens. Over the years, I've recalled the tale of the aggravated businessman when I otherwise might have been tempted to assume the worst about someone else. Being able to step back and realize that I cannot possibly know everything else that is going on in another person's life at any given time has helped me to be much less judgmental and thus better able to maintain stronger, more productive relationships.

I'd like to end this chapter with three wonderful short stories that Tony Robbins also tells. It's often through stories and parables like these that the greatest teachers help us to really understand the most important lessons.

Ruined by Revenge

One day a man was hiking up a mountain for a bit of exercise. As his excursion was drawing to a close (in fact, he was only about twenty minutes from the base camp), he heard a rattlesnake nearby and looked down to see the reptile coiled at his feet. He quickly tried to jump out of the way, but it was too late. The snake bit him, and what had been a beautiful and perfect day now took a turn for the worse.

Angered and in pain, the man immediately grabbed the small hatchet strapped to his backpack and went after the snake. He took a whack at it, but the snake avoided his blow and started slithering up the mountain. The man, following the sound of the rattle, hurried behind his tormentor even as the venom slowly began to set in. After much struggle, the man finally caught the snake and chopped its head off.

However, by now the poison was really taking its toll on the man, and he realized that his rash decision to pursue the snake had actually cost him his own life too. He was simply now much too far away from the base camp to get the help he needed. If he had only left the snake alone and spent the past twenty-five minutes getting off the mountain, he surely would have been saved.

The moral of the story is a powerful one: Too often, we spend our time and energy continuing to be angry and upset with people who have hurt us in the past. (In fact, in all likelihood the targets of our negative emotions aren't losing any sleep over their earlier actions…and they certainly aren't aware of or hurt by our animosity toward them!) All of this wasted energy, time, and often even depression over those who have wronged us causes us to become distracted from the wonderful things we could be doing in our lives. And what's more, it has been proven that people who continue to harbor these negative feelings get sick more often, too.

The Story of "Maybe"

In a village in a far-off land, there once lived a wise man. This man had one teenage son, and together they lived on a farm. In addition to farming the land, they also owned several horses that they loved. One day, the son's favorite horse, his prized mare, ran away. Before long, the other villagers heard what had happened and came to commiserate with the man and his son.

"That's terrible that you should lose such a wonderful horse," the villagers said. "You're so unlucky that this happened!"

"Maybe," said the wise man.

A few days later, the mare returned, followed by three magnificent wild stallions that she had obviously attracted. Soon, the villagers heard what had happened and came to celebrate with the man.

"That's wonderful that your horse has returned and brought three more magnificent horses with her! You're so lucky!" the villagers exclaimed.

"Maybe," said the wise man.

Some time later, the man's teenage son was training one of the three wild stallions and was thrown off of the horse. As a result of the fall, the boy broke both of his legs and for a time was confined to a wheelchair. The villagers heard what had happened and came again to commiserate with the man.

"That's so awful that your son broke both his legs. How will you harvest your crops now without his help? You're so unlucky!" they said.

"Maybe," said the wise man again.

Not long afterward the village on the other side of the river declared war on the wise man's village. This happened about once every generation and was devastating because it wiped out so many of the young men from both areas. When the authorities came to the wise man's house to conscript his son for military service, they found the boy in a wheelchair with two broken legs and therefore could not enlist him to fight in the war.

"You're so lucky," the villagers now said to the wise man, "that your son doesn't have to put his life on the line like our sons do."

"Maybe," said the wise man.

Of course, this story, and so many of your own, could go on and on endlessly. The point is that *it's not the events that happen in our lives that are important. Instead, it's how we see them and respond to them that is crucial.*

Life isn't about luck—we must all have faith in God's plan for us. Think back on your life so far. I bet you'll remember events that you were sure would be disastrous at the time, but turned out to actually be blessings. In the same way, you can look back and identify events you thought would be wonderful but actually turned out to be problematic.

An old Chinese proverb says that *in every disappointment lie the seeds of a much greater opportunity.* I would add that if you're not careful, in every triumph lay the seeds of a much greater failure. Looking back, I can tell you that in my own life some of the events that initially made me the most uncomfortable and miserable turned out to be the best for me in the long term. They were springboards for my greatest personal growth and happiness because the upset they caused me forced me to step outside my comfort zone and rise to meet the challenges they presented. The reverse has also been true—what I thought were blessings often turned out to be traps. For example, I rested on my laurels after running the Boston Marathon for the first time in 2007, got lazy, and actually wound up six months later in the worst physical shape of my adult life.

Basically, the bottom line is that when events happen to us we must not judge whether they are good or bad. *Instead, their significance will be determined by how we choose to respond to them.*

Your destiny is not the events that happen to you but the choices you make when dealing with them.

Now let's meet Joe, another protagonist used by Tony Robbins to help us learn one more vital lesson:

Faith vs. Foolishness

Joe was one of the most active elders in his church, a totally devout follower of God. In fact, Joe was in the habit of bragging to others that he had a "special" bond with God. Then one day, during a torrential rainstorm, the town in which Joe lived was flooded because the dam holding back the main river broke. The people were told to immediately evacuate to higher ground. Most did—but Joe and his followers chose not to leave, believing that God would surely protect them.

As the flood worsened and the waters filled the first floor of Joe's house, people came by in boats offering to rescue him and his followers. Everyone but Joe now fled.

"I'm not leaving," scoffed Joe as his companions boarded the boats. "I have such a special relationship with God. You'll see. God will never let me die in this flood."

But the flood steadily worsened, and Joe was forced to scramble onto his roof. A man came by in one last boat and pleaded with Joe to climb aboard, saying, "If you don't come now, Joe, I know you'll die!"

"I'm not leaving," replied Joe stubbornly. "I have a special relationship with God. I tell you, God will not let me die in this flood."

The man in this last boat once again pleaded and implored Joe, telling him that he would certainly die if he did not leave immediately, but his pleas were to no avail. The flood waters continued to rise. And rise. And soon, they rose over Joe's head.

And Joe died! He died! Joe died!!!

When Joe got to heaven, as you can imagine, he was very angry with God. And he said to God, "You have embarrassed me in front of all my friends and let me die. After all the good deeds I did for you on earth, why did you let this happen?"

And God now said to Joe, "Joe, I sent many boats to rescue you—and I even sent my own special angel on the last boat to save you. But you refused even his desperate pleas to you!"

God has a plan for all of us. But we can't arrogantly assume that we know exactly what it is. Neither can we sit around thinking that God is going to do all of the work for us. He will give us guidance and help, but we are the ones who must actually act. We must be open-minded enough to be aware of the possibilities that are put in front of us. We must be proactive. God is not going to save us. *He's going to give us opportunities to save ourselves.*

I have been listening to cassette tapes (and now CDs) almost every morning for over twenty years—and I am still astonished by how many lessons I continue to learn. I listen religiously to these motivators because I feel it is just as important to feed my mind with positive messages as it is to feed my belly with breakfast before the day begins. All of these teachers through the years have helped me to maintain a more positive outlook on life. They have helped me to reprogram my mind. My application of these lessons has turned me from the self-absorbed, worried perfectionist about whom you read in earlier chapters into a successful, happy person who tries to help everyone as best I can.

The last time I saw Tom Quirk, he was still the same admirable guy with incredible positive energy and enthusiasm. I am eternally grateful that Tom was able to influence my life in such a profound way by recommending those first Tony Robbins tapes to me. That's what happens when you choose to recommend what has helped improve your life to a friend in need (and I was definitely in need back then!). You can literally change another person's life by taking the time to care.

My introduction to empowerment had just begun, and it's a journey that I am still continuing today. And let me tell you, those first steps couldn't have come at a better time, as I was about to need all the help I could get while struggling with the challenges of my advancing career. But before I go into that story, let's talk romance.

TIPS FROM TODD:
CHAPTER NINE

- **Actively seek to learn from those you admire.** If you encounter an individual whose attitude, outlook, or life path you admire, ask him or her to share with you what sorts of principles, actions, and lessons have impacted his or her life path. The answers and insights you receive may well change your own course—and you might even acquire a mentor in the process.

Likewise, take advantage of the wisdom of well-known "masters." There are numerous authors and speakers whose messages have stood the test of time and whose areas of expertise can speak to you personally. Try to listen to audio books and audio motivational tape sets in the car, read a chapter of a self-help book before bed each night, or sign up for daily emails from a "master" you admire. You'll be surprised by the impact these lessons have!

- **Understand that your happiness depends on your reactions to what happens to you, not on what has actually occurred.** You cannot change what is past. To some extent, you can't even change the events that will happen in your future. However, what you *can* change is how you react to those occurrences—whether they are setbacks or triumphs. When you are knocked down, get back up. Always look for the positive in every situation, and also always look for lessons to learn and ways to improve, even if you're doing "well" already.

- **The difference between "good" and "great" isn't *that* big.** If you want to stand head and shoulders above the crowd, you probably won't have to work twice as hard as those currently in the lead—in fact, giving only 5 percent more will propel you forward past them. "Getting ahead" isn't as difficult as many people think…if, that is, you're not afraid of putting your nose to the grindstone. The fact is, most people just aren't willing to put forth the requisite effort for the requisite amount of time; you must stay at it until you succeed. Do not quit prematurely!

- **Know exactly where you want to go and how you're going to get there.** If your goals for life are along the lines of "Be happy" or "Be successful," you're probably not going to achieve them—because they aren't specific enough. And frankly, they won't motivate you every morning to jump out of bed in order to reach them because they aren't grandiose enough, either. Essentially, you must be able to articulate *exactly* what happiness or success looks like for you (e.g., healthy relationships with family, financial security, fulfilling work, gardening, a hobby, etc.). Beyond that, you need to sit down and figure out what steps will take you there. And then you must review this list daily. Only then will you begin to see your life truly change for the better.

- **Take control of your thoughts.** The tone of your thoughts—and words—has a real impact on your attitude and outlook…and hence on the quality of your life. When you dwell on or constantly talk about what has gone wrong, how you messed up, how stupid you are, or what you think you're lacking, you invite depression, jealousy, and unhappiness into your life. However, if you think and talk about your blessings, your achievements, your greatness, and your hopes, you will find that your day-to-day existence is much more positive.

- **Design personalized "emergency behavior" plans.** In many situations, knowing what to expect is half the battle. If a certain type of recurring situation in your life consistently causes you anxiety, determine beforehand what your ideal reaction will be. (This could be anything from a work crisis to holidays with your in-laws.) Decide what attitude you will strive for and identify related tasks you can do to be successful. This will remove the stress of having to decide what to do in the thick of things—and will give you more peace of mind beforehand.

- **Stop before assuming.** You know what they say about assuming: Don't. While you might be able to make educated guesses about what others are thinking, feeling, or going through, you'll never be able to do this completely accurately. Most people have a tendency to project their own insecurities, hang-ups, and worries onto others, and this most often causes unwarranted pain as well as misunderstandings and problems in relationships.

CHAPTER TEN

God Begins to Even the Score for Me

"There is only one happiness in life, to love and be loved."
—George Sand

Very few people go through life without desiring the company and love of another. Whether you're pro-marriage or hope to avoid it at all costs; whether you're looking for a long-term commitment or someone to have fun with for a little while; whether you want a life partner or a partner in crime—or something else entirely—you probably know more or less what you're looking for in the romance department.

I'm certainly no different. While I enjoyed looking at attractive females as much as the next guy (after I came to the conclusion that girls didn't have cooties, that is), I knew from a fairly young age that I wanted to build a long-term, loving relationship with one special woman.

My Mental Romance Blueprint

During my formative adolescent years, I quickly realized that I'm a person who goes all out in the pursuit of my goals, and thus even at that point in my life I knew that I would likely work very long hours in whatever career I chose. I also knew that I wanted my future family to be close-knit and loving, and I hoped that my children would be able to receive the same amount of parental support and attention that I had.

Now, please don't misconstrue what I'm about to say—I have the utmost admiration for women who pursue successful careers, many while also raising children and running hectic households. I really respect their drive, their tirelessness, and their devotion. In fact, overall I think that most women perform as well as or even better than most men in business. That said, since I was a teenager I knew that I would have to be—for the sake of my own self-esteem—the breadwinner in my family.

> *The phrase "working mother" is redundant.*
> —Jane Sellman

Thus, as I grew into adulthood, I'd developed a mental picture of myself married to a woman very much like my mother had been while I was growing up: a woman who focused her energy on the children and home.

Each weekend I would go out to Boston bars hoping that I might find this girl of my dreams. And let me tell you—I definitely had a physical "type," too. The dark look—brunettes with dreamy brown eyes and tanned complexions—was the charm for me. Of course, I wouldn't have turned away a blonde, a redhead, or any other version of an attractive girl who showed any interest in me whatsoever either. Yes, I had developed a relationship with Theresa, my girlfriend in Montreal, but my experience with women was still pretty limited.

So, here I was—a young man in his early twenties, working like a dog in the family business—and I wanted more. Unbeknownst to me, I was soon to get it. It was 1989, and oh what a special year this would turn out to be for me!

In March of that year, I went to Rio de Janeiro, Brazil, with two national salesmen I had become friends with while working the phones, Bill Jimmie and Jason Rizzo. After a New England winter filled with long, cold days and lots of hard work, all three of us were certainly ready for some sun and fun!

> *A vacation is what you take when you can no longer take what you've been taking.*
> —Earl Wilson

Overall, my week in Brazil was just what I needed. I had a good time from start to finish, developed a nice tan during my time on the beach, and even ran into the Atlanta Falcons' offensive line while out on the town one night. Plus, as I explored Rio and enjoyed Ipanema Beach, I struck up successful conversations with locals…including a few very attractive Brazilian beauties! I arrived home with some much-needed new self-confidence. For the first time in as long as I could remember, I was not depressed about being alone.

There She Was

My second night back home from Brazil was March 16, 1989—a date that will forever be engraved in my memory. Still recovering from my vacation, I was initially not very interested when my friend Adam asked me to go out on the town with him. Despite my protests that I was just too tired, Adam persisted and wouldn't take no for an answer. In the end—as often happens between friends—I gave in simply to shut him up.

No man needs a vacation so much as the person who has just had one.

—Elbert Hubbard

Our first stop was T.G.I. Friday's on Newbury Street. Newbury is one of Boston's most charming and well-known streets. Even though I was tired, I had to admit that I still felt the lingering effects of the high I'd experienced on vacation. My self-confidence with women had never been greater than after my experiences in Rio, and I had a nice Brazilian tan to boot. Adam and I hadn't been sitting at the bar long when I noticed an incredibly attractive woman across the room. As cheesy as it sounds, my gaze locked onto her and I ceased to notice anything—or anyone—else in the restaurant.

This young woman was just so incredibly beautiful! She had all of the physical features that really capture me: dark brown hair with gorgeous brown eyes, and the most amazing smile. And what a tan! After another drink (during which I'm sure I stared shamelessly), I approached her and started to engage her in conversation. Her name, I learned, was Yadira.

Most often it's when you're not looking for something that you find it.

As luck would have it, Yadira was actually from Venezuela. She had come to America to be a nanny in nearby Lexington, Massachusetts, for her aunt's friend's niece. Even though she had already been at the job for a couple of months, this was the first night she had been out to socialize. I found myself mentally thanking Adam for his insistence that I accompany him this night! His timing couldn't have been better.

It even seemed to me that God really had, in his way, prepared me to meet this intriguing woman just this night. After all, my recent trip to Brazil had refreshed my memory of my high school Spanish—which, I'd found, was adequate to get my points across to the Portuguese-speaking Brazilians. Now, my newly sharpened Spanish conversation skills proved vital, as Yadira spoke almost no English at that time. Plus, as I've mentioned, this night was already different from most in my past because I was feeling absolutely great about myself. Clearly, this was Fate!

> *Put your hand on a hot stove for a minute, and it seems like an hour. Sit with a pretty girl for an hour, and it seems like a minute. THAT'S relativity.*
>
> —Albert Einstein

At the end of the evening, I took Yadira's phone number and promised to call her. She seemed a bit nervous about this prospect, but not daunted. I did indeed call her shortly afterward to ask her out on a date. Again, I sensed some reluctance, but she agreed to meet me. And, at the time, that was all I cared about!

Later I found out that the only reason Yadira agreed to go out with me was because of a cultural misperception! Yadira thought I was gay, and thus a "safe" person to show her Boston. Why, you ask? When Yadira and I had met on that fateful night at Friday's, she had seen me with my friend Adam, hanging on to one another as American guys often do when out drinking and having a good time. In Venezuela, however, men do not touch at all in public, Yadira explained to me, unless they are gay—and this being Yadira's first social outing in America, that's naturally what she had assumed about Adam and me. Yes—this is definitely one of those "it's funny *now*" stories. As you've no doubt guessed, I very soon set the record straight with Yadira.

Also, as I got to know Yadira better, I found out that things were not going well for her. She was working much harder than expected, and the family she was staying with wasn't paying her any of the money they had promised.

It turned out that Yadira and I had only four dates together before she laid her concerns before her employer—and was summarily dismissed from her job! To be more accurate, Yadira was essentially thrown out into the street by this woman who, as further punishment, now kept Yadira's plane ticket as well from Boston to Miami, giving her only the return portion of her ticket from Miami to Venezuela. Yadira now had nowhere to go.

Imagine my surprise when I received a call from my brand-new love interest, telling me that she had been fired and asking if she could stay with me until she was able to sort out her situation! Looking back, I can assure you that what happened next wasn't my proudest moment. Essentially, I panicked. I was still in the process of getting to know this woman, after all, and I was very unsure of my feelings. Plus, I was certain my mother would go absolutely ballistic if she heard Yadira had moved in with me.

I suggested that Yadira stay with some of the other people she had met from her English class in Boston instead. Yadira had no choice now, and fortunately the five guys whom she knew and begged to stay with until she could figure things out treated her exceptionally well. Next, Yadira had to board a bus to North Carolina, where she stayed with other friends before finally making it to Miami (and, ultimately, back home to Venezuela).

There's Something Here

I was really upset by Yadira's departure; in fact, the intensity of my feelings surprised even me. I very soon began to understand the meaning of the phrase, "You don't know what you've got until it's gone." A little too late, I realized that Yadira and I had experienced the beginning of something special, and I now knew that I wanted to pursue it more. So, I did what many other impassioned young men have also done—I called my love interest constantly after she went back home. Thankfully, Yadira bore me no hard feelings (well, at least not too many), and we continued to learn more about one another long-distance. Gradually, I began to wonder if I might be happier marrying this woman from another country and culture.

Absence weakens mediocre passions and increases great ones, as the wind blows out candles and kindles fires.
—François de la Rochefoucauld

Within a few months of Yadira's departure from Massachusetts, I was entranced enough by her to do something completely out of character for me. In September, I excitedly hopped on a plane—after making plans with Yadira, of course—and headed to Yadira's home town of Maracaibo, Venezuela. Thank goodness that in matters of the heart—even when you make a mistake like I did—boldness and a prompt apology can earn you a second chance. I cannot express how grateful I am that Yadira didn't shut me out of her life after I failed to act the part of her strong rescuer in her time of greatest need!

I arrived in Venezuela just as night began to fall. Yadira and her brother Ramon were already waiting at the airport for me. Ramon didn't seem particularly pleased to see me. Actually, judging from the expression on his face, I thought that he might want to kill me. *Is he worried that I don't have good intentions concerning his sister?* I wondered.

To compound matters (nothing's ever simple), my suitcase had gotten lost somewhere over the Caribbean, so I now had only the clothes on my back and hardly any personal effects at all. The suitcase then took its sweet time in catching up, forcing me to spend the first few days of my trip wearing Yadira's father's clothes. Talk about a less-than-ideal way to meet the family!

Yadira and her brother now took me to the hotel I'd booked and dropped me off, much to my surprise. You see, I was expecting Yadira to stay with me at the hotel. Obviously, I had misunderstood our conversations concerning the arrangements for my trip, as Yadira now told me I was totally nuts and that her parents would disown her if she stayed with a strange (to them, anyway) man at a hotel. So I was left somewhat disappointed and alone at the beautiful and romantic Maruma Hotel.

Thankfully, things went straight uphill from there. First, because no one in Yadira's family spoke English, that week I got an immersion course in Spanish. And as I got an immersion course in Spanish, I simultaneously got an immersion course in the Venezuelan culture. And boy, did I love it!

Yadira's family, relatives, and friends were incredibly warm and generous, and they couldn't have made me feel more welcome. It turns out that Ramon *hadn't* harbored hostile feelings toward me the night he and Yadira had picked me up—his natural expression is simply a poker face that masks a great personality. I sensed immediately that here were a people and a family who had their priorities straight. They showed a tremendous love for life in which family was the most important priority. They enjoyed having fun, and put happiness above material possessions and consumerism.

On that trip I fell in love with Yadira's family's way of life. More importantly, I also fell in love with Yadira.

A Rocky Road to Happily Ever After

When I returned home, I was convinced that I had found the perfect woman for me. I was naturally ecstatic, but my family's reaction was a bit more skeptical. Actually, it was downright negative. Of course, this was somewhat understandable—my family didn't know Yadira well, and they didn't know anything about her family either. And to complicate things even more in their eyes, Yadira is Catholic while I am Jewish, and she spoke very little English. However, I was not about to let these obstacles deflect my pursuit of the woman I wanted to marry.

Initially after returning home, the going was very trying for Yadira and me as well because we had to continue our relationship long-distance via the phone. This type of communication was much more problematic than it sounds because the telephone system in Venezuela can be terribly unreliable. Heavy rain, a high volume of calls, or a variety of technical problems can knock the service out for days at a time. Not knowing this, I panicked the first time Yadira did not pick up her phone at our agreed-upon time, or on the next hundred calls I frantically made to her home during the ensuing days.

Jumping to the worst conclusion possible, of course (as you remember, this was always my way), I thought that she must be dumping me, which caused my stress level to spike until we eventually connected. I was so relieved to find out it was the phone system that was in trouble, and not our relationship!

Several months after my trip to Venezuela, Yadira visited me again in Massachusetts. We had a wonderful, romance-filled time, and while we didn't verbalize the thought to each other, I believe we both knew then that this truly was the real thing.

Over the course of the months following this visit, Yadira remained in Venezuela while I sought—and eventually found—work for her as a live-in nanny in Newton, Massachusetts. This job was only about a mile from where Adam and I were living in West Roxbury. In such close proximity, my relationship with Yadira now really took off, and we both knew it was only a matter of time until we would get married.

Although I had never been happier than I was with Yadira, my family was still vehemently against our marriage. My mother and her parents were the most vocal. While they didn't have anything against Yadira as an individual, they simply didn't think that a cross-cultural marriage between an American Jew and a Venezuelan Catholic was going to work.

The art of love... is largely the art of persistence.

—Albert Ellis

In fact, my mother's opposition to our engagement was so persistent and at times so aggressive that one day, to my shock, Yadira packed up all of her bags and informed me that it was time for me to finally choose between her and my mother. Shaken, I realized that as unpleasant as the task would be, it was time for me to put my foot down with my mother and tell her in no uncertain terms that Yadira and I were going to get married regardless of what she thought.

An Expert View on "Cutting the Apron Strings"

Letting go of a child is rarely an easy or simple proposition for a parent, regardless of whether that child is leaving home or getting married. In the case of marriage especially, the transition is influenced heavily by the personalities of parents and child, as well as by their relationship with one another.

When parents have a very close relationship with a child of the opposite gender especially, "losing" that child to another man or woman can be a challenge. Parents might be tempted to focus on (real or perceived) negative aspects of the match to justify an opinion that a marriage should not happen. Yes, it's tough to achieve emotional objectivity when loved ones are involved, but parents should:

- Make a sincere effort to get to know a child's chosen partner.
- Specifically articulate to themselves and to their child the positive qualities the partner possesses.
- Strive to find common interests, points of view, and preferences with the partner.

A selfish (even if well-intentioned) reluctance to accept a child's partner can do a great deal of damage to multiple relationships. It is important to make every effort to accept and include your child's chosen partner. That said, obstacles that might legitimately compromise your child's health or happiness (such as fiscal irresponsibility or signs of abuse) should be addressed seriously.

In an odd way, I think I was extremely lucky to have felt so lonely and depressed for significant stretches of my life already by the time I met Yadira. I believe that my relative isolation enabled me to truly and fully appreciate the precious nature of what I had found with her. If I hadn't known exactly how rare such a connection was for me, I—like so many other people I have known—might have succumbed to my family's pressure and allowed them to choose my mate for me…thus losing the love of my life forever.

As it was, though, I knew *exactly* what it was that I had found…and I was prepared to do whatever it took to keep Yadira in my life. I have since come to firmly believe that one of the most important things you can do as a parent is to simply love the person your child chooses to marry.

An Expert View on Anxiety and Relationships

An individual who is experiencing anxiety might have more difficulty engaging in a serious relationship for several reasons:

- He or she may be overly self-critical and thus have low self-esteem.
- He or she may be uncomfortable approaching and interacting with a romantic interest.

- He or she may fear certain aspects of a relationship, such as the possibility of infidelity or betrayal.

Once an individual with anxiety *has* engaged in a serious relationship, though, he or she is more likely to "hang onto" it.

- Because an anxious individual has potentially faced more obstacles in building a partnership, he or she may value it more highly.
- If overly self-critical, an anxious individual may worry about "never finding this again."
- An anxious individual may also develop an unhealthy physical and/or emotional dependency on a partner.

As Todd's story illustrates, anxiety is not ultimately a barrier to building and maintaining a healthy relationship. If your anxiety is a major part of your life, it's always a good idea to discuss your relationships—romantic or otherwise—with a therapist.

Because of my family's opposition to our marriage and the fact that Yadira was still learning English, I now had to singlehandedly plan our wedding. I even went with Yadira to pick out her wedding dress—so much for the "seeing the dress for the first time at the wedding" tradition!

To be honest, I had little patience for all of the details that needed to be considered when planning our wedding—I was caught off-guard by the myriad decisions regarding flowers, the menu, seating arrangements, etc. etc. After all, I was used to dealing with auto parts—not wedding etiquette!

By the end of this unnerving process, I was so frazzled that I almost killed the wedding site coordinator when I received word of a last-minute change. Specifically, I was told three days before the ceremony that our reserved wedding location—Boston's magnificent Bay Tower Room—was going to be given to a larger party solely for financial considerations. Meanwhile, our wedding would be moved to a smaller space down the hall. In the end—most probably fearing for his very life—the meeting room coordinator backed down, and

Yadira and I were married in one of the most beautiful spaces in all of Boston overlooking Boston Harbor.

I'd like to say that the trouble ended there, but sadly, it didn't. Turns out, the ceremony itself didn't go very smoothly either. You see, Yadira and I had agreed that a rabbi would marry us. I had always been open to marrying someone outside of my faith. However, I had also been upfront with Yadira from the beginning of our relationship, telling her that I could marry only someone who agreed to raise our children in the Jewish faith. I was very fortunate that Yadira did not feel as strongly as I did about raising Joshua in her religion. Despite our agreement, though, at that time (1991) it was difficult to find a rabbi who would perform a service in which both bride and groom were not Jewish. In the end, I succeeded in rooting out an officiant—but he was retired, and obviously getting on in years.

Well, my wedding day dawned, and all of the meticulous preparations seemed to be paying off. Everyone and everything was at the appointed place at the appointed time—except for the rabbi. As the minutes to the ceremony ticked by, I began to get more and more anxious since the rabbi was nowhere to be found. Of course, cell phones had yet to come into common usage back then, so all we could do was wait…and wait…and wait—and pray!

It was time for the wedding to begin, and no rabbi. Fifteen more minutes passed, and still no rabbi. By the time the wedding had been delayed for twenty-five minutes, I was a mess. At this point, I assumed that the man had put the wrong date in his calendar or had simply forgotten entirely about our wedding and wasn't going to show. My friends, seeing my fright, speedily brought me a couple of shots from the bar—which I quickly downed. So, by the time the rabbi did show up—a full thirty-five minutes late—I was a bit inebriated. Nevertheless, the ceremony proceeded, and in due time I was married to the love of my life. Yadira, you *truly* are!

My Wisest Decision

Yadira and I honeymooned at the well-known Trapp Family Lodge in Vermont because Yadira didn't yet have her resident's papers allowing her to leave and re-enter the country—so we saved our globe-hopping vacation plans for the future. It was the beginning of a fabulous marriage, which on October 5, 2011, will reach twenty great years.

As my family eventually got to know Yadira, they too realized just how lucky I was to have found her and how smart I was to have fought for her hand.

Yadira has been the perfect partner for me. She is incredibly beautiful on the outside, but what I treasure the most is that she is always so serene and happy. Nothing seems to bother her. In fact, I can't remember a single time when my wife has been unhappy. I know this seems impossible, but it is 100 percent true! Yes, Yadira is definitely my very greatest teacher in the art of how to live a happier life.

> *Marriage is not a noun; it's a verb. It isn't something you get.*
> *It's something you do. It's the way you love your partner every day.*
> —Barbara De Angelis

TIPS FROM TODD:
CHAPTER TEN

- **Know what you're looking for.** When looking for a partner, it's entirely possible that you'll get "lucky" and become involved with your ideal mate without really meaning to. But it certainly doesn't hurt to think ahead of time about what you're looking for in a mate. It's fine to have a physical "type," but go a bit deeper than that as well. Identify personality traits, core values, living preferences, etc. that are important to you to have in a partner. Knowing what they are ahead of time will make them much easier to spot when you encounter them in living color!

- **Know *why* you're looking for those things, too.** Avoid hastily drawing up a list of "ideals" and leaving it at that. Especially when it comes to values, priorities, etc., make sure you can articulate exactly why you're looking for these things. After all, it's these foundational qualities that will enable a relationship to endure through the rougher times…and through outside objections and threats too!

- **Don't let others talk you out of what you know to be a good thing.** The opposition of family and friends is a common theme in the romance department—just look at famous stories like *Romeo and Juliet!* The fact is, the people who care about you have an idea of the person they *think* you should be with, and don't always react well when reality doesn't meet this vision. It won't be easy, but don't let others block your happiness no matter how good their intentions might be. If you have responsibly selected your partner with your eyes wide open, remind yourself of your blessings and stay the course. In the end, you know yourself—and the type of person you need—best.

- **Don't assume that the path will be smooth.** Whether you encounter objections to your match or not, remember that you aren't living in a fairy tale world. Yadira and I encountered a host of these and other difficulties as well in those early days, ranging from cultural and religious differences to a necessary long-distance phone relationship early on, etc. etc. etc.! Other couples might be challenged by their careers, differing goals, etc. Working through these obstacles won't be easy—but if you love someone and are willing to sacrifice and compromise for him or her, you *can* make it work.

- **Get to know your partner's family.** Obviously, it's not always possible to develop a relationship with your partner's family. And just as obviously, one's family isn't always an accurate mirror of oneself. However, in many cases, a person's family's beliefs, dynamics, and priorities indicate what he or she will bring to and expect in a relationship and/or family.

- **Choose a partner who will make you better.** *Remember, people tend to become more and more like the people they spend the most time with.* Therefore, it's very important that you have a life partner who is a happy, positive person. Look for someone who tends to see the glass as half-full rather than someone who mostly sees it as being half-empty—this type of person will pull you up rather than drag you down.

- **Don't lose hope!** *If you are depressed because you think you will never meet the man or woman of your dreams, I ask you to accept my one-year challenge.* First, you must realize that the anxiety and/or sadness that stem from your fear of never meeting "the one" are probably creating a self-fulfilling prophecy. You see, people who look unhappy and depressed are actually much less attractive and thus much less likely to attract someone else.

Taking that into account, here is my one-year challenge for you: For the next year, I want you to pretend you have looked into a crystal ball and have seen that you will meet your ideal partner within the next year, 100 percent guaranteed. That being the case, you can now relax and enjoy your life, and not stress out so much about it. I truly believe if you begin going out happily as you would if you were in love already (smiling, dressing attractively, and hopefully even working out more often), you'll be greatly surprised by how differently everyone will respond to you during the next year. After all, you've got nothing to lose...and you will have a much better chance of finally meeting "the One," I promise.

- **Make sure you're on the same page.** Before you get married to your intended (*definitely* not after!), it is very important to discuss major aspects of your anticipated life together. For example: Do you both want to have children? If so, how many? What are your views on religion? If you have different religions, are you okay if neither person converts? In what faith will any children you might have be brought up? If you have family in different parts of the world or country, where will you live? What are your financial habits and philosophies? You really must try to settle these questions before you tie the knot.

- **The most important thing you can do as a parent is to simply love the person your child chooses to marry.** Although you may never have thought about it from this angle, many parents force their children to make a terrible, emotionally fraught choice. How? Quite simply, by not supporting their child's choice of a partner. Yes, please do speak up if you think your child is in a relationship that truly is physically or emotionally unhealthy. But make sure that your objections aren't based on the belief that "no one will ever be good enough," or on the fact that you don't want to "lose" your child.

  You see, when you act this way, you force your child to needlessly choose between his past (you and your spouse) and his future (the love of his life). Such a choice can force a child to say goodbye to the person who, perhaps, would have made him happiest. And conversely, parents can lose years of closeness with their child after he chooses a new love "over" them. Remember, the way in which you decide to approach your child's partner may determine whether you gain a family member or lose one.

In the Zone

"Happiness is not in the mere possession of money; it lies in the joy of achievement, in the thrill of creative effort."
—Franklin D. Roosevelt

My marriage to Yadira brought me tremendous joy and comfort. And now, with this new sense of personal fulfillment buoying and inspiring me, I set out to distinguish myself—and my family's company—to the best of my ability. In addition to guiding my team on a purely professional level, I also began to try to improve their personal well-being by passing on the lessons I was learning from Tony Robbins and other teachers.

I believe I was at my very best during this time in the early nineties when I was working incredibly hard to build the business and change the way we ran Foreign Autopart. Those were days filled with very long hours and many, many difficult business decisions, but they also transformed the company—and me—tremendously.

(Thirteen years later, in 2004, the Automotive International Association would honor me as the industry's Young Executive of the Year. And while I was, of course, deeply grateful, I can remember thinking back to the early nineties and saying to myself, "*Those* were the years when I think I was more deserving of the award because of all of the incredibly hard work I put in!")

As fulfilling as they were, though, these early years of my career also lulled me into a false sense of security because—with a great deal of outward ego success—I never realized that I was working myself into the ground, and, eventually, toward a breakdown.

The Leadership Team

By 1992, our management team was led by my father, who possesses tremendous knowledge and insight about our entire company and about business in general. Truth be told, my dad is the finest overall businessperson I have ever personally known. Assisting him in the early nineties were my brother, Roger, who excelled at the legal, governance, and purchasing aspects of the company, and myself, who was best at business development and employee motivation and management. The fourth person who rounded out the leadership team was Ann Marie Kannally, a Boston College graduate whom I had met through my friend Karl Kreshpane and his future wife, Jamie. I brought Ann Marie on board at Foreign Autopart in 1989, and by 1992 she had clearly become the number one star who made our entire headquarters gel. Ann Marie never left a stone unturned and was driven to ensure that everything was always handled as it should be. Together, the four of us made a very formidable team.

Ann Marie, Roger, and my dad were all so strong at overseeing the running of our corporate offices and warehouse that I had the freedom to do what I loved most—focus all of my energy and attention on both the people and the processes in our two profit centers: the store chain and the National Sales Department.

Change: It's A-Comin'

While assuming a prominent leadership role so soon out of college was stressful (to say the least!), in some ways it was also a blessing. First, my enthusiasm, my sense of fair play, and my ideas hadn't been blunted by a corporate hack or by sour experiences working my way up through the management ranks of some large company. Also—incredibly—almost from day one my father gave me a virtual free rein, first in the stores, and later in the National Sales Department (our telemarketing department). It turned out that his trust in me was well-placed, because I had an intuitive sense about just how we could get the most from our employees and thus grow the business.

As I've already mentioned, two of my personal strengths are—and always have been— problem-solving and what the business community now calls emotional intelligence (the ability to quickly connect with and understand people, and then to be able to further motivate each individual so that the performance of the entire team improves). I suppose my father, who knew me well, sensed that these two strengths would find fertile soil in which to grow. If so, he was right!

> *Leadership is action, not position.*
> —Donald H. McGannon

Immediately I realized that to spark true growth I'd have to change one major unwritten rule of the New England auto parts industry: traditional salary caps. You see, when I took over our store chain in the early nineties, it was virtually impossible for any of our (or anyone else's) store employees to make more than $40,000 a year. Essentially, the company owners seemed to feel that they alone should have the opportunity to make more than this amount.

This limiting system seemed unfair to me, for starters—but I also thought it was incredibly counterproductive to realizing the full potential of Foreign Autopart's employees, and thus the full potential of the company as a whole. After all, why should anyone do much more than the norm if there was nothing to be gained from the extra effort?

If a dedicated, intelligent employee in our store chain wanted to work seven days a week in order to improve the bottom line of his or her store, I felt that he or she should be rewarded for that extra effort. And so, I made an executive decision to introduce the concept of performance-based pay with no cap to the automotive market in our area. As you might imagine, everyone at Foreign Autopart was wholeheartedly on board with this new initiative (although the same couldn't be said for our competitors, who quickly looked stingy by comparison!).

We instituted a pay plan that gave generous incentives to our store managers for improving their branches' bottom lines. Meanwhile, the company still (rightfully so) got the lion's share of the increased dollars. Almost immediately, this decision single-handedly exploded our sales and profits in over 60 percent of our stores.

Maintaining Momentum: My Open-Book Strategy

It is one thing to offer generous incentives to managers and other employees, but to get the most out of people, you also need to show them the actual numbers. This allows them to fully understand the relationship between their performance and the bottom line—and thus their own pay. I am a great believer in "open-book management" because I think it helps the employee understand how his or her everyday choices and decisions affect the bigger picture. This understanding then promotes better decision-making on the part of employees for themselves and for the good of the entire company.

As part of instituting the open-book policy, I also simplified things as much as possible for my store managers by drawing their attention to the things that *really* mattered—and that made a difference. Specifically, I showed them that although we had twenty-one line items on their stores' profit and loss statements, they could affect only seven of them. I wanted them to understand that the other fourteen listed items (things like rent, for example) were out of their control and thus should be forgotten about from a manager's point of view.

The managers' mission was zoom-focused even more when I highlighted the fact that just three of these seven remaining items accounted for fully 97 percent of their paychecks. These three items were sales, gross profit percentage (or margin), and payroll. Once the managers understood this, they could purposefully focus the appropriate amount of their energies and time (97 percent) on improving just these three things—and thus their own take-home pay.

As is often the case, we at Foreign Autopart found that a basic refocusing of our attention opened the door to much more innovation too. For example, with our managers' efforts primarily working towards just these three main line items, we soon also learned that it was much easier to raise a store's gross profit percentage (GP) than its sales. From there, it didn't take us long at all to decide that we should focus more of our energies on our stores' gross profit percentages in order to increase our bottom lines. We found many creative ways to emphasize this initiative, including making and distributing T-shirts that read, "The GP is the key," for example.

A leader's role is to raise people's aspirations for what they can become and to release their energies so they will try to get there.
—David R. Gergen

Here's one very simple-yet-profound truth that we really used to our advantage in the nineties: The more specifically you focus on a goal, the more likely you are to achieve it. And achieve our goals we thus almost always did.

Now that our managers had an understanding of how best to increase their stores' bottom lines as well as major incentives to do so, we collectively increased our overall combined stores' gross profit percentage by eight whole GP points in the first half of the nineties. Plus, we were also able to increase our sales as well due to the amazing customer service we provided at this time.

And bonus: All of this collaboration had the effect of greatly reducing the "us vs. them" employee-owner dynamic that had previously existed in the stores. We were now all on the same team…and I couldn't have been happier. Also, most of us began making lots more money, too, which of course did not hurt morale!

Onward and Upward

Yes, I was pleased with Foreign Autopart's new sales trajectory… but overall, I wasn't close to being satisfied with our performance yet. (Remember my tendency to set over-the-moon goals?) That being the case, I continued to brainstorm new, innovative ways to beat the competition.

Before long, we instituted another incredibly profitable and, back then, totally unthinkable sales tactic: We began allowing our store managers to charge any price they felt was necessary for any given item and to any given account. All I cared about was each store's overall sales and gross profit percentage figures at the end of each month—so why not allow our store personnel and their salespeople to do whatever they deemed necessary? After all, who knew better than the people on the front lines just how much we could get from a specific account for a specific part at that very moment?

This strategy had several benefits. First, it allowed the stores to develop even better relationships with their current accounts because prices could be customized according to what worked best for each customer. Often this would mean that store managers could sell those specific items that customers were most concerned about at very low prices, and make up the GP on other items sold to that same customer or to other customers. This pricing freedom increased customer loyalty and therefore sales, and it also allowed our managers to make the competition look very expensive on certain key items. Along these lines, in fact, the strategy even enabled our more sophisticated and motivated managers to actually steal customers away from the competition because of this new pricing flexibility.

A Special Thanks!

I certainly don't want to give the impression that I single-handedly propelled Foreign Autopart on to bigger and better things. Far from it! After I got the innovation ball rolling, several amazing individuals stepped up and made sure the momentum didn't slacken. Todd Leach, Frank O'Regan, John Tyburski, Mario Magro, and many other top store managers and store supervisors were responsible for coming up with many new and effective profit-generating ideas. Honestly, for the most part it was these other stars who came up with the great new ideas that pushed our company forward in the early nineties. It was just my job to make sure they got life.

This fundamental shift to a much more team-oriented corporate culture enabled me to challenge my teammates as they had never been challenged before. As I've told you, I set incredibly high—some might even say crazy—goals for my store managers, but I always attached huge bonus opportunities to these goals in addition to my managers' commission plans. Also, I always gave my managers all of the tools they needed to be successful. While I do believe that showing recognition and appreciation is truly more important over the long run than money, I learned early on that if you need a certain sales goal to be met quickly, offering money trumps any other motivational method.

Leadership is understanding people and involving them to help you do a job. That takes all of the good characteristics, like integrity, dedication of purpose, selflessness, knowledge, skill, implacability, as well as determination not to accept failure.
—Admiral Arleigh A. Burke

On the other hand, my admittedly challenging expectations meant that I had to ask uncomfortable questions of the managers who now lagged behind our emerging "stars." For example, I would visit a store that was conspicuous because it consistently did the same sales every month while its neighboring stores were almost always increasing their sales.

In these situations, I tried to avoid outright criticism and blame. Instead, I would ask the manager something like this: "If your life depended on it, if you *knew* you would cease to exist for even one more day if you didn't do another $10,000 in sales this month, could you do it?"

In answer to that specific question, almost 100 percent of the managers would say, "Hell, under those circumstances, Todd, I bet I would do $50,000 more in sales!" And they were serious.

My response was, "Then why aren't you doing just this extra $10K more that we need now?"

The truth was, many of these managers simply preferred to take it easy and do "just enough" rather than to have to work harder in order to make more money. Others, I think, were afraid of failure. These individuals would rather stay in the same comfortable place than really go all out for a few months because they feared coming up short—and its implications for their fragile egos.

These managers were not sure it was possible to increase their sales, or perhaps they didn't believe they themselves knew how to. Of course, I would try to work with all of my managers in order to increase their stores' sales and/or GP percentage, but if a particular manager didn't seem interested or capable, I would move him to another location to try to mix things up a bit and to teach him some new techniques in the process. At this point, a more experienced and more motivated manager would typically take over his store—and its sales would almost immediately skyrocket.

An Expert View on
Performance-Limiting Fears

Quite often it's our fears, and not our actual abilities, that hold us back from achievement. In a workplace setting, this can be addressed by leaders or managers in several different ways:

• If an employee's effort is limited by a belief that he or she doesn't possess the skills necessary to do a specific job, leaders can help in several ways. They can:

 ○ Provide more training.
 ○ Work directly with the fearful employee for a little while in order to bolster her self-confidence.
 ○ Assure that the employee knows that if he fails on a first-time attempt at reaching a new goal or completing a new task, he won't face serious negative consequences. (Actually, this is a good policy for all employees.)

• If an employee's fear is a function of perfectionism, supervisors can set very specific, manageable, and measurable goals. This way, performance will be measured through specific and objective criteria, not generically or subjectively.

Employees themselves shouldn't "settle" for working with performance-based fears, either (although, by definition, fears might make an employee reluctant to seek change). If you'd like to empower yourself at work, start by reading self-help books or listening to motivational tapes. You might also consider asking a workplace friend for advice as to how you can improve, or talk to your supervisor about ways to expand your abilities. If these strategies are not feasible or do not make an impact, consider seeking professional help. Therapy or a regulatory medication can make a tangible difference!

For our top managers, from 1993 until around 2003, taking business from the competition was literally like taking candy from a baby, because Foreign Autopart was now honestly miles ahead of our competitors in terms of our ingenuity and, most importantly, our overall customer service.

Do not follow where the path may lead. Go instead where there is no path and leave a trail.

—Ralph Waldo Emerson

Tackling—and Transforming—Telemarketing

With all of these positive changes, the store chain was really rolling along on a wave of self-perpetuating momentum. But then, as is usually the case in business (and in life), another huge challenge was thrust upon me. In 1993, my brother, Roger, had a major disagreement with Brian Jones, the head of our National Sales Department—and Jones quit.

While I knew from experience that Jones had not been Foreign Autopart's biggest asset, his leaving was nevertheless very stressful for me as I now had to immediately jump in and run that department simultaneously to the chain. During the following year and a half, while running both the stores and the telemarketing division, I rarely worked less than seventy hours a week—and usually more—in order to handle all of my multiple obligations and in order to see to it that both divisions hit their sales and bottom-line profit numbers.

There is no doubt in my mind that I would have failed miserably had I not enjoyed the cooperation of everyone in our National Sales Department. Why? Well, frankly, I knew almost nothing about running that particular department when I suddenly became its leader. (Talk about sinking or swimming!) Another reason I didn't stall at the starting line back then was that I was also able to cash in on all of the "emotional deposits" and friendships I had made with so many of our great store employees by then too. (Again, it all comes down to *people* and, most importantly, how you treat them.)

People don't care how much you know until they know how much you care.

—John C. Maxwell

Now, with the invaluable support of everyone, I tried to do for our tele-marketing department what I had done for the store chain. First, I let every salesman set his own pricing. I also asked the salesmen to share any ideas they had for improvements and began implementing many of them as soon as possible. And to kick-start this regimen of change, I was purposefully generous with bonus money too. For example, if the department was falling behind its sales goals during any given month, I would respond by challenging the sales-people to step it up, promising them attractive bonus incentives for getting back on track and hitting their sales quotas. More often than not, we would find ourselves not only making up the needed ground and hitting our targets, but exceeding them.

> *Leadership and learning are indispensable to each other.*
> —John Fitzgerald Kennedy

Well-Deserved Recognition

As you know, it's important for me to give credit where credit is due. I hope you'll thus indulge me while I thank some outstanding members of that telemarketing sales team! First of all, Sam Bornstein has always been, for over thirty years now, our star national telemarketing salesperson. Sam has a terrific sense of humor and is an unbelievable performer. Bob Forman, also still with us today after over thirty-plus years, is tremen-dous too. And Wayne Kaufman, Ken Mizrahi, Bob Edmunds, as well as Manny Misiph also led the telemarketing sales team during my early days along with Sam and Bob. Meanwhile, Jack Creeden, another man with a tremendous sense of humor, led the support team for all of these salesmen throughout the 1990s—and still does to this day.

I was, of course, thrilled with what the National Sales Department was accomplishing, but the bottom line wasn't my only focus. I also wanted to make sure that my salespeople felt appreciated and motivated. Furthermore, I wanted them to have as much fun as possible. So in my typical fashion, I went out of my way to make sure everyone had a ball—especially when we broke our all-time monthly sales records.

For a company that's been around for decades, setting a new all-time monthly sales record is a big deal, and I treated it as one. At my suggestion, Foreign Autopart hosted lavish celebratory lobster dinners at the very best restaurants in our area when this happened for the telemarketing division, and we invited the entire team. At the top of my lungs, I would begin the meal by making a rousing toast to all of our amazing star telemarketing salesmen and to their great support people as well. My dad would usually also speak, and then Sam Bornstein, one of our top performers, would really get the party going by making a toast of his own that would have us all in stitches.

> *Recognition is the greatest motivator.*
> —Gerard C. Eakedale

From the beginning, I wanted all of my employees, both in the stores and in telemarketing, to feel like they were kings. If this was the case, I believed, they would be much less likely to ever leave Foreign Autopart for another company regardless of the size of the pay raises offered. And I was right—over the years, 99 percent of our employees stayed with Foreign Autopart. And of the 1 percent who did leave, most sooner or later asked to come back.

My successful attempts to break down the barriers that had formerly existed between the employees and the owners had an extra benefit that I hadn't even considered at first: It opened the door for my father to get to know our leading store managers and telemarketing salesmen better. Now that the "us vs. them" dynamic had been dismantled, he could speak much more often and honestly with them. This had an enormous effect on morale and profits.

You see, my father has an incredible business mind, sharpened by a university engineering degree. And he, too, refuses to leave a single stone unturned in pursuit of a solution to a problem. Thus, he and I were now working day and night to come up with creative solutions to our people's suggestions that would benefit our customers. Before long, National Sales thus really started to take off as well!

Keep On Keepin' On

There was one area, however, in which Foreign Autopart struggled for almost a decade: finding a permanent leader for our National Sales Department. As I said, I had been forced to step in on an interim basis after Brian Jones quit, but our goal was always to find a fully qualified individual to lead this department. The search started in 1994 and proved to be more difficult than anticipated.

In fact, we went through so many candidates who were not up to this task that in 2000 a competitor tested me at our Las Vegas trade show by snidely observing, "There must certainly be a problem with your management style, Todd, if you have to keep changing your telemarketing managers every six months!"

Keeping my cool, I replied in all honesty, "On the contrary, it should show you that we won't settle for mediocrity like most companies do. We'll keep searching until we find the right person to lead this critical department."

In fact, that's exactly what we did. And in 2003, almost ten years to the day since Brian Jones had quit, we finally hired the right person to run our National Sales Department. Darrell Daniels had met my wife, Yadira, back in 1993 at our local dry cleaner's store, which was then located just a block from both of our homes in Canton, Massachusetts. Yadira, Josh, and I soon became friends with Darrell, his wife, Valerie, and their two great kids, Nicole and Dylan.... and I quickly recognized what a good fit Darrell would be in this leadership role for Foreign Autopart.

It took me nearly a full decade before I was finally able to convince Darrell to become the head of our telemarketing division, and as far as I'm concerned those years of persuasion were well worth all of the effort as Darrell did an outstanding job for our company from 2003 right up through 2009.

Before closing out this chapter, I would like to tell you about two amazing women who also ran our National Sales Department for a time during the pre-Darrell era. My sister, Kimberly Macchi, and Dzintra Donato enjoyed more success than nearly every other sales manager until Darrell was appointed!

The Feminine Touch

I am incredibly grateful to Kimberly and Dzintra for the long hours, mental effort, and emotional energy they invested in National Sales. Now, I'm aware that gender-based attributes vary from individual to individual, and that they don't strictly define anyone. I know from experience, for example, that some men can be very nurturing, and that women can strongly lead just as effectively as men.

Looking back, though, I believe a portion of Kimberly's and Dzintra's success was due to the fact that they each possess qualities that tend to occur most strongly in women: the ability to personally connect with others, to be empathetic, to be flexible, to collaborate, and to nurture, to name just a few. Historically, these "feminine" qualities have been pooh-poohed in the business world. This is a huge mistake to make! Trust me! I believe that Kimberly and Dzintra were able to connect with individual employees more quickly and effectively than a typical male manager might have, and I know that they also each succeeded in unifying the team into an especially cohesive and collaborative whole.

I am pleased to see that with every passing year "feminine" qualities are being embraced further by the business world. It's true—the old "command and control" leadership model is on its way out (and it's about time, too!), and a more empathetic, community-oriented model is thankfully putting down roots.

With all of that said, I would like to take a few moments to give Kimberly and Dzintra the thanks and credit they deserve.

My sister, Kimberly, stepped in to lead Foreign Autopart's National Sales Department in 1997, a role in which she enjoyed tremendous success. Actually, I feel badly because I don't think Kimberly ever got the enormous credit she deserved at the time. For most of that year she ran a very dysfunctional department, yet she still managed to end the year with bottom-line earnings increases.

Kimberly's greatest strengths are her honesty, straightforwardness, work ethic, and loyalty. She can be tough when she has to be, but she is *always* fair. Kimberly did everything she could for the sales team, and as a result, she got their full support. It also helped that she naturally has a great relationship with our father, and was thus able to convince him to "ask" other department managers to do the right thing for her sales team. Ultimately, Kimberly made sure we did whatever was necessary for her salespeople to keep their customers happy with us. Thank you so much, Kimberly!

A few years later in 2000, I asked Dzintra Donato, my own assistant from 1996 until 2006, to step in as a personal favor to me and manage the National Sales Department for about a year. She too had both morale and sales soaring in a short time. Similar to Kimberly, Dzintra is very honest, straightforward, and hardworking, and she also inspired amazing results under difficult circumstances.

Dzintra's other main strengths are that she is incredibly concerned for everyone and patient. Thus, she was naturally very interested in every one of her salespeople, and because she cared about each of them so much and so personally, she inspired them to tap into their full potential. Also, Dzintra, like my father, is totally incapable of leaving a single problem unsolved! And let me tell you, she solved quite a few of them, because, having been in nearly all of Foreign Autopart's departments by then, she knew how they all worked and fit together. Thank you so much, Dzintra!

When both women and men bring their strengths to the workplace, business benefits.

—Nancy Clark

There's No Substitute for Talent

So, what did I learn from my decade of searching for the perfect leader of our National Sales Department? Essentially, I learned that there's no substitute for talent. Not degrees, not previous experience, not recommendations, and not business connections. Talent is something you cannot teach.

And, knowing that, I have always done whatever possible to attract the best people.

As I settled into my leadership roles at Foreign Autopart, I was initially pleased to find many examples of such talent already established in the ranks of our own employees. One of the big advantages of hiring from within is that your own employees already know your culture, appreciate it, and understand how it works. Sometimes, a star hired from another company simply can't replicate his or her stellar performance when dropped into a different corporate culture—and I did in fact see this "situational success-to-slump" pattern play out several times.

Nonetheless, this didn't mean that we at Foreign Autopart wouldn't consider recruiting top talent from outside our own organization—on the contrary! And when we did look farther afield, we'd usually offer very lucrative deals to our candidates...but we didn't stop there. If a very desired employee's current employer matched our initial offer, beginning around 2000, we would offer a signing bonus without hesitation. This made Foreign Autopart stand out positively, and also made our new recruit feel very special indeed. He or she could now go home and tell his or her family, "I just got offered a $2,000 signing bonus! I feel just like a pro athlete! Can you believe it?"

Recruiting methods and signing bonuses aside, though, here's the bottom line. Foreign Autopart was successful under my leadership not because I am a genius in all things business-related, but because I know the value of attracting and holding onto great talent.

> *The best executive is the one who has sense enough to pick good men to do what he wants done, and self-restraint to keep from meddling with them while they do it.*
>
> —Theodore Roosevelt

Focus on the Positive (People, That Is!)

Speaking of holding onto great talent, I once went to a seminar by John Baker, and boy did I get one incredibly valuable golden nugget of wisdom that day! John explained that one of the biggest mistakes American managers make is that they spend way too much of their time with their most negative employees. These are often the employees who have a ton of talent, but who are nevertheless always griping and complaining. And as a consequence, we then have very little time left to keep building up, cheering on, and "re-recruiting" our very best people. The reason for this is that we want so desperately for these talented negative people to become great employees like our current stars. Also, we almost feel guilty asking and encouraging our very best employees to do even more.

I have to say, when I came back home and took John's advice by patting my very best people on the back more and offering them bigger incentive bonuses, I found to my surprise that they could often do much more than they were already doing. Focusing on "positive" employees was time much better spent, as opposed to continuing to waste my time trying to change negative people.

Overall, my knowledge of auto parts and the industry itself was perhaps one-fiftieth of Wicks's and Jones's. How could it have been otherwise? I was a kid barely out of college when I took over their positions. But while they were more old school and believed in retaining almost total control, I took the opposite approach—I tried to be as open and transparent as possible, and I constantly asked for input and advice. (To some extent, I had to do this because I was just learning the business and was therefore dependent on my employees for their knowledge, guidance, and help!)

Beyond Business to a Life Lesson

If you treat people with respect, are fair to them, and reward them for what they do well (instead of criticizing them for what they are doing wrong), you will have happier and more fulfilling relationships. Empowering people in your business results in measurable increases in performance and monetary pay-offs, but empowering people in life is even more rewarding.

Still, my experiential education aside, my natural inclination has always been to be fair and honest, to motivate and to reward hugely, and to work my tail off. The success that resulted from these strategies led me to recognize that business really is primarily about hard work, honesty, and relationships. As you will read in the next chapter, as I continued to do everything within my power to ensure that my teammates were handsomely rewarded, having fun, and working hard, our company's sales and profits absolutely went through the roof.

TIPS FROM TODD:
CHAPTER ELEVEN

- **A wage ceiling is almost always a performance ceiling.** It's a fairly simple concept: Most people aren't going to go above and beyond if they won't be recognized or rewarded for their extra efforts. If you want true innovation, determination, and diligence, compensate accordingly. You'll find that your initial investment is returned with interest!

- **Use cash rewards in short-term contests.** It's true that appreciation and positive reinforcement create the love and loyalty that keep employees performing well through the years, but monetary rewards are the number one motivator if you've got to accomplish something in a matter of months or weeks.

- **Transparency prompts terrific performance.** If you show employees the relationship between their actions and their own pay, as well as how those actions correlate to the overall performance of the company, they will be able to make better decisions. They'll also *want* to make better decisions because they will trust you more!

- **Strive for "all for one" instead of "one over all."** If you lead through commanding, controlling, and intimidating, you might temporarily get the results you want—but never *more* than that. What's more, your team's performance will be uninspired and grudging. To unlock inspiration and achievement, make it clear that everyone at your company or in your division is part of a team. Lead through example, collaboration, and encouragement.

- **Be goal-oriented.** Set high goals for your people and offer generous monetary rewards if they are reached. Also, be sure to give your team all the tools they say they need to attain those goals, and then step aside and let everyone do what they need to in order to get to the desired destination.

- **Make sure your voice isn't the only one heard.** Part of building an "all for one" culture is making sure that every voice can be heard and is valued. No matter how much experience you have, you can still benefit from the knowledge, perspective, and ideas of your team. Encourage sharing and acknowledge all contributions.

- **Ask the hard questions.** It's nobody's idea of a good time, but asking hard questions and constructively pointing out deficiencies and weak points—as well as issuing challenges—prompts growth and discourages inertia.

- **Realize that it's a woman's world, too.** Traditionally, business (and to some extent, society as a whole) has valued masculine traits and attributes above those exhibited by women. It was once thought that emotion, the willingness and ability to compromise, and empathy, for example, were weaknesses. Increasingly, though, that is proving not to be the case at all. In fact, these traditionally feminine traits draw teams closer together and inspire them to greater achievement.

- **There's no substitute for real talent.** While it might be tempting to quickly plug holes with individuals who are "adequate" or "convenient," make every effort to continue searching until you have found the most talented, qualified person for whom you have been looking.

- **Constantly "re-recruit" your very best performers as often as possible.** Doing everything you can (within reason) to attract a valuable new talent to your team is a no-brainer…and the same should go for tried-and-true high performers. Tell employees who consistently perform well how much you appreciate them and all they do for your company. Also, think of little bonus gifts (like tickets to the movies or gift certificates to their favorite ice cream store) to show your gratitude. And conversely, do not make the all-too-common American business mistake of spending too much of your time with your negative and under-performing employees. As much as you *wish* to change them, the majority of your efforts are better spent invested in individuals who will take them to heart.

Treat Them Like Kings

"When we feel love and kindness toward others, it not only makes others feel loved and cared for, but it helps us also to develop inner happiness and peace."
—Tenzin Gyatso, Fourteenth Dalai Lama

In the last chapter, I told you how I, along with my family and colleagues, grew Foreign Autopart as a whole. In this chapter, I'd like to share with you how I invested in the company's most valuable component: its people.

I've referenced my management style several times in the preceding chapters, so I know you're familiar with its basic foundation: *It's all about people.* In fact, I would say that this deceptively simple phrase accurately sums up most of my career at Foreign Autopart (later, Autopart International), especially once I had established my niche as a leader of the company.

From childhood on, I've found it nearly impossible to proceed in any endeavor without taking into account the well-being of others. I am extremely sensitive to the feelings of the people around me, and depending on the nature of the situation, it can be difficult—if not impossible—for me to effectively proceed if I know that someone is hurt, upset, or unhappy, especially if it is because of me. This sensitive attitude certainly extended to my career, where (as I have said before) the old "It's not personal; it's just business!" idea always ticked me off.

Yes, I *did* develop an adequately thick skin in regard to competitors and prospects after my first few encounters with the likes of the cursing client in

Florida and the Missouri madman. (See Chapter 8 if you'd like a reminder of who these two difficult customers were!) However, I felt much differently about my coworkers and employees. As far as I was concerned, everyone at Foreign Autopart was part of a big family, and I made it my mission to ensure that *they* felt that way, too.

Basically, I wanted everyone at my company to be happy. In fact, being able to reward others, make them smile, and even teach them a few of my tricks along the way have always been some of the things I have found most rewarding throughout my life.

Looking back, it's sadly ironic that in earnestly working toward making others happier, my younger self was ignorant of what true happiness for *me* looked like. I was also unaware of the fact that through my own hard work, I was trying to compensate for the fact that I had never truly felt myself to be "worthy." Until my breakdown in April of 2001, I didn't realize that the anxiety I often felt throughout the nineties was an indication of a problem that was rooted deep within me, instead of in my surroundings.

Be that as it may, though, I didn't—and still don't—regret all of the long hours and energy I spent in making Foreign Autopart a very special place to work. I consider my achievements there to be some of my life's proudest contributions, and, that being the case, I'd like to share in more detail my "It's all about people" strategy. It is my sincere hope that the stories I have to tell, as well as the advice embedded within them, will inspire and help you become more successful, too.

This chapter is mainly business-oriented, but I believe its lessons can be much farther-reaching. You see, treating others generously and positively is a central component of personal happiness no matter who you are or what you do.

You Look Like You Need a Hug!

As you know, it didn't take me long as a leader to recognize that praise and reward are much better motivators in the workplace than fear and punishment. Sure, you might temporarily raise performance by terrorizing your employees, but this only builds resentment and totally erodes loyalty and commitment. Because I naturally understood that people learn and perform best through praise and reward rather than as a result of criticism, I always spent significant portions of my time searching for our people in their greatest moments so that I could then publicly "sing" about them to the highest heavens.

I also strove to create a culture in which every person really knew that I genuinely cared about each of them as individuals, too. Okay, I'll admit it: "Hugs" and "the workplace" are not usually associated with one another. But I didn't care! I have always been a natural hugger, and this was a primary way in which I let my team know that I cared about them beyond their functions as employees. Furthermore, I believe that the expression of physical closeness indicates more than words ever could that you really care.

> *Hug [in other words, show] someone your appreciation.*
> —Violet Gartenlicht

An Expert View on Physical Touch

So much of communication is nonverbal, touch being a prime example. As early as infancy, affectionate touch is used to communicate, to form bonds, and to convey security. Unquestionably, touch conveys closeness much more strongly than mere words—and for this reason, it should be used judiciously.

For adults in Western cultures, touch on the arms and shoulders in particular—as is the case in hugs—conveys friendship rather than anything more intimate. That's why it can be appropriate in a variety of settings, including, in some cases, the workplace. (Some company cultures are more conducive to hugging than others.)

Touch can evoke very powerful emotions, both positive and negative. That's why it's important to approach physical touch, such as hugs or pats on the back, with extreme judiciousness in a professional setting—it *can* forge a bond of closeness, but it can also be a potential landmine if interpreted in a negative manner.

In general, it's a good idea to ask people for permission before you hug them—and always respect the wishes of anyone who declines.

When I first started hugging my store managers, some of whom were very big men twice my size, they felt very uncomfortable. Gradually, though, they came to understand that these embraces were my way of expressing appreciation and concern for them. And once the managers got used to being hugged by their boss, they even seemed to like it. In fact, if I was ever in any doubt in the beginning as to the effectiveness of hugs, my qualms were relieved by the fact that my assistant at the time, Julie Tassinari (1990-1995), would often receive calls from managers who were concerned that I was upset with them if I forgot to hug them when visiting their stores!

The bottom line is, I have learned through the years that no matter our age or position, we all crave love and appreciation. The desire to be recognized and to belong is a basic human yearning. We all want to feel noticed, respected, and liked. Knowing that, I tried to praise my employees for good things they did every day in order to ensure that we developed and maintained a culture of respect, reward, and recognition.

The Royal Treatment Begins

I also went out of my way to treat my teammates as royally as possible. At a base level, Foreign Autopart's employees received competitive salaries, and as a result of my pay-for-performance bonus system, many were soon making great money indeed. In fact, by 1995 several managers were making double their 1992 or 1993 W-2 wages. Two especially motivated store managers were even making over six figures at this point!

While large bank accounts never hurt, I have always been aware that money isn't everything. (After all, I had grown up as a "rich kid" by most standards, and despite my creature comforts, had experienced more personal unhappiness and stress than most of my peers.) Thus, as the leader, I wanted to provide some extra perks and considerations to show my people just how much I really loved them and appreciated all of their hard work. I also wanted to prove that I was more fun and exciting than any other boss they could possibly work for "across the street." And so, my brain kicked into high gear and began devising ways to make my employees feel second to none.

The manner of giving is worth more than the gift.
—Pierre Corneille

One of the first ways in which I began to deliver the royal treatment was through sporting events. We Bostonians are lucky to live in an area that is home to four great sports teams that are almost always competitive in their respective leagues. Knowing that a good portion of my Foreign Autopart team were big fans of at least one (if not all!) of these local teams, it seemed logical to me to give them the ultimate sports fan's spectating experience. Thus, I regularly rented out the very best luxury suites for various games at Fenway Park (for Red Sox games), Gillette Stadium (for Patriots games), or the Fleet Center (for Celtics and Bruins games) and held contests for my managers, etc. (which sometimes included tickets for their families as well) to come and have an absolute blast in high fashion while watching their favorite hometown teams.

Another initiative I put a lot of effort into was our company holiday party. Yes, I knew that the stereotypical office party was characterized by mediocre hors d'oeuvres, awkward conversations, boring speeches, and perhaps some alcohol-tinged karaoke. Well, I vowed, this would *not* be the case for Foreign Autopart. So beginning in 1993, I switched our yearly party to every other year so we could absolutely go all out in our spending and throw a holiday party extravaganza. Hosting an extraordinary party every *other* year actually gave the event some extra appeal.

So, what did a Foreign Autopart holiday party extravaganza look like in the mid-nineties? We would rent out rooms at the finest hotels in Boston; for example, most often our party was held at the famous Boston Park Plaza Hotel. We always served steak or prime rib as one of our dinner choices. We would have great music, and later in the evening we would also pick names out of a hat in order to choose recipients of highly coveted prizes, such as top-of-the-line televisions and other high-end electronics. I was especially happy when employees at the lower end of our pay scale won the most expensive gifts, which seemed to happen a good bit of the time.

I was thrilled to see over time that all of the employees and their spouses really anticipated, enjoyed, and appreciated these five-star affairs, which I explicitly billed as a token of the company's appreciation, respect, and love. In addition to motivating the team to stay on top, I also believed that these fabulous parties built an "emotional bank account," if you will, with my employees' spouses. Specifically, if an employee were to come home angry or upset with me or anyone else at work, his or her spouse would at least now know the other side of continued loyalty to the company! Furthermore, each of these parties gave Yadira and me a chance to get to know and become friends with many of my employees' spouses.

The Method Behind My "Madness"

If you're thinking that using holiday parties in order to win spouse loyalty is, well, intense…you might be somewhat correct. However, I felt it was the right thing to do, and looking back, I still feel that way. You see, I was very sensitive about employees leaving Foreign Autopart. My experiences of having some of our store chain managers quit without notice (which, you'll recall, happened during my first year running the store chain) made me determined to do everything in my power to prevent such occurrences in the future. They were just too upsetting to me, both on a practical level (finding a good replacement was often a major hassle) and also on a strategic level (keeping good talent and providing organizational consistency is crucial to any company's success).

Speech Time!

Managers' meetings were another ideal opportunity for me to give our people the royal treatment and to tell them how much I loved them. Store managers' meetings were held two times a year and were enjoyed by all. We also had one assistant store managers' meeting each year. Again, we'd serve the very best food—typically steak—at all of these events. I learned early on, from my own observations and from feedback, that people's perceptions of a meeting or a holiday party, for example, are significantly influenced by the quality of the food served! Not surprisingly, the better the food, the better and more valuable our managers judged the meeting to be.

I also made sure that there were a lot of theatrics at our managers' meetings, usually thanks to yours truly. For example (as you read in Chapter 1), I would jump off tables to make my points, and sometimes I'd even get down on my hands and knees in mock begging, pleading for more sales and better results. That tactic never failed to get a laugh.

I wasn't the only one talking, though—employee speeches were also a major part of these managers' meetings. After employees moved up the store chain hierarchy and became managers, they were expected to give a maiden speech to the approximately one hundred store managers and store supervisors in attendance explaining what they did to be so successful while running their Foreign Autopart store—a rite of passage of sorts.

Speaking to this many colleagues for the first time, obviously, is a very scary and big deal, and thus I always encouraged each of these newbies to take plenty of time to plan his or her first speech. I'd even urge these employees to take the Friday afternoon prior to the event off so that they could prepare their speeches and presentations.

> *It usually takes me more than three weeks to prepare a good impromptu speech.*
>
> —Mark Twain

Even though most of my more experienced supervisors and managers honestly gave wonderfully effective speeches when asked, I—and they—were amazed by how often a rookie would steal the show. Of course, everyone pulled for the "new kids," especially as they usually started out visibly nervous—but then, it so often turned out to be the case that all of that Friday afternoon preparation and planning paid off handsomely. Unfortunately, buoyed by their initial success, many of these rookie managers now became overconfident in their public speaking prowess and completely bombed their second speeches because they simply hadn't prepared for them well, if at all. (The School of Hard Knocks strikes again!)

These managers' future speeches were, I am glad to say, always much improved after such a dreadfully embarrassing second speech experience. We all must learn, unfortunately usually the hard way, that every time you do something you must prepare to do it right if you want to succeed.

What Happens in Vegas

In the interest of being totally honest, I'd like to share with you my own public speaking disaster.

In 2004, thanks to my brother Roger's advocacy, I was slated to give a talk at the huge annual automotive show in fabulous Las Vegas! I was beyond excited, of course, and beginning on Sunday, I started inviting everyone I knew to come hear my speech scheduled for Thursday evening. However, by the time Thursday rolled around, everyone—including me—was exhausted (and some were hung over to boot!). I definitely hadn't taken the advice I usually gave to my rookie managers before their maiden speeches: to get plenty of rest!

I wasn't worried, though; I always memorized my speeches rather than using notes or audiovisual aides. I had totally memorized this one, and I had a lot of experience in public speaking by this point. When I got to the podium, however, I found that my speech was one of several talks happening simultaneously. And the walls between the meeting halls were very flimsy; thus I could hear several of the other presentations going on all at once. This was quite distracting to me.

As I was introduced and approached the microphone ready to address about 150 people, all of whom I knew as customers or competitors, and again, most of whom I had personally invited to come and hear one of the greatest speeches of their entire lives, I completely froze. Yep—I totally forgot what I was going to say.

I'm sure I looked like the classic deer caught in the headlights. Once my anxiety had kicked into full gear, combined with my fatigue and the noise distractions, it made it impossible for me to regain my train of thought. Instead of standing there and trying to fake my way through it, I simply told it like it was. I said to the audience, "I am very, very sorry, but frankly I've completely forgotten what I was going to say." And with that, I turned and walked off the stage.

Of course, I was (extremely!) embarrassed, but I also knew that people make mistakes. I was not the first person, nor would I be the last, to freeze in these sorts of circumstances. Logically, I knew that this wasn't the end of the world. I held my head high and carried on as best I could for the remainder of the event, and I even took all of my customers who had just witnessed my most embarrassing moment out for a great dinner that night, as was previously planned.

And this time, I *did* take my own advice about always learning from your mistakes. You'd better believe I now bring an outline of my speech folded up in my pocket to the podium with me whenever I speak…just to be safe!

An Expert View on "Blanking"

Even under ideal circumstances, many of us would be in danger of forgetting at least part of a memorized speech. In this case, Todd's anxiety (caused by noise distractions and heightened by exhaustion) certainly contributed to his "blanking" at the podium.

Actually, high levels of anxiety can cause temporary memory loss in a variety of situations, including everyday conversations. Unfortunately, it can be difficult to immediately recover a memory or train of thought when your mind goes blank. The experience is likely to embarrass you or make you more self-conscious, thus causing your anxiety levels to ratchet up even higher.

If you "blank," take a bit of time alone to regain your poise if at all possible. Temporarily leaving the situation can help to calm you, and deep breathing should help to manage the anxiety and get your brain focused on what it is you're trying to remember. If you are in the midst of a conversation or speech and cannot easily step away, repeat your last point. Retracing your steps can help you regain momentum.

Above all, try not to criticize yourself if your mind goes blank during a conversation, speech, or other interaction. This is a natural occurrence and is often beyond your control in the "heat of the moment." Feeding feelings of frustration and inadequacy will do you no favors in the future, and might even make a repeat episode more likely.

Todd Patkin, Public Servant?

My Vegas experience aside, I love giving speeches and honestly feel most alive and happiest when on stage. That being the case, it was natural for me to always deliver the keynote address at Foreign Autopart's annual January company kick-off meetings each year. During these speeches, I went all-out to deliver an extra-special and memorable performance, often dressing up in crazy garb and playing loud raucous music to start the meetings off with a bang. Also, we would hire a comedian to follow lunch in order to add even more fun and excitement to these annual kick-off meetings.

I will always remember, and I believe everyone else will too, our January 2001 kick-off event. My after-lunch keynote presentation actually began with a local comedian, Tom Hayes, falsely introducing himself as a political consultant. He claimed he had worked in the past for the Kennedys and other New England politicians, and he then announced how thrilled he was to be part of my run for governor of Massachusetts! It was only right that my employees should be the first to know about my political aspirations, he told the stunned audience.

At this point, I took the stage with all of the fanfare that would accompany someone announcing a real run for a major political office: balloons, loud music, and even a "television broadcast station" videotaping the event to add authenticity.

Smiling and making calming motions, I adjusted the microphone at the podium and began to speak, especially thanking my brother, Roger, and my father, Steve, for okaying all that I was about to tell the audience. I now thanked all of the employees in attendance for their support through the years, and I told them that my gubernatorial run was a burning aspiration I had harbored for a long time.

Of course, I admitted, this would require me to withdraw from the business, and also my run would cost a lot of money. Thus, regretfully, there would be cutbacks and layoffs. "Most of you, my friends here today, will either get laid off or will be asked to take very, very large pay cuts," I informed the sea of stricken faces before me. "But I know," I continued, "that because of our love for one another, you would want to do this for me and for Massachusetts."

To say that the audience was stunned would be a vast understatement. I heard a few angry grumbles, but most people were so blindsided that they simply didn't know how to react at all. Pretending to be oblivious to this less-than-encouraging reaction, I continued with my speech, which ended with a release of more red, white, and blue balloons. By this point, my "campaign launch" had lasted about twenty minutes. I finally took pity a short time later on the meeting's attendees and admitted that my run for the governor's seat was, in fact, a complete sham. After breathing a huge sigh of relief, everyone agreed that this was a hilarious hoax and that I had totally blown them all away.

The Upside of Audacity

Directly after my now-legendary "political campaign" spoof, I announced another huge (and this time real) gamble that fortunately paid great dividends for our company. At the time, however, several people (especially my father) were extremely nervous and unsure about its potential for success.

By the end of the year 2000, I felt that Autopart International (Foreign Autopart) was losing its competitive edge and thus its momentum as our competition had started to mimic many of the tactics we had instituted throughout the nineties. Plus, the country was in the midst of a recession. I took an honest look at the situation in front of me and decided that since I had been overseeing the store chain for more than twelve years by then, my management methods must have become a bit stale to my team—and thus I felt I needed to come up with something new and outrageous to get the most out of my people once more.

"Something new and outrageous" turned into a plan in which I rented three multi-million-dollar homes on Martha's Vineyard, a beautiful island off of southern Massachusetts, for fifteen weeks, costing the company over $110,000 in all. These luxurious homes would be used to motivate and then reward our best store leaders as they helped us to get our sales and GP percentages moving back upward once again. My father was understandably concerned about the size of this dollar expenditure, since we hadn't test-driven this contest on a smaller scale (which was our normal practice). He was also hesitant to shell out such a large amount of money, because the overall company profits were really slumping at this time thanks to the downturn in the economy.

In the end, I convinced my father and my brother to set aside their reservations and support my plan. And now, in the late afternoon of that same January 2001 launch meeting, I announced Autopart International's biggest contest ever to-date: The manager, store supervisor, and store road salesman of the five stores that increased the most in sales and GP (gross profit percentage) from January to April would each get to vacation in one of these luxurious homes for a week, starting in June. Each home had room for about ten people, so the winners' families and friends could take advantage of the opportunity as well.

In the Nick of Time

In retrospect, I am glad that I was able to get this initiative off the ground when I did, as my full-out breakdown was sparked in April of that year (remember, due to that very next store managers' meeting and my fractured feet fiasco)—right as this competition was ending. As you'll recall, I was completely out of commission in May and June before finally finding the right doctor in July. By the time this popular contest was gearing up for a second run in 2002, I was thankfully well, back on the front lines, motivating and inspiring once again.

In the very first year of this contest's existence, our overall store chain's bottom line increased by about $200,000. The rent for the vacation homes had already been recouped—with interest! As the years passed and the contest expanded, it easily added more than $1 million to our bottom-line profits, over and above its cost. I was amazed by how aggressively certain managers would work in order to be able to go back to their new favorite spot on earth.

And better yet, these luxury vacations became not only an incentive to our managers, they also prompted the spouses and families of the winning employees to give their continued support and commitment to our organization. Many a store leader was now encouraged by a husband, wife, or child to "win this same contest again next year!" The message implicit in this contest was that if you worked hard for the Patkins, you and your family could live like kings.

Incidentally, I had been saying for years in my speeches that if we all worked hard and smart, there would be enough money for us all to live like royalty. And believe me, when you arrived at these incredible ocean-front properties, you did feel like you had just won the lottery! Also, by year three, we had added several more weeks on the Vineyard so that we could incentivize some of our best customers to give us even more of their business as well. I am told several winning customers still talk about those amazing weeks to this day.

An Extra Special Thank-You

All of the winners (and their families) were totally blown away by the fact that they could earn something so incredibly special by simply doing their jobs to the best of their abilities. Not surprisingly, there was a tremendous amount of appreciation and excitement after the first group of winners returned and told stories about their luxurious week's vacation on the Vineyard. One expression of gratitude stood out especially for me, though.

Mike MacGregor, one of our very best superstars, took his entire family on vacation with him when his store won during the contest's first year. Soon afterward, I received a letter from Mike's grandmother, who had gone on the trip even though she was terminally ill with cancer at the time. She wrote me a wonderful thank-you note in which she said the trip had been "one of the best weeks of my entire life." I still treasure that card!

Ultimately, though, I don't think it was the chance to live like the rich and famous on the Vineyard that year that restarted Foreign Autopart's growth—that was just the icing on the cake. Instead, I believe that it was all of the intangibles—the love, respect, and the extreme gratitude and generosity that my top leaders and I had been showing our employees for years by now—that truly re-committed them to our cause. I believe that showing people love, appreciation, and respect are the three most important ways to motivate. They trump money just about every time.

Affordable Employee Appreciation 101

While I spared no expense in rewarding and motivating my team, often less expensive gestures from the heart, I believe, meant just as much. Here are a few ways to say "Thanks for a job well done!" to just about any employee, anytime. I used them all at Autopart International, and I can assure you from personal experience that they are each incredibly effective.

- **Send "love notes."** When an individual does an excellent job or achieves a goal, send a handwritten note conveying your most sincere appreciation and admiration.

- **Distribute inspiration.** If you run across a quotation or story that inspires you, don't keep it to yourself—pass it along to an employee, and perhaps, if appropriate, also mention that the quote or anecdote reminded you of him or her.

- **Tell stories.** If a team member does something noteworthy, make sure that everyone else knows about it by sending this around in an email to the chain. Remember to always praise in public as "loudly as possible," and conversely to criticize only in private!

- **Identify stars.** Consider recognizing a certain number of individuals every month. For example, I always wrote about several store managers in our "Managers of the Month" newsletter. Later, I included assistant managers, store supervisors, store salespeople, and our drivers in this letter of champions as well. My profiles for each star would often be a full page in length, lauding both their professional achievements and wonderful personal qualities.

- **Make it a family affair.** Whenever possible, engage your employees' families when praising them. For example, as I shared in a previous chapter, if an employee did something really tremendous, I would call his home, generally trying to get the answering machine. Then I'd leave a voicemail like this: "Hi, (name of spouse and kids), this is Todd from Foreign Autopart where your husband and dad works. I just want to tell you that your husband and dad is the most incredible, wonderful, amazing person in the whole world. He just broke the Nashua, New Hampshire, store's all-time sales record!

"So, please, kids, do me a favor. When your dad comes home tonight, everyone run up and give him a huge hug and tell him how great he is. And (name of spouse) I hope you too will give him a big hug and a wonderful kiss to make sure he knows how much you love him and how much he is appreciated for all he's doing for our company. Thanks, guys."

Silent gratitude isn't much use to anyone.
—Gladys Browyn Stern

The Other Side of the Coin

There is a flip side to every coin and leading others is no different. Rewarding and recognizing is the "fun" part, but leaders must also ask the hard questions and deal with employees when they are off course. Knowing that I am far from being a perfect person myself, I always tried to show my employees respect and understanding when they made a misstep. In fact, I would often surprise people by choosing to look at the positive side of a very negative experience, usually focusing on what they, and perhaps even our company, could learn for the future from their errors.

Let me give you an example of this. One of our better store managers, Billy Diamond, wanted to invest $10,000 in a new brake pad line. I wasn't convinced that this was a good idea, but Billy went ahead anyway with my permission, largely on the grounds that the pads could be returned in four months if their sales were disappointing. When the brake pads arrived, Billy ripped off the labels because they included the phone number of the local competitor from which the pads were drop-shipped to him. As it turned out, the pads were not as good as Billy had hoped, and therefore he wanted to return them. However, he discovered that because he had ripped off all of the labels—which included the barcodes as well as his local competitor's phone number—they now could not be sent back.

I think Billy was expecting me to yell at him and maybe even fire him—or at least to take the company's monetary loss out of his own paycheck. Perhaps such an angry response on my part would have actually been simpler on Billy emotionally. Instead, though, I told him that he had just learned a very important lesson…and besides, everybody makes mistakes. In a short space of time, I assume, Billy had gone from feeling really bad and guilty about what he had done to being extraordinarily grateful because of my enlightened attitude. Hopefully, he also felt that he now needed to work extra hard to make up the money that he had cost our company.

Here's the moral of this story. Quite simply, I believe that employees must not be afraid to make mistakes. If they constantly dread a misstep, they will never really go for the gold by trying new outrageous things for their customers. And as many experienced businesspeople will tell you, great innovation is the real fast track to huge business success today!

Also, despite all of the warmth and praise I gave people, I would be totally shocked if anyone who ever worked for me said that I was a pushover as a boss. On the contrary, because I tend to believe so much in people, I get extremely upset if I feel a person is letting himself or herself down by not going all-out or by not taking personal responsibility for disappointing results. And when I do feel these strong emotions deep in my gut—especially about people I love and believe in—I have to express them. My team knew that I could be as firm and as stern as I needed to be, and that I wouldn't pull any punches out of pity. Even when it was uncomfortable, they'd always get the truth from me.

Now, I know I've told you that I am very sensitive to others' feelings and emotions; however, that *doesn't* mean that I would "sell out" in order for my employees to like me. On the contrary, I wasn't terribly bothered if someone whose performance was disappointing didn't like me because I held his or her feet to the fire. I wasn't after popularity. Instead, I wanted respect. My goal was to motivate my employees to be the best they could be, and if we became friends, all the better. But friendship was *not* my priority.

Respect is the key determinant of high performance leadership.
How much people respect you determines how well they perform.
—Brian Tracy

Good Advice from the Gridiron

Bill Parcells, the great NFL coach, said that he never felt bad if one of his players didn't like him. His leadership style epitomized "tough love." He called triumphs and mistakes alike as he saw them, and didn't tolerate deviation from his instructions. He wanted his players to respect him and give him 100 percent all of the time, and he was quite willing to act as a mentor to those who were receptive. That's how I felt as a leader, too.

It turns out that Coach Parcells was, of course, on the right track. After they retired, many of his players said that he was the best coach they ever had. While it was true that some of them didn't like Parcells while they were playing for him, they later came to realize that it was because of him and the lessons that he had taught them that they had become much more successful and happier than many of their peers. Likewise, my goals were to inspire respect, loyalty, and commitment, and to make all of my people better and happier for the rest of their lives, too.

From time to time (as all managers must), I would need to have a difficult talk with a great employee—most often a rookie manager or assistant manager with huge potential who had just gotten off track or made a serious error in judgment. I needed to let these folks know in no uncertain terms that they were on thin ice, but I didn't want to upset them so much that they would quit or allow lasting negative feelings to further affect their performances.

Normally I could see these "talks" coming from a mile away, so a week or two before I planned to call up an employee to schedule our difficult meeting, I would send that individual some tickets to an event that I knew he or she would enjoy. It could be to a sporting event, a concert, or a night at the theater—whatever I knew would mean the most to him or her personally. This strategy might seem counter-intuitive, but the fact is that I *did* value each of these individuals a great deal; otherwise, I wouldn't have decided to go through the stressful (for both of us) experience of conducting a "you need to improve" meeting in the first place.

By treating an employee extra-special with these tickets, I knew that when we met for our difficult talk, she would be in an appreciative mood, would want to please me, and most of all would recognize that I really respected and cared for her as a person, even though I felt the need to address an uncomfortable issue.

At other times, I needed to ask a great employee—usually a manager—to do something inconvenient, even though he or she might currently be putting in a stellar performance. Often, this involved transferring to another store to improve its performance, or just stepping in temporarily if another store was experiencing specific short-term difficulties. Obviously, asking a manager to work at a different branch could be extremely disruptive to his or her life. For example, it might mean a longer commute, longer hours, or working in a less pleasant environment—and sometimes, even relocation.

Under these circumstances—even when I really couldn't afford to give the manager in question a choice (with the exception of a relocation, which I would never force someone to do)—it was certainly my preference for him to *choose* to do what I was requesting. Therefore, I always presented what I needed, explained how much it would help the company and mean to me personally, and then I allowed the individual employee to sleep on whether to accept the move or not. I wanted him to *own* the decision, because when someone is "on board" of his own volition, he is much more effective. On the very, very rare occasions in which the employee didn't now volunteer, I would then ask more directly, or even say, "I am sorry, but I need you to do this for the company."

Judgment Calls

It didn't take me long in my position to learn to recognize employees who didn't take responsibility for their own decisions, as well as those employees who were resistant to change that was necessary. By and large, I knew, these were people who would never fulfill their potential and would not add much to our corporate culture. Such employees are almost always detrimental to their companies, much like having a sulking player on the bench of a sports team. One person's negativity and lack of motivation can ruin the whole team's chemistry.

Ultimately, I was forced to let most of these "toxic" employees go, but I *did* retain some who had other redeeming qualities. I then continually tried to motivate these individuals, and once in a while, my efforts were rewarded by unexpected change after a long period of resistance. Doug Chris, one of our assistant managers, is a wonderful example.

Doug was a tall, strong guy with a very tough exterior. More than once, I remember him telling me, "Todd, I'll work hard for you but I don't want to hear any more of this Tony Robbins stuff. I'm not into your cult-like ideas."

This rejection, of course, didn't stop me from trying to shift Doug's surly and skeptical persona. After all, I knew better than anyone just how much change was indeed possible! One particular day as I was extolling the virtues of positivity, Doug burst out in a louder-than-usual voice and said, "Todd, my grandfather was always negative, my father was *totally* negative, and I am thus destined for the same. So just give me a break! I'm not going to change." Doug continued to make his case and remained very negative, often saying that everything bad happened to *him*. For example, if it was raining outside, it rained more on him than on anyone else.

Clearly, Doug wasn't going to change anytime soon. In fact, I think that he actually enjoyed feeling sorry for himself, which, he figured, was his "right" due to his "inherited" negative personality. And then Doug had a son. About a year after his son's birth, we met. This time, I didn't go into my customary positivity spiel. Instead, I congratulated Doug and told him how special fatherhood was. We talked for a little while. In the course of our conversation, I confided, "You've proven to me that I can't change you. But do you really want your son to grow up like you, cynical, negative, and unhappy?"

I could tell from Doug's face that I had hit a nerve. Pressing my advantage, I added, "You know, Doug, you were right—studies do show that kids grow up to be like their parents, not how their parents *tell* them to be."

Now Doug, the big tough guy with the hard exterior, broke down and admitted, "No, I don't want that for him. I don't want him to be miserable like me. I want him to be happy. I want to change for him. Todd, please help me to change for my son."

Of course, I was all too happy to share everything I had learned with Doug. And a lesson I had already known from my own personal experience was reinforced that day: *People will always do more for their children than they will do for themselves.*

These sorts of personal encounters with my employees were honestly the aspect of my job that I enjoyed the most. Making money for money's sake, as I've said, gives me very little satisfaction. What *does* give me satisfaction is being there for others when they are in need. Sometimes, I'd even go to an employee's home in the evening if there was a problem I thought I could help with. For me, being a leader is about helping people to become better dads, moms, sons, daughters, brothers, sisters, and friends. I tried to do that by encouraging our people to make changes in their lives that would lead to more personal happiness.

> *If you don't like something, change it. If you can't change it, change your attitude.*
>
> —Maya Angelou

Emphasizing Service

If my approach to my employees was all about developing the right relationships, I was also insistent that my employees in general—and our store managers and sales supervisors in particular—worked hard to develop the same types of relationships with our customers.

To foster the relationships that would inspire customer loyalty, around 1997 I told my store managers that they needed to act more like the saleswomen you see at Bloomingdale's. In other words, they needed to take a truly personal interest in their customers. At first, this proposed strategy did not go over very well at all! We were selling car parts, general sentiment ran, not perfume and designer duds.

Eventually, though, my store employees embraced the need to be more sensitive to their customers' feelings and to show tangible signs of appreciation for their patronage. For example, many store managers now got into the habit of writing thank-you notes and sending birthday cards to their most loyal customers. I believe that the feeling of being valued and appreciated that my people got from my letters and messages helped them to see the benefits of likewise writing these notes to their own customers as well.

From a managerial standpoint, I also knew that if my team was willing to build better face-to-face relationships with our customers, this would bring us more business *and* it would cause our customers to be less price-conscious. I truly believe that business and life are all about relationships, and the more you invest in them, the more you get back.

TIPS FROM TODD:
CHAPTER TWELVE

- **Harness the power of the hug.** Use your best judgment, of course, but if you and another person (friend, family member, coworker, etc.) are comfortable with physical touch, show your appreciation and affection with a hug! Often, hugs show that you care more effectively than words ever can!

- **Don't stop with dollars.** While you'll rarely meet a person who would say no to a monetary bonus, realize that there's value in thinking outside of the bank, too! When you show your appreciation to employees through time spent with them (it's the same with kids—time is more important than money), thoughtfully considered gifts, and personalized events, you will develop much deeper bonds of loyalty. Why? Because you will have demonstrated that you care on a more personal level. Showing employees (and other people, too!) love, appreciation, and respect motivates them more than money just about every time.

- **Say thanks.** Expressing gratitude isn't expensive and it isn't time-consuming—but its impact can be tremendous. Whether you're verbally saying "thanks," writing a note, or singing another's praises, you are investing in that person's self-esteem, motivation, and loyalty.

- **You're not a bird, so don't wing it.** Regardless of what you're doing, how often you've done it before, or how good you think you are at it, *prepare.* You won't regret putting forth at least a modicum of time and energy to ensure that your bases are covered. Winging it is a recipe for disaster!

- **Keep calm and carry on.** Face it: We all mess up. Whether it's forgetting the words to a speech or burning the casserole at a dinner party, we all make mistakes that cause us to feel, well, foolish. When this sort of situation occurs, remember that you're not the first and you won't be the last to wear these shoes, and strive to maintain as much composure as possible. *How you handle yourself during and after a bad* *situation shows your true colors and personal power more than anything else!*

- **Express criticism constructively.** When you withhold suggestions and criticism, you don't do anyone any favors; however, derisiveness, anger, and too much negativity are equally unhelpful. When others operate in fear of doing something wrong, their work will be timid and uninspired. However, the freedom to make a mistake unleashes ingenuity. When expressing criticism, always try to point out positive qualities or successes to balance out the bad stuff and suggest methods for positive improvement. *And remember, always criticize in private and compliment in public.*

- **Respect the power of...well, *respect.*** There's a big difference between respect and popularity when you are in a leadership position. If your number one priority is to be liked, your ability to lead with decisiveness and firmness will be compromised. Instead, focus on motivating and guiding your team with integrity. You'll get the results you want...and your team will, in the short or long run, appreciate your commitment and respect you for it.

- **Get others on board.** If you are in a position of leadership or authority, focus on winning your group's buy-in. If they understand why you have made the decisions you have and agree based on their own understanding and reasoning, they will be much more invested in achieving the outcome you've envisioned. In short, people must own the decision in order to be motivated to implement it. And here's a bonus: The sense of purpose that comes from owning a decision will enhance their self-esteem.

- **Clean out the toxins.** In a workplace environment (and again, when *any* type of relationship is involved), be vigilant for "toxins." If you spend time with a person who is constantly negative, cynical, deprecating, malicious, etc., these attitudes will begin to infect you, too. Of course, try to offer positive advice and perspectives if you feel comfortable doing so. However, if any "toxic" individual is uninterested in changing, remove yourself from his or her presence as much as possible. And if you are in a leadership position, honestly consider the effect this person is having on your team and act accordingly. Remember that one source of negativity can drag an entire group down.

Since I have spent a significant portion of my life in the corporate world, I would like to set forth here some of the core tenets of my business philosophy. I truly believe that the following strategies are effective at every level of leadership. You'll recognize many of these truths from what you've already read...but I do believe they bear repeating!

Twenty-Three Truths I've Learned about Leadership...and Life

- At its heart, every issue or problem is always about people.
- *People don't care how much you know until they know how much you care about them.*
- You can train almost anyone to do almost anything if they are motivated to do so and are treated well.
- Remember that appreciation and rewards inspire great work—fear of criticism or punishment inspires only adequate work.
- There's no substitute for talent—not technology, not finances, and not reputation. So make sure your outstanding team members feel incredibly appreciated, valued, and cared for! Yes, it is not only okay, but necessary, to treat your top performers extra-specially!
- Get to know your people. Not just what their job functions are, but what their dogs' names are, how many kids they have, and where they go on vacation. Personal connections inspire loyalty!
- Don't be fooled by the idea that "it's business and not personal." It is *all* personal, and the sooner you realize this, the more successful—times 100—you will be. After all, I believe that other than your immediate family (husband or wife and kids), in America, because of how much time we all spend at work, our coworkers really become our extended family...even more so than our real ones (mom, dad, brother, sister, in-laws).
- Set high goals...and then give your people the tools and the freedom they need in order to do what it takes, including going outside the box, to reach them.
- If you know you need to have a difficult discussion with an employee who is important to your company, consider sending him or her a nice

note and even a gift a few weeks prior to this conversation. This will let him or her know that while you are actually criticizing his or her actions, you still truly care for him or her.

- When you know that you will have to require someone in your company to do something very important that is less convenient for her (for example, working in a different location to help that particular store grow), it is always best to first *ask* the employee if she would be willing to do this as a favor to the company and yourself. Later, if she refuses, you can always *tell* this employee that you are sorry, but she must do this for the company.

- The phone is a wonderful invention for many things. However, unless you are literally hundreds of miles away from an employee with whom you must have a difficult and/or emotional conversation, make every effort to meet her face to face. Do not have such a conversation over the phone.

- Make sure your people know you desire and encourage ingenuity by celebrating what you can learn from mistakes that are made—so long as the same mistake is not made twice.

- Encourage everyone on your team to exercise, even if it's just a little bit every day. They will enjoy less stress and more restful sleep, which fosters a more positive attitude. Quite simply, exercise makes you feel better about yourself, as well as everything and everybody else around you.

- Take time to write your people regular thank-you cards telling them how great they are and how much you love and appreciate them. Yes, I often use the word "love" in my notes, even to my most "manly" store managers. Honestly, everybody wants to feel appreciated and loved, even if they themselves are uncomfortable using the word or writing it in a letter.

- Don't be afraid to be outrageous when thanking and praising your team! For example, I would often call my employees' homes during the day if they had experienced an amazing sales month. I hoped to get their home telephone voicemail or answering machine so that I could tell their children and spouse the great news on the machine. I'd say something like, "Your husband and father is the world's greatest, most incredible, most unbelievable manager. *Please* give him the biggest hugs and kisses and tell him how proud you are of him when he gets home." Believe me, ten years later I know that the many managers who got these calls from me to their houses remembered returning home that evening much more than any large bonus checks they may have received that quarter from me!

- Whenever possible, include your employees' families in gatherings, contests, etc. When spouses and children are directly on the receiving end of the benefits your company provides, they'll be more supportive of you when the going gets tough…and they'll also encourage their mom/dad/spouse to work hard and win again!

- Don't hold too tightly to people who don't want to be on your team and thus become negative no matter how talented they are. Always remember that one negative person can pull down a whole group of otherwise positive people.

- You have to walk the walk as well as talk the talk. There is nothing more damaging to your credibility—and to your team's morale—if you do not do what you say you will do as well as what you ask others to do.

- The higher up on the "food chain" you are, the harder and longer hours you should work.

- Realize that the buck stops with you. Take ownership of and responsibility for everything that you have even the slightest control over.

- Remember that if you do what you enjoy and are best at, you'll be successful. But if you also do your very best at what you *don't* enjoy and aren't so good at (assuming these tasks are also important to your job), you'll truly be a top one-percenter in your field.

- Don't let your pride cost you sales or bottom-line profit dollars. It's always better to let a customer feel good at the end of an interaction, even if you think he or she was indeed the one who was wrong.

- "Wow" your customers as often as possible. At Foreign Autopart, we would aim to absolutely astound our best customers with appreciation for their business. For example, we would send ice cream trucks around in the summer so that we could thank them with their choice of a cool treat on a hot day.

Politics for Sale

"In order for people to be happy, sometimes they have to take risks. It's true these risks can put them in danger of being hurt."
—Meg Cabot

As you've read, my lifelong search for happiness played out largely in my personal life and in my professional life. As I strove for self-improvement and self-fulfillment (with varying levels of success), I tried to pass on what I'd learned to my loved ones as well as to my colleagues, employees, and clients. But I didn't stop there. You see, even before my breakdown and subsequent breakthrough, I understood on some level that I have an inherent need to achieve goals and to help others outside of my work and home.

Realizing this, I set off to conquer new worlds. First up was politics.

Some people thrive on the twists and turns of political races and legislative debates. In fact, they sometimes seem to be more familiar with the issues and policies than the elected representatives themselves! Other people, though, don't even want to touch a campaign sign or governmental news report with a ten-foot pole, whether from apathy, disgust, or something else entirely.

Personally, I have always been somewhere in the middle of those two extremes. I think it's important to know what's going on in legislative chambers, but until I found myself being invited into the thick of things, I never thought that I would personally be involved in the world of politics. Here's how it happened.

Patkin Politics: A Short History

For the first three decades of my life, I was never very political. Neither politics with a big P (government, economic policy, and so forth) nor politics with a small p (for example, manipulative games at the office) ever interested me. Essentially, I'm too direct to operate in those circles. I'm always upfront and honest, and I prefer to tell people exactly what I'm thinking and how I'm feeling. (No, I'm not saying there are no honest, direct politicians; just that the politics "game" is generally multi-layered and is played with an eye to the near and far futures, as well as to one's allies and rivals. Not exactly short, sweet, and straightforward!)

> *There are many men of principle in both parties in America, but there is no party of principle.*
> —Alexis de Tocqueville

Furthermore, power per se doesn't particularly interest me. Influence, yes; power, no. (You've just read my professional philosophy: I like to help my team grow, not control their every move.) Sure, there were occasions growing up—especially the times when I was feeling bullied and picked on—when I dreamed of having power so that I could strike back at my nemeses, but those were adolescent fantasies that are common occurrences during the teen years when individuals have more emotions and passions than ways to channel them.

At home, we didn't talk much about politics while I was growing up. For one thing, my dad was a Republican, and my mom was a Democrat. Perhaps that's why there wasn't much political debate in our house—the subjects were too contentious and too potentially volatile. However, we would sometimes talk about Israel when hostilities broke out in the Middle East. There was much more agreement about that subject. My parents, and later my siblings and I, all agreed Israel needed to do whatever was necessary to survive. When those who share your history and heritage are fighting for survival, it certainly simplifies the political agenda!

Not surprisingly, I planted my first political flag in Republican territory. With little life experience of my own to draw on, I did what many young boys do: I followed in my father's footsteps! Beyond my dad, Ronald Reagan also influenced me as a teenager because he seemed strong and dependable, a virtual John Wayne who was in control in the White House! And on the flip side, Jimmy Carter had earlier soured my view of the Democratic Party because he seemed weak and ordinary, more John Doe than John Wayne. At the age of fourteen, I was deeply affected by the Iranian hostage crisis, and I was disturbed by Carter's seemingly inept failure to free our hostages.

Once I came of age, I almost always voted in the major elections. And while I related more to the Republicans in my early twenties, by the time I was thirty I had come to realize that I identified more with the Democratic Party. Ultimately, I was more drawn to this agenda because I have a strong sense of empathy for the marginalized and the poor, and I believe that government (federal and otherwise) should do more to help this sector of society.

An Expert View on Heritage and Party Affiliation

Clearly, not *all* members of specific ethnic or cultural groups stand on the same political platform. Especially in a free, media-dominated society like ours, there's room for individual thought and opinion (as evidenced by the varying opinions within the Patkin family itself!). By and large, though, it's interesting to note that many Jews identify primarily with the Democratic Party. That's because Jewish heritage, culture, and tradition are characterized by community spirit and social justice. Helping others and providing for the disadvantaged is ingrained in the Jewish psyche, which predisposes many (like Todd) to identify with a Democratic agenda.

Politics, it seems to me, for years, or all too long, has been concerned with right or left instead of right or wrong.
—Richard Armour

Still, I don't think I would have actively entered the political fundraising realm had I not begun to become bored with my career by the late nineties. Now, don't get me wrong: Up to this point, my time at Foreign Autopart/Autopart International had been a difficult, wonderful, stressful, exhilarating ride. I had spent over ten years reaching for the stars, urging, motivating, cajoling, harassing, loving, and driving my team to fly higher and higher. And now here we were, launched, speeding through the stratosphere with a self-sustaining trajectory headed straight for the moon.

My professional goals had all pretty much, to be honest, been achieved— and now I needed something new to inspire and drive me. In other words, helping politicians was about to be the next rung on my self-fulfillment ladder, which already included good grades and work triumphs. Not yet having experienced my breakdown breakthrough, I hadn't learned to love myself by this time and was thus still in need of ways to stroke my always-fragile ego.

An Expert View on Challenges and Self-Esteem

Have you ever noticed that (for the vast majority of us, anyway) "sitting back and doing nothing" doesn't feel as good as we think it will? That's because we're happiest when we're pursuing fulfilling challenges. In large part, happiness comes from feeling good about yourself, and you feel good about yourself when you're meeting your obligations and creating new goals for yourself.

Think about it like this: When you avoid issues, responsibilities, and problems, at some level you know you're not doing everything you could or should. So even if you're kicked back on the couch watching your favorite show while enjoying an ice-cold soda and bag of salty chips, you'll probably be unable to *completely* relax…and your self-esteem will slowly erode.

So a commonsense remedy for low self-esteem is to a) make sure you do what you're supposed to be doing so you don't have to endure that nagging, self-esteem-sapping sense of guilt, and b) always be working toward a meaningful goal beyond your immediate obligations. When you've taken on a big challenge, there is often a justified sense of pride because you're proactively tackling the big stuff, regardless of the outcome.

Here's How It Happened

In terms of personal achievement, I had found myself at a temporary standstill around 1999-2000. I knew I needed to do *something* new, but I had no idea what that something should be. What would get my juices flowing once again? At first, I turned intuitively to charities. I've always been drawn to reaching out to others and trying to make a difference in their lives, and now I had the time and the money to do so.

So I visited several different organizations whose missions I agreed with but didn't feel that I would be a good fit for any of them. These charities (understandably) wanted to capitalize on my business acumen and quickly overwhelmed me by asking if I would run major fundraising events and/or take on key leadership roles right out of the gate. While I wanted to help, I didn't want to become burdened by time-consuming and stressful obligations—or be responsible for significant organizational matters—before I could become acquainted with these charities on my own terms. Also, I didn't yet have un-limited time on my hands—remember, I was still running the entire sales op-eration of our company! (Later on, though, I *would* get more heavily involved with charities—I'll share that story with you in Chapter 16!)

Since the charitable path wasn't panning out as I had envisioned at this point, I turned to a good friend for advice. Peter Berenson has been our fam-ily's accountant and close friend for a very long time, and he also has unusual business flair and general savoir-faire. Yes, Peter is certainly not a stereotypical accountant in that while he is of course a "number cruncher" with a logical mind who (I am sure) derives much happiness from seeing two columns of numbers balance, his interests don't stop just with figures. He also has an excel-lent understanding of the world and people around him. So I decided to talk with Peter about what else he thought might be a good fit for someone with my interests and abilities.

We began by discussing other charitable opportunities, moved on to differ-ent roles within the business community, and finally ended up with politics. In the course of our conversation, Peter mentioned Steve Grossman, a successful businessman who was running as a Democrat for the Governorship of Mas-sachusetts. I was intrigued by Peter's incredibly flattering description of Steve, and soon I was researching Steve as a person and as a gubernatorial candidate.

Steve Grossman: Survey Says…

Steve Grossman's list of accomplishments is incredible, combining business success with a long family tradition of civic involvement. He was a founding board member of The Massachusetts Institute for a New Commonwealth (MassINC); a trustee of Project Bread, an organization dedicated to alleviating and preventing hunger in Massachusetts; and an advisor to ACCESS, Boston's leading provider of financial aid, advice, and scholarships.

Steve has been chairman of the board of Brandeis University, trustee of the Museum of Fine Arts in Boston, an overseer of the Dimock Community Health Center, an advisory board member of the Women's Lunch Place, and former campaign chair of Combined Jewish Philanthropies. Steve was also the chairman of the Democratic National Committee in the nineties. In short, Steve Grossman is amazing: a completely sincere, tirelessly dedicated, and amazingly talented individual.

Also, when Peter Berenson himself became chairman of the board of trustees of the Massachusetts School of Professional Psychology, he was proud to award Steve an honorary doctorate in 2008, saying, "Steve is a passionate advocate for social justice and religious and racial harmony and has a deep history and interest in politics. Not a day goes by when he isn't somehow involved in feeding the hungry, healing the sick, and giving a voice to the oppressed."

In my own experience, what I most love about Steve is his humility and humanity. He never loses personal contact with his friends or those who are working for him, never takes them for granted, and always seems genuinely interested in their well-being. In fact, Steve often calls his friends at the end of a long day or long week just to see how they are doing. As someone who is a natural connector myself, this has always made a deeply positive impression on me.

So very early in the year 2001, at my request, Peter set up a lunch meeting between Steve Grossman and me. Before our food had even arrived, I had ascertained that Steve was everything I had hoped he would be. In person, I was able to confirm that Steve is incredibly smart and has an amazingly high energy level. I'm sure it also helps his rate of achievement that he needs only four hours of sleep each night.

By the time our lunch checks had come, I was convinced that working to help Steve's campaign was just the exciting challenge I had been looking for. (Also, as you'll recall, I was still in the process of dealing with the loss of Yadira's pregnancy at this point, and I hoped that this new endeavor would provide me with something reinvigorating on which to focus.)

Very quickly now, during February and March, I began to accomplish quite a bit on Steve's behalf. Inspired by his integrity as well as excited by his candidacy and my fundraising challenge, I started to raise as much money as possible to help fund Steve's run for the governor's seat. I immediately called on all of my friends, family, and acquaintances, familiarizing them with Steve and asking them for contributions.

Giving and Receiving: My Original Fundraising Philosophy

I used to be surprisingly comfortable making solicitations, in large part because I truly believed in the causes for which I worked. (Steve Grossman's campaign is a prime example of this!) Furthermore, I believed in a friendship model based on generosity and mutual giving. Simply, I will do anything that is in my power for my friends, and I expect that, similarly, they will do whatever they are able when the tables are turned. So especially when I was working to help the less fortunate or to effect positive change, I used to feel that it was the duty of everyone I knew to thus contribute when I asked them to.

Throughout the years, this belief caused some amount of tension between myself and several of my family members and friends, because to be honest, the total amount of money I asked for and received on behalf of various charitable and political causes really started to add up! And, on the occasions when a friend or family member in the past protested yet another of my solicitations, I used to get upset with them. This is no longer the case, though. First, I understand now that we all live our lives according to different sets of "rules"—thus I shouldn't take it personally when another person's "rules" don't line up with my own. Secondly, to be honest, I realize today that my political fundraising was done to a large extent just to fulfill my ego needs and get a lot of "atta-boys."

A Campaigning Crash Course

It was during Steve's campaign that I learned firsthand of the difficulties a challenger—even someone as accomplished as Steve Grossman—faces when trying to get elected to public office. First, all political candidates have to win their own party's primary. In this case, Steve was one of no fewer than six candidates trying to win the Democratic primary. And money is the ammunition with which you fight a political campaign. Ergo, you need *a lot* of money to win both the primary and the general election.

In Massachusetts, a traditionally "blue" state, the winner of the Democratic primary slugfest usually faces off against a Republican challenger who has not had to fight a primary contest. This is due, I believe, to a combination of the following: 1) Republican contenders willing to play the long odds of being elected by a largely liberal populace are few and far between, and 2) the Massachusetts Republican Party seems to intelligently realize that their only chance of winning elections is to have but one contender hoarding his or her money and resting until the start of the general election.

Meanwhile, the Democrats in Massachusetts almost always viciously battle each other close to the death in the primary, depleting the winner of money, energy, and other resources before the general election even starts.

It was no different for Steve, who put up a good fight. Also, Steve was hurt badly when quite unexpectedly another strong Jewish candidate entered the primary, thus splitting the powerful Jewish vote. In the end, he left the race in July because he knew he couldn't defeat the Democratic front-runner, Shannon O'Brien, who was herself then no match at all for the well-rested and extremely well-heeled Republican candidate, Mitt Romney, in the general election.

Working on Steve's campaign was an eye-opening experience for me; first, I never realized the long odds and difficulty involved in winning a political race. Also, the whole experience was very exciting, to say the least, if a little disappointing in the end. There was one huge positive outcome for me though—Steve Grossman and I became good friends, and our great relationship continues to this day. Incidentally, fabulous news: Just this November (2010), Steve was elected Massachusetts' state treasurer. Great job and congratulations, Steve!!!

Onward and Upward—for Awhile

In addition to my friendship with Steve Grossman, I was to be the recipient of another legacy from his campaign; I was well on my way to developing quite a reputation within the Massachusetts Democratic Party as a capable fundraiser. Thus, by the following summer, I was back in the political fray once again.

Steve Grossman himself asked if I would help with Howard Dean's campaign after he entered the 2004 presidential race. After researching Howard and his platform, I accepted the challenge and once again launched into raising a good deal of money for Howard. If you followed that election closely, you might recall that Howard Dean actually started off quite strong and was favored early on to win the nomination.

Unfortunately, Howard was undone by the media's spin on his speech following the Iowa caucuses. Getting into the spirit of the moment and trying to be heard over the enthusiastic crowd, Dean let out an exuberant yell. Before long the media had taken his excitement completely out of context and presented him as unprofessional, unstatesmanlike, and clearly not presidential material.

Howard Dean's abrupt removal from the spotlight was another disappointing political lesson for me. If you've been involved in a political campaign, you know how closely candidates (and their teams!) have to monitor themselves for fear that the media will take a small gesture or a soundbite and effectively finish off their races. It's a tremendously difficult balancing act. You don't want to appear too bland, safe, and boring, but if you risk being spontaneous, you can really hurt your campaign.

Leading up to the New Hampshire primary, I visited the Dean campaign headquarters in Concord, New Hampshire, which was a truly great experience. There was a definite thrill of excitement in the air, as well as a sense that we were all working for something much bigger than ourselves. Unlike the campaign for Steve Grossman, however, after the race petered out, I lost contact with Howard Dean and the other major players on his team. For this reason, in retrospect, his campaign didn't seem as personal or as worthwhile as Steve's run for governor had been for me.

> *Apparently, a democracy is a place where numerous elections are held at great cost without issues and with interchangeable candidates.*
>
> —Gore Vidal

Can't Take Another Strike!

By this point my reputation as a political fundraiser had really been established—I had been Steve Grossman's number one fundraiser and one of Dean's top five in all of New England. Hoping that my momentum would continue, Steve, along with his friend Alan Solomont, now convinced me to support Massachusetts Attorney General Tom Reilly's run for governor in 2006. Alan, like Steve, has a long history of helping Democratic candidates. Most recently, Alan played a major role in President Obama's amazing 2008 victory. Also, at the time of this writing, Alan is the U.S. Ambassador to Spain.

Steve and Alan were wholly convinced that Tom Reilly was going to win the governor's seat, and their certainty won me over as well. So off I went again pitching to my family, friends, and acquaintances for more money; however, this time on behalf of Tom Reilly. By now, I was becoming more than a little self-conscious about constantly pressing people for money. I was concerned that my appeals were beginning to impact some of my relationships. In a nutshell, it's one thing to raise money for a winner but another to raise money for a loser. And so far, I was 0 for 2. However, Reilly was way out in front and, finally, it looked like my candidate would at last prevail.

Except, he didn't. The reality is, no matter how high you're flying, in politics you're always only one mistake away from disaster. And in an attempt to make political capital but against the advice of everyone on his team, Reilly announced that he was going to appoint a fairly unknown woman as his candidate for lieutenant governor. To make a long story short, this woman turned out to be a poor choice, and then when the ensuing controversy was handled even more ineptly, a bad situation was made even worse.

> *In war, you can only be killed once, but in politics, many times.*
>
> —Winston Churchill

I was now 0 for 3, and Reilly disappeared off my radar completely. In the wake of this loss, I was left feeling very flat and discouraged. Now I promised myself that I would be extremely choosy about whom I would raise money for in the future, if I ever did so for anyone again!

> *We'd all like to vote for the best man, but he's never a candidate.*
>
> —Frank McKinney "Kin" Hubbard

Back on the White House Campaign Trail

Well, they do warn you to "never say never." This saying proved correct in my case once again, when in 2007 I was approached by Steve Grossman to help Hillary Clinton's presidential run. Interestingly enough, Alan Solomont, who had always backed the Clintons in the past, immediately decided to support Barack Obama instead. Based on his observations as a college professor, Alan said he sensed the strong desire of the students and others for real change in America, and he was convinced, therefore, that then-Senator Barack Obama had the best chance to become the next Democratic candidate for president.

Personally, I've always been very impressed with Hillary Clinton, who I have met several times in Washington, D.C., and in Jerusalem (and, by the way, that opinion has not changed after "working" for her and raising money on her behalf). Also, I firmly believe it is vital for America that we have more women in our highest political offices. So, how could I refuse the offer to help her cause? The innate wisdom of my decision was confirmed by Hillary's behavior during her campaign. I saw her many times during this race, and no matter the circumstances, she was always incredible.

Also, on a more personal note, whenever our paths crossed, she was always very quick to thank me for all I was doing for her, and she even remembered the details of my family. On one occasion I even received a personal phone call from Hillary to thank me for everything I was doing on her behalf. Of course, this special "touch" meant the world to me, recharged me, and inspired me to work even harder for Hillary's cause.

At the beginning of the 2008 electoral campaign, it truly looked as though Hillary Clinton would win. I wondered what that could mean for our country and, more selfishly, for me. In the midst of my ruminations, about one month before the Iowa primary, I was invited to come to Washington, D.C., to speak with Hillary's campaign people. To say that I was honored and excited is a vast understatement. Earlier in the campaign I had told Hillary that I would love to do more to help her win the presidency, and thus I wondered whether I was about to receive an offer to somehow do just that.

On the appointed day, I dutifully flew down to Washington, D.C., hoping that I would be given an important role in Hillary's campaign. Perhaps I would be brought on board in some sort of assisting role, or with my love of public speaking, maybe I'd even be asked to travel the country making speeches on Hillary's behalf! As it turned out, though, these were pipe dreams. The meeting for which I'd been asked to fly down to D.C. was extremely disappointing and, frankly, very unnerving to me.

Charged with excitement and ambition, I met one of Hillary's lead people in a Washington restaurant, eager to hear why exactly I'd been asked to fly down. To my increasing shock, though, I found the ensuing discussion totally outrageous. In fact, this man was so cocky and arrogant that he simply spent thirty minutes reassuring me that there was absolutely no way, according to his polls, that Hillary could possibly lose the primary. Furthermore, he told me, "This is the easiest campaign I have ever been asked to run. In my mind, in fact, we've pretty much already got it won."

All he wanted me to do, it turned out, was what I was already doing: raise money for Hillary from my friends and family. I left the meeting with a very bad feeling. Not only had the trip been a complete waste of my time and money, but now I was also beginning to feel that we might very well lose the election.

I had already learned at Autopart International time and time again that there is no place for complacency in any organization, no matter how well you think you are doing. And to underscore this knowledge, I couldn't help but think how strongly Steve Grossman, Howard Dean, and Tom Reilly had started—only to be forced to drop out of their races. Nevertheless, I continued with my fundraising efforts, figuring that Hillary had at least a 50-50 shot of winning. And unfortunately—once again—my hopes fell flat.

The Clinton Loss (As I See It)

As you're no doubt aware, Hillary Clinton did lose her bid to become the Democratic presidential candidate in the 2008 election. This, I believe, was due to several unfortunate circumstances. First, the debacles within the party in Florida and Michigan really hurt Hillary's chances. (Essentially, since both of these states held their primaries before their set January 15th voting days, Democratic voters in these states lost the right to have their votes counted in the primary.) Also, soon-to-be President Obama's superior organization in the states that held caucuses rather than elections greatly influenced the outcome.

But overall, I believe that the media unfairly affected this election the most. From the very beginning, Hillary was bashed mercilessly, while it seems to me that the media took comparable aim at President Obama only after the race had already effectively been decided in his favor. And yes, as my gut feeling had suggested, the early overconfidence of Hillary's top people did not help either!

The Glow Fades

Understandably, I became even more disillusioned with politics after this presidential and congressional election cycle, and thus I began distancing myself from the world of politics. My experiences as a political fundraiser had really opened my eyes to truths I hadn't fully seen on news reports or in articles. I had put so much of my own time, effort, and emotional energy into raising a great deal of money for the candidates I believed in, and all to no avail. It was now clear to me how strongly (and unfairly, in many cases) the media influences politics. I also saw a system in which career politicians and incumbents are almost impossible to remove from office, even by outstanding people whom I believe would do a far superior job for their constituents.

And yes, I saw firsthand and close-up that politics really is all about money. As a politician, it's necessary to always keep at least one eye on your next election, which means ensuring you have enough money to win it. In order to raise enough money, you have to be constantly wheeling and dealing. And in turn, you often become beholden to those people and companies who can raise the most money on your behalf. It is simply our system, I believe—and not necessarily our politicians—that has caused, in my opinion, our politics to become corrupted.

Politics is supposed to be the second-oldest profession. I have come to realize that it bears a very close resemblance to the first.
—Ronald Reagan

Despite my ever-growing frustration with politics, I did surprisingly decide to give it one last shot in 2009. I did so for three reasons. First, I frankly had too much free time on my hands; I was very bored and looking for a challenge. And secondly, in September of 2009, Massachusetts Attorney General Martha Coakley called me herself and asked me to be the chairperson of her campaign cabinet during her attempt to become the very first female senator from Massachusetts. Finally, my decision was clinched by the fact that—as I've already mentioned—I am passionate about getting more women elected to political offices in America (and throughout the rest of the world). I believe that a more equal balance of women to men will always yield better government and, more specifically, also a better chance for peace.

Thus, I committed myself to yet another match in the election ring. If you are not a political junkie, I'll go ahead and tip you off as to how that turned out: Scott Brown! Need I say more?

> *I think it's about time we voted for senators with breasts. After all, we've been voting for boobs long enough.*
> —Claire Sargent, Arizona senatorial candidate

As the chairperson of Martha's campaign cabinet, it was my job to work with those people who had promised to raise at least $50,000 for Martha's bid for senator. I now threw everything I had into this task of helping Martha win, every bit as much as I had thrown of myself into making Foreign Autopart great in the early nineties. And thus, I was quickly promoted to one of Martha's three VPs of fundraising. In that position, I can honestly say I had a tremendous experience during the primary from September through December 7th of 2009.

I now had the opportunity to work alongside two incredible women, Beth Boland and Representative Katherine Clark. And as had been the case with myself, my dad, my brother, and Ann Marie at my company, the three of us—Beth, Katherine, and myself—really made a perfect team as we each had very different but very complementary strengths and styles. Also, we led a dream team of about one hundred campaign cabinet and steering committee members who were all incredibly committed to Martha. And we had the best candidate, too! Thus, we collectively raised more money by far than anyone had initially thought possible. And Martha now beat her three extremely qualified Democratic challengers handily. This was a huge win, and we were all incredibly relieved and thrilled!

And then, within just three days of our primary victory, as we were all still celebrating, I very personally saw firsthand just how ugly politics can be!!! In vying for more of the limelight for themselves during the upcoming general election, some people within the campaign with whom I had been working and who I thought were my friends (not Beth or Katherine, let me hasten to clarify) now very underhandedly succeeded in pushing me out of my leadership role.

This callous act came totally out of the blue for me, and I felt humiliated and extremely hurt. I had selflessly put so much time into helping Martha and the whole team for the past ninety days (approximately), and just like that, I was kicked to the curb. This act was so distressing to me, in fact, that it brought back memories of how poorly I was treated in high school by the likes of Jeff Israel and Karen Clark, and it literally left me shaking.

All of us who are concerned for peace and triumph of reason
and justice must be keenly aware how small an influence reason
and honest good will exert upon events in the political field.
—Albert Einstein

It is important for me to make it clear here that I do not believe Martha herself had anything to do with this ugliness whatsoever. Furthermore, I know objectively that the people who caused my pain and pushed forth this decision did not pursue this course of action to intentionally hurt me. This was about their egos, not about me, in my opinion. However, I cannot help but feel that this poisonous jockeying and maneuvering for power, without any regard whatsoever for someone (me) who had just put in (on average) thirty to forty hours per week for the past three months for his candidate, was absolutely indefensible. As a boss, I would never have tolerated such behavior from my employees. But I have been told that this type of behavior is par for the course when working on political campaigns. So after this last very personal blow, I decided once and for all that politics is simply not the place for someone like me. I should have listened to my wife sooner—I am simply too sensitive a person!

Also, I would like to add here that I still have the utmost respect for Massachusetts Attorney General Martha Coakley as a person and a public official, and was very saddened by her loss in the general election. I truly believe that Massachusetts and America are worse off for her not being in the Senate today.

An Expert View on Changing Course

When something is important to you—and *especially* if you've poured a lot of time and/or money into it—it can be hard to admit that your present course of action just isn't working out. Nevertheless, it's important to have the ability to stand back and look at the big picture. If a pursuit or endeavor isn't taking you in a direction you want to go, it's unhealthy to continue out of habit, stubbornness, or ignorance!

It's true: We don't always have the luxury of changing course when we'd like. (For example, you may need to stay in a hated job a while longer because you have no other current offers.) To a large extent, though, most of us have a variety of options at our disposal. We just fail to look at the big picture, or else we have trouble summoning the courage to deviate from the unhealthy but "safe" familiar.

I believe that we can all learn something valuable from Todd's decision to leave politics behind, despite having devoted a great deal of time, energy, emotion, and money to that endeavor. Todd is a person who throws his heart into what he does, who gives everything the best shot he has. And so, at the conclusion (no matter if it's positive or negative), he can say that he has done precisely as he should…and then he can move on to something else. Likewise, we should all try to:

- **Do things wholeheartedly.** If you put forth a half-baked effort, then your results will most likely be mediocre as well. Furthermore, when you give the best you've got, you can't logically reproach yourself for not "doing more."

- **Always recognize that there is an alternative.** In a nutshell, if you're still breathing, you're not finished. You've got options. It won't always be easy or instantaneous, but you *can* pick yourself back up and keep moving forward.

- **Take time to stand back and look at the big picture.** In a great many endeavors, many of us can't see the forest through the trees, as the saying goes. If you're doubting whether you should continue a particular pursuit, it helps to ask an objective party for an opinion.
- **If you do end up changing course, look for the lesson.** Reassure yourself that all your hard work was not wasted. After all, you learned something new about the world, about other people, and hopefully about yourself.

Another Avenue

From the time I first entered the political arena helping Steve Grossman back in 2001 until now, I have found ways to develop both my charitable and political work. Ultimately, I have figured out how to be involved charitably without being overwhelmed, and although today I am thoroughly disenchanted with our political process, I learned long ago never to say never about anything in my life. *And recently, as this book illustrates, I have begun to focus more and more of my time on developing my new passion: helping people learn how to live much happier lives.*

TIPS FROM TODD:
CHAPTER THIRTEEN

- **Think for yourself.** It's natural to let the opinions of family, friends, and your community influence you—especially in your younger years when you are still gaining life experience in the "real world." However, make a habit of re-examining what your values and priorities are and deciding how you think they should manifest themselves in your life. Then, make sure your actions reflect who you want to be. In terms of politics, for example, it is commendable to change your political party for your principles' sake, but not vice versa.

- **Stay motivated.** Don't underestimate the vital importance of always having a goal to work toward. If you feel that you are losing interest in your current endeavor (whether it's a job, a hobby, or something else), look for new alternatives to engage your interest and energy. Without a mission or task to inspire you, you run the risk of becoming ineffective, stalled, dulled, and even depressed.

- **When voting, look at a candidate's character.** Every American ought to know the importance of being an informed voter. It's our responsibility as citizens to vote, even if we do so only out of respect for all of our veterans who died so we could live in the greatest democracy on earth. Also, we should take the time as voters to think about what we want to change and what we want to stay the same. For our votes to have their full effect, we've got to know what issues and priorities the names on the ballots represent.

  I think that voters should take their research a bit further, though. As much as possible, research the character of the candidates in which you're interested. Do their private lives reflect the values they supposedly represent? Do they genuinely seem to care about their communities and their country? Do they, as people, possess qualities worthy of admiration? If the answers to these questions are negative, think twice about giving them your support. Politicians who are mostly motivated by money and power don't truly work for their constituents.

- **Give if you can.** In a perfect world, political campaigns would not be powered to an overwhelming extent by money. However, that's not the system we live in. The fact is, all candidates—whether they're corrupt or sincere—need money to stay in the race. So if something is important to you, you may want to consider donating to the campaign of a political candidate who represents those interests. Even if it's only a few dollars here and there, you *can* make an impact. Also, of course, giving of your time (volunteering at a phone bank, making door-to-door visits, etc.) is a great help to candidates as well.

- **Watch what you say.** Thankfully, most of us are not as closely scrutinized as political candidates. Still, an ill-advised or thoughtless statement can wreak havoc on our personal and professional lives. Be especially vigilant about what you express in a permanent form: on video, online, or via email. What is done on the spur of the moment can have lasting and irreversible ramifications. If you *do* say or write something you quickly regret, immediately call the other person and apologize sincerely. Most often, this will fortunately do the trick!

- **Guard against overconfidence.** You've heard about the walls of Troy that couldn't be breached and the mighty Titanic that couldn't be sunk, right? Well, "couldn't" clearly turned into "was." Whether you're dealing with a political campaign that's "in the bag," a promotion that's "as good as yours," or a do-it-yourself project that "can't be messed up," be careful not to let your confidence edge out good sense, proper preparation, and double-checking for mistakes!!!

Set Free

"It's pretty hard to tell what brings happiness.
Poverty and wealth have both failed."
—Kin Hubbard

Over the years, I've learned that the pursuit of happiness can sometimes require us to change direction as we go through life. In other words, our happiness journeys rarely follow a straight path: There are crossroads, exits, twists, and turns. What's more, changing course is rarely an easy transition. Striking out on a new path—even if you're doing so to remain true to yourself—requires you to leave your comfort zone.

For that reason, a majority of the time it's much easier to say that you *want* something to change than to actually go about changing it. But that doesn't mean you shouldn't try! I've discovered several times in my life that the most valuable changes are often the most challenging to effect.

When you are through changing, you are through.
—Bruce Barton

Exit Strategy

As you know from reading about my breakdown and multiple forays into the charitable and political realms, after almost a decade and a half at what was now Autopart International, I was first pretty beat up from all of the long hours I had put in through the years, and secondly, I had honestly become quite bored with my job. So the question was, how was I going to transition out of the company without hurting Autopart International and my own wealth too severely?

After all, I held perhaps the most vital position in the company. I couldn't exactly hand in my two weeks' notice and leave without it really weakening the company and hurting the people I cared about. No, I'd have to make my withdrawal much more gradual and structured than that, and I'd have to do it in a way that (hopefully) wouldn't cause a rift with any of my family members.

And so, in 2004 as my boredom with the business increased, I devoted more and more thought as to how I might create an exit strategy for myself from Autopart International. Since A.I. had enjoyed amazing growth over the past few years, the idea that *now* might be an ideal time for my family to sell the entire company began to resonate increasingly in my brain. I was concerned, however, that both my father and brother were still enjoying the challenges of running the company, and I wondered specifically what my father might do with more free time if we sold the business outright.

With these thoughts in mind, I searched out a friend for advice. Jason Chudnofsky was the clear choice to bounce my ideas off of, since he had run several businesses that he then sold. After listening to my idea, Jason confirmed my view that we should consider selling Autopart International now. He explained to me that there is an optimum time for every business to be sold, and if you miss your window of opportunity, you can really suffer in terms of the value you receive for all of your years of hard work building your enterprise.

Because things are the way they are, things will not stay the way they are.
—Bertolt Brecht

Jason felt that with the consolidation currently taking place in the automotive aftermarket industry and our position within it, now was probably indeed just the right time to look for a buyer. His logic and grasp of the bigger picture certainly had me convinced, so I asked him to meet with my father and my brother to explain his view based on his experience. Of course, Jason was happy to talk to them, and to my utter delight (and frankly, surprise), after listening to him, both my father and Roger said they were open to looking around discreetly for a buyer.

As it happened, my father was more amenable to selling the company than I had expected, for as he explained, he was growing weary of the wide variations of the business's bottom-line profits from one year to the next. It worried him that even though Autopart International's performance was excellent most years, we still fell prey to much smaller profits during softer markets.

Ever the pragmatist, Roger looked at the situation logically. If now was the time we would be able to get the most money for the business, he decided, we should definitely look into a sale. Our decision was now made, and while we didn't feel any major pressure to sell the business, if and when the right offer came in, we all agreed we would take it.

Setting Things in Motion

With the prospect of selling Autopart International now a distinct possibility, I actually began to have some concerns myself about what I might do after a sale. After all, Autopart International had been the only thing I had known for my entire work life. I had dedicated the past fifteen-plus years to supporting my employees and driving the business higher and higher, and until fairly recently, I had relished and loved almost every minute of it. Sure, I knew that I wanted to try *something* different, but I hadn't yet been able to figure out exactly what that would look like. *Well, first things first,* I told myself. *We've got to get the business sold…and then I can figure out where I want to go from there.*

> *Slow and steady wins the race.*
>
> —Aesop

Thankfully, my father, Roger, and I weren't alone as we moved forward with our new plan. Jason and his colleague at the time had generously offered to do some due diligence research for us and had received interest from a group they knew in Japan. This attention right out of the gate served as a catalyst, causing us to focus more of our attention on readying the business and ourselves for a potential sale.

We decided to have a low-level meeting with the Japanese group. Roger, who is an excellent CEO, was willing and even excited to handle the negotiations. The Japanese feeler offer turned out not to be tempting at all because we valued the business at that time to be worth significantly more. It was clear we and this group could not get together, but the experience gained from these early negotiations was incredibly valuable. Specifically, Roger was able to work with and learn from Jason concerning how to properly position our company for a sale. This time of Roger being "mentored" by Jason would prove invaluable for us very soon.

One Step Forward, Two Steps Back

Next, we attracted the interest of a Canadian group who had just acquired one of our larger New York-based competitors—with around three hundred stores. The discussions here were more serious than the ones we'd had with the Japanese company. Although in the end nothing came of them, they were once again great training for Roger. Also, Roger's experience as a lawyer (he worked as an attorney from 1989 to 1991 before joining Foreign Autopart) as well as his basic thinker's temperament and knowledge of our business made him the perfect person to sell our company.

Gifts for a Purpose

There's no doubt in my mind that God gives everyone specific gifts. Roger is so much more patient than I am. He is also better able to hold any potentially distracting emotions in check for as long as it takes to hammer out the nuts and bolts of a situation. These gifts thus enabled him to master the negotiations of selling our company, while to me they very frustratingly just seemed to drag on and on. And eventually, because of Roger's patience and some huge "luck," a fabulous third suitor entered the picture when the time was just right. I don't believe anything really happens just by coincidence!

While all of these preliminary negotiations were going on, first with the Japanese and then with the Canadian companies, my charitable work (which I'll cover in the next chapters) and a few other non-business-related causes I was getting involved in were creating more and more tension between Roger and me.

Roger felt that I was letting him, our dad, and the entire company down by spending so much of my time back then on outside pursuits. And in all honesty, he was right: I really *had* lost interest in the company, and I was the first to admit it. From the inception of our plan to sell Autopart International, I had been upfront about my personal desire to move on. But I should not have been moving away from my everyday duties at the company as much as I was at this time.

This conflict finally came to a head one Thursday morning just as I was leaving the office to attend the Wealth & Giving Forum at the Greenbrier Hotel in West Virginia. This event matched up perfectly with my emerging charitable interests, but obviously Roger didn't share my priorities. Our disagreement erupted into Roger (very much out of character) yelling at me just as I was literally walking out the door en route to the airport. This loud disagreement (I was yelling too, as you've probably already guessed by now) was certainly one of our most contentious moments to-date, and of course I went to the event anyway.

An Expert View on Familial Conflict

There's no question that many a dispute has been primarily fueled not by present circumstances but by past history...*especially* when said dispute is between relatives. Without a doubt, you've got a lot of shared past with and preconceived notions about your family members. That's why things that wouldn't be an issue between strangers or uninvested parties—or at least would be a manageable one—often become full-fledged fights between spouses, parents and children, and yes, siblings.

While Roger had a valid point when he confronted the departing Todd (as Todd himself points out), it's unlikely that the argument would have escalated into a yelling match had the two men not been brothers. You see, it's common to have the same base argument over and over again with family members, just with different surface content. And most of the time that argument is really about control, as seems to be the case in this instance.

It is very important to consciously examine your relationships with siblings in particular as you move through adulthood. Don't waste time needlessly fighting and re-fighting childhood battles. Be aware of issues that are likely to push your siblings' (and your own) buttons *before* the battle starts so that you can remain (relatively) calm in the thick of things—or better still, avoid the conflict altogether.

Our siblings push buttons that cast us in roles we felt sure we had let go of long ago—the baby, the peacekeeper, the caretaker, the avoider...It doesn't seem to matter how much time has elapsed or how far we've traveled.

—Jane Mersky Leder

By the time I arrived in West Virginia, I had more than calmed down enough to enjoy what I'd come for. The sessions at the Wealth & Giving Forum were interesting and covered philanthropic topics such as how best to choose which charities to support, how to effectively pool the donations of several donors for a single charity, and so forth. I listened to all of this valuable information avidly and took copious notes, unaware that the forum's biggest gift to me was yet to come.

The second evening of the forum, I found myself sitting next to a friend at dinner, Mark Solomon. Mark's company (CMS) was one of the lead sponsors of the forum, which meant that he knew almost everyone at the event. He also knew how much I wanted at that time to sell Autopart International, so looking out for my interests, he asked if I knew Ed Smith. Ed, he explained, was on the board of Advance Auto Parts, and he was sitting at the very next table to us.

I glanced to the side, and told Mark that I definitely didn't know Ed. I was excited by the possibility of meeting such a big name in my industry, though. Advance was, and still is, the second-largest autopart retailer in the country by sales volume. At that time, Autopart International was around number forty based on store count, albeit number one in terms of the number of autopart stores specializing in imports—one of the fastest growing segments in the industry at the time.

After hearing that I hadn't yet been introduced to Ed, Mark walked me over to his table. In the course of the introductions, Mr. Smith admitted that he had never heard of Autopart International, which didn't surprise me much. His company was a big domestic retail parts supplier, and, we, until recently, had been a relatively small imports-only wholesale parts supplier (remember, we'd just expanded to domestic parts in 1998).

I now quickly familiarized Mr. Smith with Autopart International and told him that we had fifty-five wholesale autopart stores in the Northeast. Then, after a mental deep breath, I took the plunge and asked Mr. Smith whether he thought his company might consider buying ours. In response, he simply asked me one question: whether our stores did any retail business. I told him that, truthfully, we really did none to speak of. That revelation effectively ended the business end of the conversation. Ed told me that Advance was interested in buying only companies with retail stores and he wished me well. That, I thought, was that. We were back at square one.

More Than a Coincidence

The next weekend, Yadira, Josh, and I went away. And when we returned home, Ed Smith was not only on our voicemail answering machine asking me to return his call, but his phone number also showed up another time or two on our caller ID. I couldn't imagine what Ed would want so urgently from me. I presumed it was something to do with the forum we had just left four days before, so I picked up the phone and returned his call.

After the usual pleasantries, Ed got right to the point. He asked me, "How could you, Todd, have possibly known that on my first day back from the forum, I would receive in my mailbox the announcement for the next Advance Auto Parts board meeting...and that one of the main agenda items for our meeting is that we need to begin looking for a wholesale auto parts chain to acquire?" And guess who was the number one company in that category at that time? Yes, you guessed it: Autopart International!

At first, I couldn't believe what I was hearing. This seemed more like a serendipitous dream than reality. Later that night, though, things began to make more sense. It occurred to me then (and I still believe) that God seems to work these things out all the time for me. I thought back to the many "coincidences" that had changed my life for the better, including meeting Yadira on the one night in my life that I hadn't even wanted to go out looking for a wife because I was feeling so great about my recent trip and myself, and finding the perfect leader for our National Sales Department due to a chance encounter my wife had at the local dry cleaner's.

Yes, I reflected, *something bigger than chance is definitely at work here.* And sure enough, that call with Ed was indeed the beginning of the relationship that eventually led to our selling Autopart International to the perfect company at just the right time.

Serendipity. Look for something, find something else, and realize that what you've found is more suited to your needs than what you thought you were looking for.
—Lawrence Block

After almost a full year of Roger brilliantly negotiating with Advance's team, we arrived at an agreement. We—the Patkins—were to get the equivalent of one year's gross revenue, so long as we met certain earn-out targets. That figure amounted to more than we had ever, in our wildest dreams, thought possible. Again, I must say that my brother, Roger, deserves all the credit in terms of the negotiations. He was, quite simply, amazing—the perfect man for the job!

When things were finally made official, I was beyond ecstatic. Yes, I couldn't believe how much money we were getting…but more than that, I was free!!! I could now explore all the other avenues life had to offer, and hopefully find a new passion that would carry me excitedly through the next stage of my life. A huge weight was lifted from my shoulders, because truth be told, part of me had believed that I would always be trapped at Autopart International by my family obligation to make sure the business remained profitable.

It's Not Over Until It's Over

There was one thing I had forgotten, however: *Never count your chickens until they hatch.* Sure enough, just forty-eight hours before my dreamed-about-for-years deal was due to be officially signed, my dad called me with some blood-curdling news. I remember his exact words very clearly.

"Todd, the deal might not happen."

Totally blindsided, I couldn't believe my ears. I had been kept totally in the dark until now! How was this possible? Apparently, our attorneys were so confident of resolving this one last issue that Roger had felt no need to concern me with it. And now, here we were just forty-eight hours away from signing a blockbuster deal that would give me my freedom and more money than I could ever have imagined, and it was slipping away. In the blink of an eye, my dream was on the verge of falling through my fingertips.

> *Those who expect moments of change to be comfortable and free of conflict have not learned their history.*
> —Joan Wallach Scott

The problem that threatened to sink the deal had to do with our computer software license. You see, the company that provided it had recently changed hands itself several times, and thus we needed a signed third party consent from Oracle, the most recent buyer, allowing us to transfer the computer software license over to Advance. We had been told repeatedly that this consent was forthcoming, but changes in personnel at Oracle seemed to be causing delays. And without the signed consent—something that sounded so simple, in theory, to obtain—the deal was in jeopardy.

My father was prudently unwilling to go ahead until we had this third party consent, because without it we could be responsible for the cost of a multi-million-dollar computer software conversion; a brutal switchover that could even put us in jeopardy of being out of business temporarily while we got the new system up and running.

Needless to say, I was extremely upset. Actually, "freaked out" might be a better way to say it, because for a few minutes I couldn't string two coherent thoughts together. As soon as possible, though, I forced myself (as Tony Robbins, I believe, had taught me subconsciously to do over the years) to calm down enough to address the problem logically. I now asked myself, *Who do I know who could help us?* After all, the advice and guidance of trusted friends and mentors had become a mainstay for me in many uncertain situations in the recent years.

Since 2000 especially, I am fortunate to have made many new connections, and indeed friends, who have proven very helpful and increased my capability when I have been confronted with critical situations. I also believe that God gives us experiences and brains so that we can figure out how to solve crises whenever they arise on behalf of ourselves, our friends, and our families. Thus, I continued to prod myself, saying, *Todd, with all that you have given and done for so many people throughout the world, there must be someone you can call to save this deal. Think, think, think!*

It was then that a possible solution hit me over the head like a brick.

You Reap What You Sow

First, I called my friend Steve Grossman to ask if he thought it was appropriate for me to call California Congressman Tom Lantos at his Washington, D.C., home; it was late by the time this brainwave hit me, and Tom was an extremely respected United States congressman. Tom had occurred to me as our possible savior because he and I had recently become very close while I was raising money for Jewish causes, and I knew that Oracle (which was headquartered in San Francisco) was within Tom's congressional district.

After hearing my plan, Steve told me he thought I was a genius to think of Tom, and he assured me that in his opinion I'd be absolutely crazy *not* to call on anyone in the entire world—even at this time of the evening—if he or she might be able to help me save such a tremendous, once-in-a-lifetime deal for my family.

Thus reassured, I took a deep breath and called Congressman Tom Lantos at approximately 11:00 p.m. the second Tuesday night in September 2005 and asked him if he knew anyone at Oracle. To my mild surprise, Tom quickly answered my question with one of his own: "Todd, do you know who the founder and CEO of Oracle is?"

Bemused, I responded that I did not. Still using a conversational tone, Tom told me that this individual was Larry Ellison. Next, Tom asked me what seemed like an even stranger question: "Do you know who Larry Ellison asked to be the justice of the peace presiding over his recent wedding?"

Again, wondering if Tom was even on the same page as me, I admitted that I had no idea. And then it all became clear. Through a loud and heartfelt laugh, Tom told me that the justice of the peace at Larry Ellison's recent wedding had been none other than himself! All I could think was, *Wow!*

In short order, Tom told me to relax, and instructed me to have my brother and father sign the deal with Advance. Tom said that he would personally speak to Larry when he returned to California the next week, and he assured me 100 percent that everything would be fine…in fact, he personally guaranteed it! Who was I to argue with that?

After this pressing concern had been laid to rest, Tom told me before hanging up that he probably got an average of five requests a month from various people who hoped he would go to bat on their behalves in order to get something, usually big money for their causes, from Larry Ellison. Tom had, he said, refused every one of them until now. But for me, because of our relationship and the fact that this deal was so important to my family, he would make this his only exception.

I was incredibly grateful, not to mention honored. Plus, I really felt like a hero, saving the deal in the final hour for myself and my family!

> *You have to sow before you can reap. You have to give before you can get.*
>
> —Robert Collier

In the end, a signed third party consent from Oracle did come through with not a minute to spare, and so Tom never had to have that conversation with Larry. For me, though, that wasn't the point. The fact that Congressman Tom Lantos was willing to make that call for me—and the fact that I had the ability to save the deal in this way—was all that mattered. If I had ever needed proof that making sincere connections with others was the right thing to do, this was it. I had reaped the kindness I'd sown, even though I had initially developed my friendship with Tom not thinking of future gain. Again, I smiled as I looked up at the heavens, realizing God surely was on my side!

In its final terms, the deal with Advance Auto Parts called for my brother, Roger, to stay on as the CEO of Autopart International, which would now be run as a separate stand-alone division within Advance. My father was to take the role of senior advisor, and both he and my brother still capably fill those positions to this day. I stayed on for about a year to make sure the transition proceeded as smoothly as possible, but at the end of that time I felt that I had met all of the challenges that this particular business had to offer me. I was ready to move on, knowing that my patience and hard work had helped my family's company to be sold at the best possible time and for the very most money.

Thanks to the Team

Selling Autopart International for such a wonderful profit was a real team effort. Roger handled himself in an absolutely outstanding manner during the year-plus negotiations. My father's experience and wisdom were also, of course, invaluable. And because of the commitment of Ann Marie Kannally and so many others, the company continued to run smoothly and successfully even though Roger and several other top managers were very occupied in hammering out the deal.

A Heartfelt Goodbye

Once the sale of Autopart International was finalized, I was completely filled with a sense of relief and joy, albeit one tinged by a small amount of regret and trepidation. I knew that life had just changed irreversibly for me. The day I left Autopart International was very emotional. After all, while I knew in my heart that moving on was the right thing for me to do, it was difficult to let go of more than a decade and a half of hard work and fabulous friends. In farewell, I wrote the following letter to all of the employees.

To all my friends:

Always remember that God's gift to you is your life. And your gift back is how you live it! And always remember you are going to die. Yes, one thing we all know for sure is that one day we are all going to die, *** So Live!!!*** And live now, today!!! Who knows? Your day could be sooner than we would all like it to be!!! Make every day your masterpiece! Paint beautiful, bold colors on your landscape, not dreary, ugly depressing ones. **Be outrageous***! Trust me, it is more fun, and something tells me that in Heaven they will get a kick out of it when viewing your life on Judgment Day!!! Hell, I know I'm going to Heaven and you all know that I'm as wild as they come! Well, it is time to sign off now and say goodbye one last time. But know just two more things: Every day I told all of you as I am now that I love you—I really meant it and do mean it now with my whole soul. And lastly, and probably most important of all, always, always, always remember* **whether you think you can or you think you can't, you're right!!!**

Your friend and brother for life,

Todd Patkin

PS: If you ever need me for anything, call me day or night! My cell number is XXX-XXX-XXXX.

Looking back, I realize just how important the successful sale of our company was in the scheme of my entire life. From living life as an insecure, not very happy young man before joining the company, I was now leaving eighteen years later with the tools, confidence, and time I needed to live the happy life helping others I had always dreamed of!

An Expert View on the Fleeting Nature of Success

With good reason, Todd was immensely proud of his role in growing his family's business. A business success of this magnitude is certainly a big metaphorical dragon to slay, and it unquestionably improved his self-esteem and mood for a time. It's important to note (as Todd himself found out), though, that over the long haul, even a big success like this isn't enough to guarantee everlasting contentment.

Scientifically speaking, here's why: When you have a novel, passionate experience (like a big success), it is processed in the right hemisphere of the brain. However, as time passes, the information and experience are transferred to the left hemisphere, which is characterized by far less emotional feeling. Thus, the information becomes much more routinized, leaving you once again wanting more.

Experiencing success is a bit like falling in love. There's an initial infatuation, over-the-moon, magical phase, but it fades over time. And when that happens, you'll need to move to the next big challenge to find fulfillment.

Full Speed Ahead—Literally!

Now I moved out of my office at Autopart International and set up shop right across the street. The plan was to become much more involved with my various charitable endeavors.

Shortly thereafter, I also signed up to run the following year's Boston Marathon. I did this because, quite frankly, I was extremely concerned that without all of the positive reinforcement I had gotten from my work and my great relationships at Autopart International, I might become depressed and fall apart all over again. And believe me, another spiral downwards into a breakdown was the last thing I *ever* wanted!

Thus, from May 2006 to April 2007, I spent a lot of time in training, running the back streets of Foxboro and Sharon, Massachusetts. When I began training in May, my "distance" running topped out at just three miles. I had a long way to go before getting to twenty-six and change! This physical challenge was the perfect stretch goal for me during this transitional period of my life.

I ran the one hundred eleventh Boston Marathon on April 16, 2007, and had a terrific day. I was able to run the whole race fairly comfortably even though, as my friend Gary Marino had joked about his run two years earlier, by the time I finished in 5 hours 44 minutes and 54 seconds the winner had probably already showered, shaved, cashed his check, and was flying back home over the Atlantic. I finished 20,069th, but I felt like a true Number One.

Treasured Marathon Memories

While the entire Boston Marathon will always remain with me because it was such a triumphant day in my life, three very specific memories stand out. First, I remember the amazing Wellesley College girls who cheered everyone on so loudly you could actually hear them from more than two miles away in both directions. Wellesley's students take incredible pride each year in how motivating they can be for all of the runners.

Secondly, I have to chuckle when I think back on the last segment of the race, beginning at mile nineteen. At this point in the course, runners hit three (in)famous inclines along Commonwealth Avenue known as Heartbreak Hill. Even though it is "technically" against official race protocol, most first-time runners are actually encouraged by veteran marathoners to have a friend jump in to keep them going for the last seven miles beginning at Heartbreak Hill.

My good friend Foster 'Buster' Ball from Autopart International, a marathon runner in his own right, must have not been thinking very clearly that day. As planned, he jumped in fresh to join and inspire me as we approached the hills. However, instead of gently guiding me across the finish line, Buster literally sprinted up the hills and nearly killed me as I tried to keep up with him! In truth, he probably did help to improve my time, but he definitely jeopardized the overall race for me, because at one point I was dizzy and seeing stars, and we still had five miles to go. Yes, certainly another "it's funny *now*" situation.

Undoubtedly, though, my most treasured moment of that whole day was when my son, Josh, jumped in to finish the last three hundred yards with me so that we could cross the finish line together.

The marathon was a wonderful challenge, but I knew that I could never derive complete life satisfaction just from running long races and staying in shape. I would need something more fulfilling. So, the essential question I'd been pondering for awhile hadn't changed: How and where could I find challenges and fulfillment similar to those that developing and growing the business had given me for the past eighteen years?

> *We all have changes in our lives that are more or less a second chance.*
>
> —Harrison Ford

TIPS FROM TODD:
CHAPTER FOURTEEN

- **Know when to let go.** Almost all good things must come to an end sooner or later. (After all, change is inevitable!) In many cases, it's your choice as to whether you're proactive about that change, or caught up in it unwillingly. If you are open to new ventures and opportunities, you'll be better equipped to see when to let the old ones go. Furthermore, being excited about what's coming will make leaving the familiar easier. On the other hand, if you refuse to face reality, you invite regret and hardship.

- **When making a change, consider others.** You shouldn't allow others' desires to dictate everything about your life—but you *should* consider how your actions and decisions will affect those around you, especially those you care about. If you are considering making a change—big or small—that might affect others who are important to you, do your best to make the transition as smooth as possible for them, too. Often, this simply requires lots of conversations and more planning ahead.

- **Also, don't rush it for yourself.** Once you've made a decision, it's tempting to barrel full steam ahead. After all, now that you've decided to make a change, you want that change to happen *now!* Remember, though, that patience is a virtue. By taking the time you have to fully consider how to proceed and where to go, you'll end up at your desired destination—or somewhere even better, like we did when we sold our close-to-fifty-year-old company.

- **Trust the process.** Whether you believe (or not) in a specific Higher Power or perhaps the benevolence of the universe as a whole, try not to despair if at first things don't go your way. Often, the very best things that happen to us are the result of seemingly insignificant decisions or encounters—or even the result of things we've tried to avoid. Timing truly is crucial—but the *right* timing isn't always the timing we ourselves would choose. Remember Tony Robbins' wise words: "God's delays are not God's denials."

- **Treat others well, and your actions will come back to you.** You shouldn't befriend, help, or otherwise support someone under the auspices of friendship for the express purpose of getting something back in return. However, that's often exactly what happens! When you give of your time, aid, and caring freely, you might be surprised by when and how your kindness is returned.

God and the Promised Land

"Many people have a wrong idea of what constitutes true happiness. It is not attained through self-gratification, but through fidelity to a worthy purpose."
—Helen Keller

As you've just read, during my final years at Autopart International, I felt myself becoming increasingly disengaged with a life that revolved mostly around business, achievement, and the bottom line. And as I've also shared, I began to spend more and more of my time and energy on charitable endeavors. However, you might be surprised by what truly opened my heart to giving during this time. Let me give you a hint: I became a truly impassioned giver in large part through the one "cause" I vowed in my youth I'd never, ever support financially. Yes, you guessed it—the State of Israel!

It's true. God used this land to which I am connected by faith and heritage to move me much closer to self-acceptance. And even more wonderfully, God used my relationship with Israel to make me realize once and for all that He has a plan for my life and that He is in control.

Ultimately, my charitable involvement with Israel caused me to revise how I see myself and how I can contribute to the world. And because I tapped into a new source of fulfillment and perspective, I grew much closer to reaching my ultimate "happiness journey" breakthrough: truly learning to love myself.

Israel and Me: Off to a Slow Start

We all say things we don't mean, and we're all proven wrong time and time again throughout our lives. Specifically, I would venture to say that almost all of us end up eating quite a few words we uttered in our youth. And I'm certainly no exception!

As you'll recall from Chapter 3, my experiences with Israel as a young man weren't exactly positive. In my youth I resented the ushers at our Temple who continually asked my father for money for Israel during the High Holiday services each year. And my ill-fated teenage trip to Israel itself ended with me feeling disappointed and disillusioned, and even a bit resentful—prompting me to swear that I'd never raise a single penny to help that nation. As far as I was concerned at the age of nineteen, Israel was on its own.

Keep your words sweet—you may have to eat them.
—Stephan Grellet

Talk about famous last words! I no doubt would have become furious back then if I'd been told just how close my relationship with my spiritual homeland would eventually become. Now, I feel a deep connection to the State of Israel and its people, and I take advantage of every opportunity I have to strengthen, preserve, and honor the heritage and history I share with its citizens. And, of course, I do whatever I can to ensure Israel's future survival!

So how did such a disgruntled teenager turn into an impassioned advocate? Well, the transformation certainly occurred over a period of years. But most obviously I can trace it back to an encounter with someone I deeply loved and respected: my maternal grandfather.

Grandpa Max's Wish

In December of 1999, I visited my grandfather Max and my grandmother Ruth in Florida just after Ruth had suffered a major stroke. Understandably, this was a very emotional and difficult time for Max. He was concerned about Ruth, of course, but also he was terribly upset with what was happening in Israel.

You see, this was the time of the first Intifada when Israelis were literally being blown up in their own streets by Palestinian suicide bombers. Max felt that American Jews needed to do more to help their brothers and sisters overseas. In fact, as he put it, "we" were turning our backs on Israel. So when I told my grandfather that I had just decided to give more money away than ever before—in fact, I had resolved to write my first-ever $10,000 check to one single inner-city charity after listening to Mother Theresa's motivational tapes about the importance of tithing—Max asked me to seriously consider giving this money instead to an Israeli cause.

At first, I was taken aback, and my thoughts immediately flashed back to my horrific teenage trip to Israel. But I kept silent and considered what my grandfather had suggested. I knew that Israel was very, very important to Max. I also had to admit that the things I'd learned about giving from my growing involvement in local charities had opened my mind to helping *anyone* who needed it. No one, I felt, should be "punished" by being denied help simply because of where they lived.

Finally, because Max—a grandfather I loved and admired—was the person asking, I found that I couldn't refuse this request. So began my support of a country I had once sworn to never, ever help financially.

And also, although I didn't know it yet, I was embarking on a journey that would bring me closer to God and to myself. In fact, I wouldn't be surprised if God had nudged my grandfather to talk to me about giving to Israel in the first place.

The Check's in the Mail

After some consideration I decided that I wanted my contribution to provide psychotherapy for parents who had lost a child during the Intifada. After all, I couldn't imagine what it would be like to lose Josh under any circumstances.

The real question was thus, "Which Israeli health-related organization could I find and trust to give the money to?" I was very mindful of my father's long-held concern that you can never really be sure where charitable donations end up unless you are actually a part of the team disbursing them. My father had read of too many examples in which charitable donations went primarily into the pockets of the "organizers" of the charity and never actually reached the needy.

Here, God intervened in my life again. Incredibly, the very day following my return from this time with my grandparents I had a scheduled luncheon meeting with a man named Bob Golden. At the time, Bob was attempting to convince me to join the B'Nai B'rith New England Sports Lodge, an organization of Jewish men and women that raises money through different charitable (mostly sporting) events each year and gives the proceeds primarily to youth services.

During our lunch, I told Bob that I wanted to donate $10,000 to Israel in order to help families suffering from the loss of a child in the Intifada. Bob's eyes widened in surprise, and he leaned forward to tell me that I wasn't the only person to mention donating to Israel recently.

It just so happened, Bob told me, that Steve Handler (the president of the lodge at the time) had recently been in Israel and had suffered a minor accident while there. He was treated by Magen David Adom (MDA), Israel's emergency medical, ambulance, blood, and disaster service. Steve saw firsthand the great work that MDA does. Also, he learned all about its critical importance to Israeli society, especially now due to the Intifada. On his recommendation, therefore, for the first time the lodge was going to directly donate some of the funds it had raised to an Israeli cause—in this case, MDA.

I was sold. Yes, I had originally wanted my money to specifically provide psychotherapy to parents who had lost a child, but after listening to Bob describe what MDA did, I was now convinced that it would use my donation just as beneficially. After all, MDA is clearly a critical service, and I knew that a large part of its mission at this time was to help Israelis suffering from all sorts of problems stemming from the Intifada. And most importantly for me that day, Bob said he personally knew the people at MDA, and therefore could promise me that 100 percent of my money would go directly to the people who were most in need.

Immediately, right then and there at the lunch table, I wrote out a $10,000 check for MDA, gave it to Bob, and felt really great doing it! I've since come to recognize that a sense of certainty and peace like the one I experienced at that moment shouldn't be discounted—in fact, it might be a nudge or an affirmation from your Higher Power.

The "Plan" Expands

Later that same afternoon, I went to the gym for a workout. And as I often do when exercising, I went into what I call my "Superman" mode of thinking. When this happens, I honestly do begin to feel like Superman—truly unstoppable—as the endorphins in my brain really start to flow. Suddenly, things that may have seemed impossible just thirty minutes before appear to be completely within my power to accomplish.

An Expert View on "Superman" Moments

To some extent, we've all probably experienced a "Superman" moment like Todd's during which we were convinced we could do anything. While the resulting grandiose plans may sometimes look fanciful or downright ridiculous after the excitement has died down, there's a perfectly rational scientific explanation for this phenomenon.

Specifically, when you get very excited, your limbic system—the area of the brain that's responsible for emotions—becomes over-aroused, and your feelings are amplified. Furthermore, when your limbic system is working overtime, the impact of your brain's frontal lobes is minimized since there is a feedback loop between the two areas. Because the frontal lobes are where decisions and plans are made *and* where self-control and inhibition are located, your judgment is truly impaired when you're feeling manic. In the heat of such a moment, you're apt to think that anything really *is* possible.

There is one more interesting aspect to "Superman" moments that, thankfully, doesn't apply to Todd's story. Our brains contain a part called the thalamus, which filters out sensory information and allows for an orderly flow of input to consciousness. If the thalamus doesn't work well—which it doesn't when the brain is amplified by positive emotion—you are flooded with input. In trying to make sense of this informational overload, you'll become very creative. Here's the catch, though: If the mind becomes super-active and stays super-active for an extended period of time, you can literally blow a fuse. This is where the line between creativity and insanity is crossed! (It's worth noting, though, that this "blown fuse" is normally a temporary phenomenon.)

Fueled by the excitement of my donation to MDA, I began to think that if I could give $10,000 to this organization, then other people living in the Boston area—people with much greater means than myself, like the Krafts (best known for their ownership of the New England Patriots) and the Firemans (owners of Reebok at the time), for instance—could surely donate $100,000 each. I began to feel, as I was pumping iron, that it was now my calling to raise much, much more money in the coming months for MDA. Unable to contain myself, I called Bob Golden on my way home from the gym and told him of my new plan.

Essentially, Bob thought I was nuts.

I am happy to report, though, that his initial assessment was short-lived. The very next morning, to my complete surprise, Bob called me and asked to talk. He said that while he was lying awake in bed the night before, he too began to feel more and more strongly that this ambitious fundraising plan was indeed something that we ought to do. Crazy as it seemed, Bob confided, something deep within him was telling him to "go for it" with me. Once again, I believe, God was at work.

In actual life every great enterprise begins with and takes its first forward step in faith.

—Friedrich Schlegel

So off we went. First, we called American Red Magen David for Israel (ARMDI), MDA's American fundraising office in New York, and set up a meeting with its president, Ben Sachs, and his then-assistant Susan Bloot.

A "Crazy" Commitment

Two weeks later, Bob and I left Boston for our ARMDI meeting in New York. On the airplane I told Bob that I was going to pledge to raise $1 million for ARMDI. Once again, my huge goals and self-confidence shocked Bob into momentary speechlessness! When he had recovered his voice, Bob implored me not to make such a pledge because he felt that the number was way too high. Also, he asked me to keep my ego and trademark enthusiasm under control, as he wanted Ben and Susan to think that we were serious people—which, of course, we were.

"And for God's sake," Bob implored me, "Todd, please don't tell them, like you tell everyone else, that you think you are one of the chosen ones to make a significant difference in this world during your time on earth."

Bob was right—I *did* tend to tell people that God had a special plan for me. Most days, augmented by my daily doses of motivational tapes and books, as well as by exercise, I believed it...although occasionally, doubts about whether God *truly* knew who I was tended to creep in.

"I can restrain myself on both the goal number and my beliefs," I assured Bob. Thus mollified, he settled back in his seat to relax for the remainder of the flight.

Once we arrived at the proper New York building and offices inside, we met with Ben and Susan. The meeting started with Ben laying out ARMDI's two main immediate needs. He explained that ARMDI had to raise $1 million as soon as possible for a new hospital wing that had to be built in Israel, and they also needed $310,000 to refurbish an emergency medical station in Kiryat Gat, the "silicon valley" city of Israel.

My response to this statement was immediate. "Okay. We'll take responsibility for raising the $1 million." Bob was shocked!

> *Set your goals high and don't stop till you get there.*
> —Bo Jackson

And soon, I was explaining that I could handle this responsibility because I believed God had tasked me to do great things just like this one, throwing in for good measure that I was a direct descendant of the famous Rabbi of Vilnius, Lithuania: the Vilna Gaon. Ben, being an eighty-year-old meshugener (Yiddish for "a good type of crazy person") himself, loved talking to me about my sense of God and purpose in my life. He shared that he also believed that certain individuals were chosen to make a greater difference in every generation, and now that he had met me, he had no doubt that I was one of them.

In a nutshell, Ben and I spent a good portion of the rest of the meeting having an absolute ball discussing our like-minded spiritual philosophies while Bob and Susan looked on in horror and bewilderment, respectively!

Once the meeting concluded, Bob admitted that even though he was very uneasy about the million-dollar goal, he was still totally fired up about the project. We both returned to Boston on the wings of excitement, thinking of all the people whom we could approach to give money to this vital Israeli organization made even more critical by the Intifada.

The Sports Lodge's board now officially appointed Bob and me to be co-chairs of this monumental fundraising challenge, and soon we were on the phone exhorting our friends, families, and colleagues to dig deep into their pockets.

At this point I also visited the one very wealthy Jewish person I knew from my own childhood. Jim Salmon, the owner of a nationally known company, was genuinely interested in my enthusiastic pitch asking him for $100,000. Unfortunately, though, he had already given away his generous allotment of money for charity for the year and couldn't make any further commitments. Discouragingly, every other well-known wealthy individual I also called on at this time had the same response.

After six weeks of very, very hard work, Bob and I had raised only $35,000 from ourselves, our families, and our friends, and the Lodge members had raised another $15,000. We had given this project everything we had, calling everyone we could think of, and we still had $950,000 to go! I felt like such an idiot!!!

Desperate Times Call for Inspired Measures!

After Bob's and, really, my initial failure, I had just about given up hope that we would ever be able to round up any very significant amount of money. Then in December of that year, I unexpectedly got invited to the Sports Lodge's executive board's year-end dinner at the Legal Sea Foods restaurant in Chestnut Hill—this was a surprise because I wasn't an executive board member at this time. I sat next to a gentleman named Russ Stein—and in retrospect, I'm sure that this seating arrangement was divinely arranged! You see, Russ told me that he admired my enthusiasm for the ARMDI project, but felt that Bob and I were going about raising the money all wrong.

First, Russ told me, we should be more reasonable in our goals. At this point, we should focus on raising the $310,000 for the Kiryat Gat Medical Station project instead of the million dollars for the hospital wing. I had to admit, given where we were at the time, that Russ's logic certainly made a lot of sense.

Russ wasn't finished, though. He also suggested that I now make a list of all the wealthy Jewish people I knew of and try to raise half of the remaining money needed for the project from them. Next, the Sports Lodge should stage some sort of fundraising event and invite as many people as possible in order to raise the rest. Prior to this, other than asking the three or four most well-known Boston families, I had not focused on other wealthy Jewish people whom I did not know personally. Russ's new approach made sense to me, especially since it would now give me a new list of prospects to work.

> *There is no one giant step that does it. It's a lot of little steps.*
> —Peter A. Cohen

Over ten years later, I still very clearly remember my drive home from Legal Sea Foods that night. I was listening to Tom Petty and the Heartbreakers on the radio. I was feeling inspired by my conversation with Russ, but I was also still terrified. For the first time in my life, it appeared I would not be able to keep a promise I had made, and one that was now so public to boot! And then, just as the panic was really starting to take hold of my mind, Tony Robbins' words for just such a situation popped into my head.

When you don't know what to do and are feeling helpless, just do something. Anything. But just do something and do it immediately.

Okay. I knew Tony was right—standing still wasn't going to do me any good. But what "something" should I do? The only really wealthy Jewish person I knew was Jim Salmon. Who else *could* I call? As Tom Petty and the Heartbreakers finished their song, a crazy thought formed in my mind: *Nobody eats more Legal Sea Foods clam chowder than my wife and me.*

Clam chowder might seem incongruous at first, but I figured that it would be as good of an opening line as any with which to call a very wealthy Jewish person I didn't know at all and ask him for a lot of money for MDA. Turning the radio off, I promised myself, Tom Petty, and Tony Robbins that night as I drove home that the very first thing I would do the next morning was to call Roger Berkowitz, the owner of Legal Sea Foods. I had never met Roger before. I was certain that he didn't know me from Adam—but I was going to call him, introduce myself and my cause, and ask him for a lot of money!

Divine Intervention

As I drove to work the next day, I was horribly apprehensive and anxious about calling Roger Berkowitz. I absolutely, positively dreaded the idea of calling someone I didn't know at all out of the blue and asking him for a substantial chunk of change. The closer my car got to the office, the more nervous and uncomfortable I became. Despite my feelings, though, I forced myself to get out of the car and walk into the building, determined to make this phone call. That's when God intervened again in my life!

And believe me, God's intervention this time was completely mind-blowing!

Now, I know that what I'm about to tell you sounds nearly impossible, but *I promise you it happened exactly like this*:

I entered our Sharon headquarters, walked over to my mail slot, and reached in to get my mail as I did at the start of each of my work days. I opened the first letter on the top of the pile…and nearly passed out.

The letter I was holding was actually a personal letter from Roger Berkowitz—yes, the very same Roger Berkowitz I was just about to call!—requesting my attendance at a fundraiser in Boston for a woman named Katrina Swett who was running for U.S. Congress from New Hampshire. Attached to Roger's letter was a photocopied similar request from Elie Weisel, the famous Jewish Nobel Prize Laureate, also asking me to come and support Katrina. In his letter, Mr. Weisel explained that Katrina's father, Congressman Tom Lantos, was his good friend and fellow Holocaust survivor.

The envelope containing this invitation must have been lost in the mail for a week or two because the post office's marked date over the stamp was over ten days old, and now the event was only three days away.

A coincidence is a small miracle in which God chooses to remain anonymous.

—Anonymous

I looked up at the ceiling in the direction of God, feeling light-headed with unbelievable gratitude and finally sure in the knowledge that I really did have the biggest possible power on my side. I now knew for certain, in my mind, that there was indeed a God and that He was squarely in my corner! I began to realize that I was not in this fundraising endeavor, or in my life as a whole, by myself. All at once, I felt that I'd been inspired and freed. It was no longer "all" up to me! How else, other than through God's intervention, could such a miracle have occurred? This, much more than placing a phone call, would be the perfect opportunity to introduce myself to Roger Berkowitz and explain to him in person my mission.

Seventy-two hours later, at Roger and Elie's request, I drove to what would be the first of many political fundraising events I would attend. Despite the divine intervention that I was certain had transpired, I was still quite nervous, and so I arrived early. I headed straight to the bar to get myself some liquid tranquilizer and found myself standing next to a tall, attractive, blond woman who turned out to be none other than Katrina Swett herself. During the evening, I spent time getting to know her and some of her children who were then ages eight to fifteen. Later, both Congressman Tom Lantos and Massachusetts Senator John Kerry spoke on Katrina's behalf. As the evening drew to a close, I knew I'd better not waste this opportunity to approach Roger Berkowitz about a contribution to MDA.

In the end, this conversation was a good deal less painful than I had feared. Roger was very gracious and asked me to call him the next week for a donation. You can bet I heaved a big sigh of relief!

Tom Lantos was also standing next to Roger, and I seized the opportunity to ask him to help MDA as well. "I'll always do anything I can for Magen David Adom, and so I'd be honored to help you," the Congressman responded.

That evening was the turning point of our fundraising campaign.

Four months later, Bob Golden and I co-chaired a spectacular fundraising event at the beautiful new John Joseph Moakley Courthouse in Boston. Tom Lantos was our keynote speaker. With this event as our catalyst, we quickly raised another $160,000. Now we were within striking distance: approximately $100,000 away from our new goal of contributing the $310,000 to refurbish the Kiryat Gat Medical Station.

One Last (Huge!) Jolt to the System

Just as it looked like the worst was behind us, the next shoe in this story dropped. An ARMDI representative contacted Bob and me out of the blue to tell us that the project might be taken away from us. Blindsided, we couldn't believe what we were hearing after all of the hard work we had put in, especially considering the fact that we had already sent in $210,000 towards the project and told all of our supporters that they should feel incredibly proud because their gift was helping to revitalize such an important medical station for the people of Israel!

Essentially, we learned, another group had visited ARMDI's offices recently and wanted the Kiryat Gat Medical Station to be named after them. They were willing to personally guarantee their $310,000 within the next four months. ARMDI was under pressure to meet its deadline and therefore had to ask us to personally guarantee this week, in writing, that the remaining $100,000 would be paid within 120 days, or regretfully, the project would have to be given to the other group.

Once we regained our equilibrium from the shock, Bob and I tried to figure out what we could do. This was certainly not something we ever thought was even possible!!! And taking on another $100,000 personally for this project was a steep prospect for both of us.

After a few days of feeling discouraged, however, I realized that I could not give up this campaign under any circumstances. Bob, myself, and so many of the other Lodge members had worked so hard to raise the money for this project. I couldn't let them all down, and we simply *had* to succeed on behalf of all the other individuals who had already contributed to this great cause as well. Plus, after all that had already happened, I had good reason to hope that God wouldn't allow Bob and me to fail. So in the end, I personally guaranteed the remaining $100,000 myself, even though by this time I had already donated over three times the amount of money my wife and I had agreed to give to this project in the beginning.

Now even more under the gun, we all redoubled our efforts. Bob especially, being a real mensch (Yiddish for "man of character and integrity"), really went all out with me at this point so I would not get stuck with any part of this $100,000 bill. Thank you, Bob! Within just two more months we hit the $310,000 mark! More than ever, I now realized that sometimes you just have to put yourself personally on the line, especially when you have reason to believe that God has your back.

Great deeds are usually wrought at great risks.
                                                    —Herodotus

Recently, Bob Golden and I had lunch and he told me that our MDA project is one of his proudest life achievements. That alone makes me feel great. Also, having recently visited the refurbished Kiryat Gat station where

I was able to speak to many of its very appreciative staff, I feel secure in the knowledge that all of our efforts to ensure success in this project were totally worthwhile.

Because of the successful completion of the Kiryat Gat project, I am also more comfortable with *myself.* As I've mentioned a few times before, working on this project convinced me that God is real, that He is in control, and that He has a plan for me. With that kind of divine affirmation, I have realized, I really don't need accolades or "atta-boys" to feel validated. God can, has, and still does use me—just as I am—for His awesome purposes.

It is my hope that you, too, will come to develop such a relationship with your Higher Power. Because when you do, you—like me—will have found the final piece of the puzzle when it comes to loving yourself. After all…when you fully know that God accepts and loves you, how can you *not* accept and love yourself?

A Brush with Holiness

In addition to my serendipitous encounters in the charity sector, I also had a very spiritual experience around this time—one that wouldn't have occurred had I not made the "crazy" decision to raise all that money for MDA. During the MDA fundraising event that Bob Golden and I chaired at the John Joseph Moakley Courthouse, I met the Rebbe (Grand Rabbi Y.A. Korff) and Rebbetzin Korff. (The word "Rebbe" is Yiddish for a spiritual counselor, the holiest of the holy rabbis. "Rebbetzin" is Yiddish for the wife of such a rabbi.)

A Kindred Spirit with an Open Mind

The Rebbe and Rebbetzin Korff come from long ancestral lines of the great Jewish rabbis. Since I met this couple, a special friendship has grown between the Rebbetzin, who is a strict Orthodox Jew, and myself. I, of course, follow Reform Judaism. Our relationship is possible only because the Rebbe and the Rebbetzin are willing to have friendships with people who view their religion and the world differently than they themselves do.

Around 2003, the Rebbetzin told me that she wanted me to fly up to Montreal to get a blessing from the Tosher Rebbe because she knew I was struggling with the idea of selling my family's company and with the question of what I should be doing with my life. She felt that such a blessing would give me a large amount of peace since the Tosher Rebbe is considered by many orthodox Jews to be one of the holiest Jewish people on earth. I agreed.

I visited the Rebbe at a time when I was feeling especially exhausted. I was also a little apprehensive about our meeting because not only am I a Reform Jew, I am also intermarried. I was surprised and flattered, therefore, when the Rebbe, after looking at me, touching the top of my head, and asking me a few questions with the help of an interpreter, invited me to bathe in his own personal mikvah (holy waters). Later that morning, the Tosher Rebbe further honored me by asking me to stand beside him as he handed out cookies (blessed food) to all of the people, children first, within his community in a special, holy ceremony. I have since been told that both of these things that the Rebbe asked me to do are incredibly rare—in fact, they are "one-in-a-million" honors.

Be careful how you interpret the world: It is like that.
—Erich Heller

More Help from Above

In addition to these three mind-blowing "coincidences" (the first being the timing of my meeting with Bob Golden just as I was looking for an Israeli charity I could trust with my first large charitable gift, the second being Roger Berkowitz's letter showing up the very hour I was about to call him totally out of the blue, and the third being the Rebbe's very special treatment of me), I had one other experience around this time that I also view as a sign that God has a very special plan for me.

As you know, around the end of 2001 I was beginning to look for new challenges because I was losing interest in the business. During this search I repeatedly heard and read about Habitat for Humanity's great work building homes throughout the world for those in need, and I had also heard that the true hero behind Habitat was Millard Fuller. It was Millard's vision and drive that launched the organization, initially to his own very severe economic detriment.

I was so intrigued by Millard's story that I decided to try to find out where he was speaking in the next year or two. Well, "coincidentally," literally just a few days after making this decision I opened a magazine—either *People* or *Time*, I believe—and saw a full-page advertisement for Habitat for Humanity that listed Millard Fuller's upcoming speaking engagements. I was again floored (and I do mean floored!!!) when I read that the four places he would be speaking in the next eight months were Melbourne, Australia; London, England; San Francisco, California; and Centerville, Cape Cod, Massachusetts. And his Centerville appearance was just six weeks away!

Now, the Centerville appearance seemed absolutely bizarre to me because Centerville's year-round population is probably less than ten thousand people. Not one to look a gift horse in the mouth, though, I immediately picked up the phone and dialed information to get the number of the church in Centerville that was listed as the place Millard was scheduled to speak.

Little did I know that I was about to embark on a lengthy adventure. It seemed that Millard's talk was a closed session, but the church receptionist was nice enough to add that she had heard that Millard would also be addressing a large group of Boy Scouts somewhere else in the same town. I must have spent at least forty more minutes calling the Centerville police, fire, and school departments—but to no avail. No one had heard anything about this second talk. Now I felt that I had done all I could do, and unfortunately would have to put meeting Millard on the back burner for now.

Well, perhaps *I* put this meeting on the back burner, but God certainly did not. He must have really wanted me to meet Millard, because about one week later I was having lunch with a friend who told me that another buddy of his was traveling to Cape Cod, Massachusetts from Georgia with his entire Boy Scout troop during the following month for a retreat. At my

request, my friend looked into the itinerary for the Boy Scouts…
and sure enough, I found out that they would be hearing Millard speak!

I now called this Boy Scout leader from Georgia and asked
him whether there was any way I could get a seat for Millard's
talk. He told me it would be his pleasure to arrange it for me.
A few weeks later when I arrived in Centerville, just forty-five
minutes from my home, to hear Millard speak, it seemed to me
that a seat in the very front row next to Millard's wife, Linda,
had been divinely placed just for me—just as it had when I was
seated next to Russ Stein at that fateful Legal Sea Foods dinner
in the middle of my ARMDI fundraising. I had already read
about Linda's own bouts with depression, and so during the
intermission I engaged her in conversation about our common
enemy. We became so interested in one another's stories, in
fact, that Linda tried to re-work the schedule so that I could be
the chauffeur for Millard and herself as they travelled back to
the Providence, Rhode Island, airport that afternoon. Millard
and Linda are wonderful people, and I'll never forget my meeting with them that day. Afterward, I was happy to donate to
this worthy cause and to attend Habitat's local annual charity
fundraiser for the next few years.

Now, you may say that I am deluding myself—or just plain foolish—to
think that all of these coincidences and unique honors that have happened to
me mean anything or are indicative of some Higher Power at work. Perhaps
you are right. None of us can be certain. To me, however, that is not the point.
You see, I believe that the way in which we view events is almost always more
important than the events themselves. Essentially, if you see events in your life
as blessings, you will feel special, and you will thus be empowered to do great
things. Your perspective on things really can change your life!

An Expert View on Synchronicity

Without a doubt, perception is reality. If you believe that there is an order or meaning to events, then this view is going to direct your thoughts, feelings, reactions, and behaviors. Indeed, belief in synchronicity very often leads to positive (or at least adaptive) thoughts, feelings, and behaviors. From a scientific standpoint, therefore, synchronicity isn't about the existence of a Higher Power so much as it is about the existence of belief. And belief can be a hugely powerful influence in your life.

In Todd's case, this story is very interesting because it is totally opposite from his previous life of worry and anxiety. Historically, his belief that bad things were going to happen literally drove him nuts. Here, though, his belief that God was helping him enabled him to be more adaptive and drove him on to achieve great things.

God's Ultimate Plan

While my fundraising for the MDA campaign concluded in 2000, its ramifications are still affecting me today. You see, during my quest to secure donations, I had approached a man named Jeffrey Davis for a contribution. After listening to my pitch, Jeffrey brilliantly turned the tables on me, and soon *I* actually wound up giving money to *his* favorite charity: Jewish National Fund (JNF). It's not surprising that I was persuaded to do so: Jeffrey was the president of JNF for New England at that time!

JNF: Preserving a Nation

Jewish National Fund is an amazing organization with which I am very involved today on both the local and national levels. JNF focuses on developing and preserving the land of Israel. More specifically, in my opinion, JNF is currently working on two of the most important and exciting programs for Israel's very survival and for peace in the Middle East.

One of these programs is called Blueprint Negev. Here, JNF is helping to build up infrastructure in southern Israel so that more people will choose to move there (to the Negev specifically). Blueprint Negev's goal is to attract over 600,000 people from northern Israel and other parts of the world to live in this region on which it is focusing. And so far, it's working!

Another absolutely vital project is the JNF Parsons Water Fund (named after a good friend of mine, Natan Parsons, who recently passed away). This project is designed to ensure that Israel and all of its neighbors with whom it makes peace, will have enough water for the next hundred years. Israel has commitments to provide the Palestinian Authority with 14.5 billion gallons of water and Jordan with 13.2 billion gallons of water each year already as part of these two peace settlements—quite a large volume for a desert region!

It wasn't long after I was introduced to Jeffrey Davis and JNF that I was invited to tour Israel with JNF's CEO, Russell Robinson.

I'll be honest; I had some trepidation about going on this trip due to my awful first teenage visit when I was nineteen, and also because of all of the news clips on television showing the horrible terrorist acts taking place in Israel at that time. Yes, for awhile now I had been working hard to raise money for a vital Israeli medical station, and I felt genuinely concerned about the Israeli people's welfare and future. But as for actually going back to the Middle East? Well, that wasn't something I had seriously considered for two decades. I eventually agreed to make the trip, though.

Fortunately, this visit to Israel couldn't have been more different from my first. Everyone I met—the politicians, the army personnel, and the citizens themselves—were all fantastic. I was overwhelmed and inspired by the relationships I formed there, and I immediately upped my pledge to JNF to donate a very significant amount over ten years.

Then, in my mind, God personally "spoke" to me again in September 2005 during the very week my father, brother, and I sold our company. Just forty-eight hours after our deal with Advance Auto Parts had been signed, Russell Robinson received a phone call directly from Prime Minister Ariel Sharon himself urging JNF to immediately raise $12 million as a matter of extreme national importance. Jewish families were being forced out of their homes in Gaza, and many still needed to be housed elsewhere.

Twelve Million Dollars Worth of Trouble in the Gaza Strip

When the Israeli government decided in 2004 to remove all Israelis from Gaza in an attempt to restart the peace process with the Palestinians, the region's residents were asked by the government to fill out a census report. This way, the authorities would know how many people they would have to relocate and just how much housing they would need. It was a good plan in theory, but many of Gaza's religious residents didn't believe that their own Jewish government would actually throw them out of their homes in favor of the "enemy," and thus they did not bother filling out the census. So now, there were thousands of these religious Israelis who literally had no roofs over their heads. Therefore, more money was very urgently required.

To me, what needed to be done was clear. (And of course, Sharon Freedman, the New England JNF executive director extraordinaire, could not have agreed more.) I immediately wired all of the money I had promised to Israel through JNF in one lump sum, as opposed to my ten-year pledge. Yes, I wired one very large sum to Israel. Am I nuts? Perhaps so. But I was convinced, just as I had been when Roger Berkowitz's invitation arrived within minutes of me preparing to call him, that this was a direct wish from God. After all, it had come to me just forty-eight hours after my bank account had grown exponentially. In fact, prior to the company's sale, I would not have been able to give this amount of money to Israel even if I had wanted to.

I believe that, through all of my past experiences, God had been "priming" me for years to make a difference in this very way. And I am proud to be a participant in all of the good that can come from "surrendering" to the greater plan.

My Thoughts on Provision

I know that my family and I have been blessed financially, but to me, the point of this story isn't the money I gave. It's that when you are open to doing God's will, He will provide for you. I believe that if you contribute what you can (whether it's money, time, energy, advice, or compassion) when you see a need, God will make sure that you don't run dry. As I have said before, I don't believe that God gives any of us our gifts to be hoarded. He wants us to share them! And when you do, you will be rewarded tenfold in terms of your own personal satisfaction and happiness—and often, more gifts will come back to you, too.

Dream On

You meet many amazing people and make great friendships when you are giving to wonderful causes and allowing God to direct your path. And sometimes you find yourself in places you never expected to be—like backstage with one of the all-time legends of rock and roll and a grieving yet impassioned woman on a mission! But let me start at the beginning…

Marvin Markowitz, owner of Factors Deli in Beverly Hills, is, like me, a major JNF supporter. One day in early October 2006, I got a call from Marvin regarding Karnit Goldwasser. Karnit, he explained, was the wife of an Israeli reservist Sergeant-Major Udi (Ehud) Goldwasser. Udi, along with another soldier named Eldad Regev, had been taken hostage by the Hezbollah terrorist organization on July 12, 2006, while they were patrolling the Lebanon border. This event sparked the Israeli-Lebanon conflict that raged during the summer of 2006.

Marvin asked me to help him raise $100,000 within two weeks for Karnit so that she could continue to travel throughout America and Europe keeping the issue of her husband's captivity in the public eye. Willing, of course, to do whatever was in my power to aid this brave soldier and his devoted wife, I agreed.

About three months after I helped to raise this money for Karnit, I learned that she would be coming to New York to speak at the UN. Figuring that she could use a fun night out as a distraction from all of her suffering, I invited her to an upcoming Aerosmith concert taking place in the New York area, at which I knew I could get her backstage to experience the thrill of meeting Steven Tyler, Aerosmith's lead singer extraordinaire. (I have a connection to Steven—he actually came to my fortieth birthday party! But that's another story.) Karnit told me that she would indeed like to go to the concert.

On the evening of the show, I picked up Karnit and her sister-in-law Rotem. Although I was hoping that the evening would be an opportunity for Karnit to forget about her grief for a little while, she begged me all the way to the show to push Steven to ask for Udi's release during his performance. Of course, I agreed that Steven publicly asking for Udi's release would be very powerful, but I doubted such a plea would really make a difference—and I doubted that it would ever happen. Nevertheless, I told Karnit that as far as I was concerned she was welcome to ask Steven for this favor herself.

Once backstage, we met John Seidl, Steven's manager at the time, whom I already knew. Part of John's job was to be the gatekeeper for his employer, so when I told him about Karnit's plan to ask Steven to help her publicly that night, John wasn't very happy at all and told me to pull the plug on this plan. After all, this wasn't scheduled, and Steven was due on stage in less than two hours!

I didn't know what to do. I didn't want to anger John or Steven, of course, but on the other hand, Karnit was a desperate woman whose husband was being held hostage by terrorists thousands of miles away. Knowing what I did of Karnit's resolve, I took her aside and explained to her that this was her chance…so she should really go for it, and with full theatrics, in order to make sure her plea to Steven was successful.

You've got to go out on a limb sometimes because that's where the fruit is.

—Will Rogers

And what a couple of minutes it was—watching this meeting between Karnit, the extremely loving and impassioned wife, and this megastar really was incredible! Steven had already gone through his pre-performance preparation and even had his make-up on, and I doubt that he knew very much about Israel, Lebanon, or Hezbollah. I'm almost certain he hadn't heard of Udi. To Steven's immense credit, though, he listened intently and totally focused on Karnit, visibly moved by her story. He was extremely sensitive to the pain she was experiencing, which was very poignant to witness.

After Aerosmith had been on stage for about an hour, Steven stopped the music and told the crowd that this evening he wanted to dedicate tonight's performance of Aerosmith's mega-hit "Dream On" to Udi Goldwasser, the Israeli soldier being held hostage in Lebanon, and that he hoped Udi would soon be released. Karnit cried uncontrollably through the whole performance of the song, and confided in me that Aerosmith was her husband's absolute favorite band. As for me, I felt so happy that I had been able to make this happen for Karnit and so proud that I could make such an improbable connection work in a way that few would have thought possible. Dream On, indeed!

The next day, the *Jerusalem Post* covered the story of how American rock sensation Steven Tyler dedicated his smash hit "Dream On" to Udi Goldwasser, the Israeli soldier still being held hostage in Lebanon, while his wife, Karnit, sat in the crowd. Thank you so much, Steven! You really are a great person.

Sadly, two years later in 2008, Udi's body was returned to Israel in a prisoner swap. It is likely that Udi was killed the very day he was captured.

Where Love Lives

Although seeing Steven Tyler make a public appeal for Udi Goldwasser's release stands out in my mind as an electrifying highlight, it certainly wasn't the end of the road in terms of my ongoing relationship with Israel. Specifically, a group of young people at the Yemin Orde Youth Village have captured my attention and my heart, and remain very important to me to this day.

During my campaign to raise the money for MDA, I first learned about the Yemin Orde Youth Village in the Carmel Mountains in Northern Israel—and several years later, I was able to visit it in person. Many of the children who come to Yemin Orde from over twenty different countries, I learned, have been separated from their families and are far away from their native lands and cultures. Yemin Orde is dedicated to giving these children the highest quality of care and education, and since its creation, Yemin Orde has occupied a unique position among Israeli youth villages. Namely, it remains open 365 days a year, it provides an extremely high ratio of staff to students, and it continues to assist alumni after they have left the village, providing support to its students throughout their army service and scholarships for those who want to attend university or paraprofessional studies.

Several very prominent American businesspeople are the driving forces today behind Yemin Orde financially. Personally, I am pleased to have served Yemin Orde by sitting on the executive board as the vice president of fundraising. And, of course, I am proud to donate money myself to Yemin Orde.

Whenever I visit the village during my trips to Israel, I always speak to the kids who live there. I tell them how wonderful and valuable they are. Many of the children, I have been told by the staff, do not believe that they have the same opportunities that other children their age who come from more stable or prominent backgrounds do, so I tell them I truly believe that they can be whoever they want to be if they have faith in themselves and work extremely hard to achieve their goals. I tell them about my depression and my breakdown, and I assure them that just because they are going through difficult times they shouldn't assume that God doesn't love or care about them.

In fact, I say, I believe—which I truly do—that He (God) is purposefully making them stronger now so that they can achieve even greater things in their later years. And as a member of Yemin Orde's executive board, it is my gift to be able to help ensure that future opportunities are, in fact, available for most of these great kids.

Yemin Orde is, quite simply, love in its purest form. In terms of helping children in need, it is the most wonderful charity with which my wife, Yadira, and I are involved. What founder Chaim Peri, his colleagues Susan Weijel and Benny Fisher, and their team of angels do for so many children is truly remarkable. And now our most exciting project yet—Yemin Orde Educational Initiatives—is spreading Yemin Orde's successful philosophy and love throughout most of the other thirty youth villages in Israel as well. If I had my wish, people from countries all over the world would visit Yemin Orde and become inspired to establish villages just like it for their own displaced children.

What Is...and What May Be

Ultimately, incidents like Udi Goldwasser's murder are constant reminders of the turmoil and insecurity in which many people in the Middle East live. I must admit, I remain skeptical that these conflicts can be ended once and for all, but that doesn't stop me from doing everything I can to make peace and prosperity in Israel a reality—and progress such as I have seen at Yemin Orde gives me hope that my efforts, as well as those of many others, are not in vain.

Additionally, I have contributed—sometimes even helping to set up whole new programs—to other Israeli and Jewish-related charities and causes, including the American Israel Public Affairs Committee, The Saban Center at the Brookings Institute, The Media Line: the Mideast News Source, Hebrew College, The Wexner Fellowship Program, and ELEM—Youth in Distress in Israel.

I have been honored, too, in the country in which I was so miserable during my first visit. JNF beautified the famous main street in Tel Aviv, Rothschild Boulevard, and dedicated half of it in recognition of my family and me, for which I am extremely proud and incredibly humbled. The other half of the street is dedicated to Estee Lauder.

At the Kiryat Gat Medical Station and Yemin Orde, my family is listed on beautiful donor plaques. My family is also prominently mentioned at JNF's American Independence Park, which overlooks the hills of Jerusalem.

These honors and awards are wonderful, but what matters most to me is that Israel remains a strong and independent Jewish state, and that I am now able to help so many people both in Israel and America with my time, my creativity, and yes, of course, my money.

Ultimately, realizing that God truly exists, that He is paying attention, and that He is actively using those who are open to Him (or to any Higher Power) helped me to begin a new leg of my happiness journey…one that I am still on today. Accepting myself and God's plan for me has truly changed everything, as it has caused me to learn that making a difference in other people's lives is really a key to my leading a very happy and fulfilling life. And as I hope my story has demonstrated to you, I truly believe that when you are trying to make yourself and the world better, the pieces to a brighter tomorrow *will* eventually fall into place for you, too.

TIPS FROM TODD:
CHAPTER FIFTEEN

- **Give confidently.** Whether you are thinking of giving your time, money, talents, or something else, don't let fear hold you back if you are moving forward with open eyes and prudence. Your gifts do no one any good unless you use them!

- **Always do your due diligence on behalf of your dollars.** Donating money to worthy causes is a wonderful and laudable thing—but before writing a check, look thoroughly into the charity's certifications and public records. Unfortunately, money donated to some less-than-honorable organizations does not end up in the hands of those who need it most. Also, your money can be squandered away to an unnecessary extent on overhead costs if a charity is not well run.

- **Keep your eye on the goal, but be flexible.** Often, we become so attached to a specific end result that we blind ourselves to other wonderful opportunities. By simply being flexible, you can have the most effective impact on the greater good. For example, if I had held rigidly to my idea of donating money to Israeli parents who had lost children due to the Intifada, I might never have become involved with the multitude of other charities and organizations I was introduced to through MDA. Remember that alternate opportunities are often put in our paths for a reason!

- **Don't ignore coincidence.** No matter what your religious beliefs might be, I firmly believe that coincidences are often more than what they appear to be. When you meet the right person at the right time, receive help from an unexpected quarter, or learn something that alters your circumstances for the better, I think that you are receiving a sign that the path you are on is a good one. Keep your eyes open for moments of synchronicity—they may be a sign telling you that you are on the right (or maybe the wrong) path, and they may also be signaling to you that it is time to re-double your commitment to a specific cause or to a specific person.

- **Keep an eye on your perspective.** You can't change what happens to you...but you can change how you think about it! In fact, your interpretation of events can determine your present mood and your future opportunities. If you choose to see events in your life as blessings, you will be filled with more happiness, self-confidence, and purpose...and you'll be much more empowered to achieve great things as a result!

My Passion

"If you haven't any charity in your heart, you have the worst kind of heart trouble."
—Bob Hope

Without a doubt, my new relationship with Israel marked the beginning of a fresh phase in my life. Finally, I was no longer dependent on business successes and pats on the back to feel good about myself. I knew that I, Todd Patkin, really did have a place in the grand scheme of things, and I was fired up to make a positive difference in the world around me.

Because of this important shift in my thinking, priorities, and worldview, I soon decided that I simply wasn't doing enough. And so, in the years before leaving Autopart International, I became more and more involved with meaningful charities—a pursuit that grew to consume nearly all of my time after the company was sold. I felt (and still do feel) that I had an obligation to share my resources, knowledge, intellect, and love with the rest of the world.

As I embarked on my journey down this exciting and challenging road, I expected my efforts to make a big difference in the lives of others. What I *didn't* expect was how big an impact these efforts would have on me.

You see, giving has played a large part in enabling me to maintain my current outlook on life. This attitude, in addition to my relationship with God, has helped me to grow from being a goal- and success-driven individual to one who fully understands that the only kind of life worth living is one based on love and connection. Giving also helped me to be more spiritual because it caused me to realize—more strongly than ever before—that the destinies of all people on this earth really are intertwined.

A History of Giving

As you know, I have always been a giver in some way, shape, or form. As a child, for example, I used to be almost *pulled* to the new kid in the class so he wouldn't feel so alone and out of place. As a business owner, I similarly found myself wanting to help my employees with their personal issues, and as a husband and father, my constant goal is to show the loves of my life how much I value and cherish them.

My point is, reaching out to others has always come naturally to me. I sometimes wonder if the great sadness and depression I've experienced at various points in my life have somehow expanded my capacity to also feel greater love and compassion for others. Whatever the case, I can categorically say that my relationships with others have consistently been the high points in my life.

Quite simply, I truly care for everyone, regardless of race, religion, wealth, or background. I even feel for people whom I have yet to meet. (In fact, to be able to help people I may not ever personally encounter is one of the main reasons I've written this book!) I feel that the purpose of life is to be productive, and no matter who you are, you can best do that by helping another soul. (And when you do decide to reach out, I've found, your own selfish desires tend to lessen.)

> *Not what we say about our blessings, but how we use them, is the true measure of our thanksgiving.*
>
> —W. T. Purkiser

That said, for a majority of my life I didn't have the time I needed to devote myself, heart and soul, to reaching out to others. First school and then my career claimed the fruits of my time and energy. As I began to feel more and more disengaged at Foreign Autopart, though, I finally began to purposefully focus on this interest.

I'll be honest: The changes that giving made in my life didn't happen overnight. In fact, this aspect of my personal evolution took several years. I truly believe, though, that after four decades of feeling the need to prove myself, connecting with others in this way (both in Israel and in the United States) is what finally enabled me to become more comfortable and relaxed with who I am. And here's why.

Taking It to the Next Level

As I got involved with helping various organizations and individuals, I didn't *just* write a check and then walk away—I got invested. I gave advice, spent time, formed relationships, engaged my emotions, and became a part of things that were larger than myself. At long last, I truly began to see how I could fit into the bigger picture. I began to define myself as Todd Patkin, the individual—not as Todd Patkin, whiz kid in the Autopart International family.

The point is, it's relatively easy to write a check. In fact, I'd classify donating money as "Level One" giving. Don't get me wrong—financially helping a worthy organization or individual is wonderful, laudable, and necessary. It's something you should feel proud of doing, and I'm not trying to downplay it at all. I'm just saying that, ultimately, opening your wallet is a one-time deal that probably won't have a direct impact on your life or mindset in the weeks, months, and years to come.

"Level Two" giving on the other hand can be, well, *intense*. To clarify, I'm talking about getting personally involved in a charity, whether that means serving on a committee, writing a newsletter, or actually working one-on-one with the people you're seeking to benefit. It's not always easy to deal with clashing personalities and keep your patience, to see real hardships up close and personal, perhaps even to resist your own darker impulses to be self-righteous or to try to control the lives of people you're trying to help.

The great news is, giving is also deeply rewarding. When you stick around to see how your check (and/or those of others) gets spent, you get the privilege of witnessing people's triumphs and transformations from a front-row seat. You get to know all sorts of individuals, and learn all sorts of encouraging things about human nature and the world that you never would have suspected otherwise. You get to share in moments of joy, inspiration, compassion, and growth. You get to realize just how blessed YOU are, and you develop a sense of gratitude that infuses every breath you take.

In other words, Level Two giving is a messier yet much richer experience, and that's where the personal growth comes from. Oh, you might get a momentary "glow" from writing a check, but that quickly fades. The lessons you learn from hands-on giving last a lifetime. So while monetary giving is very important and necessary (and indeed, something I continue to do), it can't function as a substitute for putting in hours of your time and really getting down in the trenches of giving.

As I share the highlights of what I've learned about giving with you in this chapter, I hope you will be as inspired as I have been! Also, you will see that, as is the case with any new endeavor, becoming more philanthropic was very much a learning process for me.

No Need to Turn Your Life Upside-Down!

Before I go any further with my story, I want to make it clear that I'm not saying you can't make a difference if you don't follow my lead and quit your job! Yes, this was my path, but it's not in any way the "only" one. When it comes to helping others, a little truly can go a long way. What matters most is that you *start*, and that you feel connected to the cause you're helping. Your involvement, plus the way you see yourself and the world, will grow from there! (I'll share more about this subject when I tell you about my Twelve Weeks to Living a Happier Life, which make up Part Two of this book.)

An Expert View on Giving

Turns out there's something to that "warm fuzzy feeling" you get when you give your time or money to others. In fact, to some extent our brains are actually wired to help other people! Specifically, there is a part of the brain called the mirror neuron circuit. It underpins empathy by enabling you to understand what others are thinking, sensing, or needing. Even though you might not be experiencing negative circumstances directly, you still have a reasonable idea of what the other person is feeling... and because of that, you might be prompted to help out.

There is no question that helping others creates a positive emotional response that is felt through the reward centers of the brain. (Actually, this is the same part of the brain that is stimulated by sex, money, and drugs!) So why, exactly, does giving fall into this pleasure-giving category? Well, all social animals (and even lesser species) show some cooperation and empathy. These things are most likely hardwired in nature since they encourage adaptability and even the survival of the species. We are all dependent on others to some extent—so "helping out" is actually in our own best interests!

My First Big Project: Operatunity

I first encountered many of the causes with which I've become most heavily involved by what society calls "chance." (Personally though, I believe that nothing so arbitrary as coincidence entered into the equation—there's a reason for everything!) First among these "chance" charitable encounters was my introduction to Operatunity, one of the organizations that helped draw me into "full-time" giving. And as you'll see, I didn't bother with slowly learning to swim in these new waters—I jumped straight into the deep end! Here's how my relationship with Operatunity began.

One day in 2003 I was flipping through the *Boston Globe*—nothing unusual there, as I routinely skimmed the paper. However, on this particular day an article about an amazing woman named Andrea DelGiudice caught my eye. According to what I read, Andrea grew up in Southeastern Massachusetts, finished high school, and headed to New York in search of operatic fame—and she then made the grade after tireless hard work and persistence. Highlights of her career included memorable performances with Luciano Pavarotti and Placido Domingo, as well as singing throughout the revered opera houses of Europe.

Once Andrea's daughter Alexia was born, though, her ambitions changed somewhat. Instead of living the life of a globetrotting opera star, Andrea now wanted to bring the wonder and joy of opera back to America; specifically, to the underprivileged children living in our country's inner cities. Andrea felt that a whole new audience could benefit from the virtues, lessons, and beauty of the art form she loved so much.

As I continued to read the *Boston Globe* article, my admiration for Andrea grew, and I was excited to learn that Andrea had created a program for children living in Brockton, one of Massachusetts' poorer cities. And I wasn't at all surprised to read that as the children of Brockton fell in love with Andrea and the program she had dubbed Operatunity, Andrea fell in love with them as well.

Each year, Andrea rewarded the Operatunity kids for all of their hard work by staging a one-night performance of their annual show at the majestic Wang Theater in Boston. To cover the associated expenses, Andrea would find a local business owner to underwrite this performance. However, reported the *Boston Globe*, this year the Wang Theater performance was being cancelled at the final hour. The sponsor for 2003, a local Chevrolet dealership, was reneging on its promise citing difficult economic times.

Now, I have to be honest: I still know virtually nothing about opera. In fact, at first I was confused reading the story, thinking that Puccini was a pasta, not a composer. That being established, it wasn't the art form that attracted my attention but the fact that, simply put, a rich business owner was "screwing over," in my mind, these inner-city kids to save what was probably in the neighborhood of just $5,000 to $10,000.

These circumstances, I felt, were unacceptable. While I couldn't force the Chevrolet dealer to spend money, I *could* try to save the event through my own charity. I wanted these underprivileged kids to have the opportunity to showcase their talents, but most importantly, I did not want them to once again feel powerless and abandoned by the more privileged sector of society.

Thus inspired, I reached out to Andrea and met with her. I was quite impressed by her exuberance and enthusiasm, as well as by the impassioned response she elicited from children who would normally be about as far removed from opera as you could imagine. Andrea and her budding opera stars had been working so hard on their performance that it was inconceivable to me that they might not get their chance to perform for one night under the bright lights of the Wang Theater. Obviously, the show had to go on, so I underwrote that year's performance myself. When I saw the kids practicing for their big debut, I was overwhelmed by the gleam in their (and their parents') eyes and the excitement in the air, and I knew that I had done the right thing.

An opera begins long before the curtain goes up and ends long after it has come down. It starts in my imagination, it becomes my life, and it stays part of my life long after I've left the opera house.
—Maria Callas

Something to Sing About

Now that I had met the kids, I was hooked. I wanted to help Andrea do more. And over the next four years, that's exactly what we did: We grew Operatunity. Personally, through my own donations and fundraising, I made sure the organization had the resources it needed for this expansion. I certainly hadn't envisioned doing something of this magnitude when I first picked up the phone to call Andrea, but nevertheless, I couldn't have been more excited.

Quickly now, Operatunity moved to a new venue with far more space. And Andrea hired another truly remarkable teacher to join her. Dori Bryan began teaching the children dance and acting at this time, too. Soon, over seventy-five students were in the program with as many as fifteen on full scholarships. Of course, it was great to view these children learning about the arts from such revered teachers. But my true enjoyment and reward came from seeing our young people so happy, and from the knowledge that they were also becoming so much more confident and self-assured as they learned these different skills and built so many new bonds of friendship.

In fact, from the very beginning, I had told Andrea and Dori that I could be involved with Operatunity only if one of their main goals each and every day was to build up the children's self-esteem and overall happiness. As sports had done for me, I wanted the performing arts at Operatunity to serve as a place where kids could forget about the worries and anxieties that might be plaguing them at school or back home. And yes, it would be even better if through Andrea's and Dori's wonderful guidance and love, some of our students began to feel more worthwhile and special, too.

Skill and confidence are an unconquered army.
—George Herbert

Andrea and Dori did an absolutely wonderful job of preparing the children for the stage and, I believe, for their lives too, and I really had a ball assisting them. In fact, Operatunity helped me to discover that I really am the most alive and happy when I am interacting with kids and trying to make them feel the best they can about themselves.

Too Much of a Good Thing

Unfortunately, though, my connection to Operatunity was so strong that it prevented me from seeing what became an insurmountable stumbling block.

You see, I was so invested in helping Andrea, Dori, and all of Operatunity's children that, for too long, I almost singlehandedly shouldered the program's financial burden. This wasn't sustainable. (The funding I provided, as well as that which I was able to raise from family and friends, together made up over 95 percent of Operatunity's operating budget each and every year.)

Although I had told Andrea from the beginning that she would have to gradually take over the fundraising and budgetary responsibilities (I could commit to contributing substantially to the organization for only three years), she was never appropriately encouraged or taught to do it. Because I gave Andrea nearly all the money she needed each year for the first four years (and yes, I did commit to one extra year when I realized Operatunity was heading for trouble) without complaint or, I suppose, enough conversation, there was no transitional period for allowing other "givers" to take over.

This was a difficult but important lesson in philanthropy for me, and I hope it can be for you as well. Whether you're donating your money, your time, or your creativity to an organization, make sure the burden doesn't fall solely on you. As I've said before, we humans are interconnected, so making the world a better place needs to be a total group effort!

Teach a Man to Fish

Many philanthropic mentors had been telling me that I was making a mistake by "simply" giving all of the money that various charities asked me for. Instead, it is actually more helpful for the charity, they said, to offer to match raised funds. (Teach a man to fish...) I have learned that these more experienced philanthropists were absolutely right. When a donor provides matching funds, the organization is still forced to raise money. If it raises nothing, you give nothing. In this way the charity must gradually learn to fend for itself. This wouldn't be the last time that the manner in which I gave money, while well-intentioned, had some unintended negative consequences.

Despite Operatunity's inability to continue at such a high level, I am pleased that Andrea is continuing to teach many of the same children, albeit in a more intimate and smaller setting. Furthermore, I am deeply gratified that Operatunity has helped so many children improve their self-esteem, develop a passion for the performing arts, and find untapped talent within themselves. Thank you, Andrea and Dori, for all of your tremendous work!

The Value of an "Operatunity"

Recently, one of the fathers of an Operatunity student sent me an e-mail and attached a video clip of his son, Colin, playing one of the lead roles, Javert, in *Les Miserables*—the final show of his high school career. Colin's dad was rightfully proud of his son's incredible performance. His note to me read,

"Thanks for your support of Operatunity. Without it, he would have not had Andrea as a teacher, and Colin almost certainly would not sound like he does."

And he might never have found his special talent, either.

While my involvement with Operatunity didn't end as I had hoped, I did learn some helpful lessons, and one thing is for sure: I was now hooked on helping. And I do still derive an incredible amount of satisfaction from knowing that so many young people expanded their worldviews and feel so much better about themselves today because of their "Operatunity."

Even as I was in the midst of helping to grow Operatunity, I became involved with another favorite charity that's a part of my life to this day.

A Wonderful Walk: The Million Calorie March

While I was at Autopart International, I used a talent agency, Harmon-Marino, to book some of the funniest comedians and to provide technical support for many of our company's corporate meetings. Gary Marino, the founder of Harmon-Marino, and I soon became friends as well as business associates—and it was this friendship that sparked one of my favorite "causes" of all time.

In 2003, Gary asked if he could meet with me to discuss his own personal journey. Gary was a man on a mission, or more accurately, a large man on a difficult mission. You see, Gary is a self-confessed food addict who had hit rock bottom in 2000 when he weighed in at 397 pounds—or as he likes to say, "just a Super Bowl party away from four hundred pounds."

Faced with some serious medical issues such as sleep apnea that caused him to sometimes fall asleep while driving and depression over his weight, Gary had simply had enough. He wanted to regain his health and his life, so he started putting together a dream team of professionals (a nutritionist, a gym trainer, a psychologist, etc.) to help him figure out how best to lose the weight that was dragging him down.

> *You must begin to think of yourself as becoming the person you want to be.*
>
> —David Viscott

Gary took his dream team's advice to heart, gritted his teeth, and pushed forward. And as the pounds dropped off, he became determined to make his quest more than just a personal triumph. Essentially, he realized that although he was working on his own personal success story, many others were not. He was deeply disturbed by the reality that America is facing a growing epidemic of childhood obesity, and he was especially upset by the fact that millions of kids were growing up just like him, destined for obesity, misery, and perhaps even an early death.

Thus fired up to make a difference for more people than just himself, Gary began to look into what his options might be. He saw that there were charity walks and runs for all sorts of medical conditions from cancer to Alzheimer's to You Name It, but at that point in 2003, there wasn't yet one for childhood obesity. So Gary set about developing the concept of a walk that would raise both awareness and money for the fight against the increasing epidemic of childhood obesity in America. As the wheels in his head kept turning, it soon became clear that this wasn't going to be just any walk. This would be a long walk. A very long walk—from Jacksonville, Florida, to Gary's home city of Boston, Massachusetts: about 1,200 miles.

With my sensitivity to suffering and devotion to living a healthy, active lifestyle, I was immediately inspired by Gary's idea after he finished explaining it to me that day in 2003. Specifically, I really liked three aspects of Gary's initiative. First, he was taking on a huge personal challenge. I like to help people with huge dreams if they themselves are also willing to put it all on the line in pursuit of their goals.

Secondly, if successful, this walk would certainly help two of the populations that concern me the most: inner-city children and people suffering from depression. (Obese people of any age are almost always very unhappy with their circumstances.)

And third, I'm a diehard devotee of exercise. I was thrilled to be able to promote this totally accessible way to fight everything from high blood pressure to depression, as well as childhood obesity. Really, there could hardly be a cause that dovetailed more perfectly with my interests!

Gary's walk, of course, would cost money since it would take about four months to complete, and would require a support road team as well as an administrator to manage the many logistical challenges of a charity walk of this nature, including food and accommodations along the route. Gary had already formed Generation Excel as a 501(c)(3) charitable organization that would collect and later distribute the contributions received along the walk.

Initially, Gary thought he would find the answer to his money needs in the form of corporate sponsors. Boy, was he wrong! Gary told me that he had personally sent out more than two hundred letters and made hundreds of phone calls to corporations in the diet industry, all of whom publicly touted their desire to team up with people who had great new ideas about how to help the weight loss cause. Guess what? From the multitude of inquiries he sent out, Gary got only one single reply. And it was a "no." So much for putting your money where your mouth is, Corporate America!

I was very impressed with Gary's commitment, persistence, and compassion, and as I have said, we were already friends. Therefore, after Gary convinced my inner businessman for the third time that he had tried every other possible funding avenue, I personally donated a significant sum of money and raised the rest from family and friends. These funds now enabled Gary's dream of the Million Calorie March to become a reality.

In 2004, believe it or not, Gary did actually walk every step of the way from Jacksonville, Florida, to Boston, Massachusetts. I was there at the kickoff, along with many of Gary's closest friends. The first steps of the walk, as well as others later on throughout the journey, were shown live on *Regis and Kelly* to an audience of millions. The walk was also featured in *USA Today* and *People* magazine, and was mentioned by hundreds of other media outlets. In total, it is estimated that the Million Calorie March reached over 70 million people!

On the Road with Gary

During his Million Calorie March, Gary walked fifteen miles a day, six days a week. He also stopped at YMCAs and various other health centers along the route. And after four months, he had walked every inch of the 1,200 miles.

I joined Gary on the road in South Carolina for four days and sixty miles, and I had an absolute ball. What made the walk so special for Gary and his "guests" like me (who accompanied him on his journey for a few days at a time) were the amazing encounters we had with everyday Americans. So many individuals we met were genuinely enthusiastic about Gary's mission, and many were willing to share personal details from their own lives concerning weight loss and battles with obesity.

The interpersonal dynamics within the Million Calorie March support team were also very interesting and added a ton of color to the whole event. These subplots, comprised of the relationships between Gary and the road team members, their differing and sometimes even extreme philosophies, the ups and downs, and the comedy of the whole trip—as well as these meetings with everyday people on the road—were all recorded on camera by one member of the team: Dan Jones, a young man just out of college.

Phase Two: The Silver Screen

When the Million Calorie March was over, Gary actually became quite depressed. It's possible that his depression was a result of the letdown that came from not doing nearly as much physical activity, combined with no longer being in the limelight. Or perhaps, as was the case with every single one of the astronauts on America's first mission to the moon, Gary got depressed because he had just reached the only goal he had set for himself for almost the past five years.

Also contributing, I am sure, was the fact that the march had failed in one of its most important missions: It hadn't raised much money to support Gary's dream of being able to set up programs through his Generation Excel charity to help the future fight against childhood obesity.

Now, as you have read, I know about depression. And I really wanted to help Gary get out of his funk. To get the ball rolling, I took my friend out to lunch and convinced him that we could and should make a fabulous movie about his recent Million Calorie March. Immediately, Gary got excited about the idea (you see, like so many of us, Gary just needed a new challenge), and over the next twenty-four months he—along with the ace production team he put together—did an amazing job creating a truly informative, entertaining, and impressive documentary. I was the funder of this project once again, while Gary and his team nearly killed themselves in the studio 24/7.

Captain Kirk to the Rescue!

On more than one occasion, I had to pull a rabbit out of the proverbial hat in order to keep this movie project alive. Most notably, I had to call on William Shatner—yes, Captain Kirk himself!—and ask him to phone the powers that be at Disney ABC Domestic Television. You see, we were having trouble gaining the rights to ninety seconds of footage of Gary with Regis and Kelly. Of course, we wanted to use that interview in our film!

I had been introduced to William Shatner through the Jewish National Fund when we had both been working on a JNF therapeutic horseback riding project together. Bill Shatner had even invited me to visit him on the set of *Boston Legal* when I was in California the previous year, which I did. Now Captain Kirk was indeed able to take us where we had not gone before, as he quickly got the approval, allowing us to use the *Regis and Kelly* footage. Thank you so much, Bill!

Our final product, appropriately titled *Million Calorie March*, was shown at several film festivals across the country and was even submitted for consideration for a FREDDIE award. The "Freddies" are the medical world's equivalent of the Oscars. Each year, they are given to the best visual media in health communications in thirty-two different categories. The winners represent an array of formats from short public service announcements to longer documentaries like Gary's ninety-eight-minute movie, and are made by a variety of production teams ranging from independents (like ours) to cable giants such as CNN and Discovery Health. *Million Calorie March* was entered in the Diet and Nutrition section for the 2008 awards.

And guess what? We won!!!

The awards ceremony at the Ritz-Carlton in Philadelphia on November 14, 2008, was really special. I attended this event with Gary and with my good friend (and co-writer of this book) psychologist Dr. Howard Rankin, who is also featured in the movie.

What was most surprising to us that weekend (being relative novices in the medical and health fields) was just how prestigious and difficult to win a Freddie award actually is. We didn't appreciate its significance until we talked with some of the other winners, who told us they had been working ten or even twenty years, and had often produced as many as fifteen different films, in order to attain their lifetime career goal of winning a Freddie.

Our team was taken aback even more (as well as proud and amazed) when one of the judges, an endocrinologist from Ohio, told us that our entry was "by far the runaway winner" in our category. It was an appropriate expression to describe this movie about a walking campaign, because after the march and losing a total of 150 pounds, Gary did indeed run (albeit very slowly) the Boston Marathon in 2005. Gary, you are truly amazing and an inspiration, my friend!

Effort only fully releases its reward after a person refuses to quit.

—Napoleon Hill

It was gratifying and rewarding to get such recognition for a project that was fully four years in the making. My only disappointment is that even though almost every one of the several thousand people who by now have seen *Million Calorie March* have absolutely loved the movie, the economy's effect on the independent film industry has kept our movie from securing worldwide distribution at the time of this writing. However, considering the two recent TV offers we have received, we remain hopeful that the *Million Calorie March* movie and the story of the march will one day again inspire millions of people.

The March Continues

The real continuing story, however, is how Gary's Generation Excel has grown following his Million Calorie March. Gary was approached by Blue Cross Blue Shield of Northeastern Pennsylvania to head up a campaign called the Million Pound Meltdown. That campaign ran for two years in 2005 and 2006, reached hundreds of thousands of people, and logged more than 52,000 pounds lost!

In 2008, Gary headed up a similar campaign for Blue Cross Blue Shield of North Carolina called the Million Step March in which Gary led hundreds of executives and employees of Blue Cross on a 600-mile trek across the state of North Carolina. In addition to the walk, the campaign included sixty live events and rallies in a seventy-five-day period! Large campaigns like these have enabled Generation Excel to fund hundreds of other obesity awareness events and initiatives. In this way, the money that helped launch the Million Calorie March, along with Gary's tremendous enthusiasm, compassion, and steward-ship, has cascaded down to help thousands of people. Now that's what I call a great investment in helping others! And today, Gary is close to kicking off a walk similar to the one he did in North Carolina in our own home state of Massachusetts.

If you had told me only ten years ago that I'd be instrumentally involved in an ongoing project like Gary's, I'd have loved the idea…but I doubt I would have believed such a change in my life was possible. And yet, here I am! Many of the obstacles and setbacks I experienced on my journey with Gary (and Operatunity as well) would have devastated me in a business context…but I've found a new resilience after seeing my efforts impact lives, and not just the bottom line. I've learned that success can mean helping just one person, and that "winning" isn't limited to arriving first at the finish line. In short, giving has opened my eyes to just what a life well spent can look like.

Merritting Attention: From Outrage to Inspiration

It's interesting what leads people to support a particular cause. You read something in the paper that touches an emotional chord (like what hap-pened to me with Operatunity) or you meet someone inspiring (like Gary Marino) and you just want to be a part of their journey. But other times, more complex emotions drive you to get involved.

Like anger over a perceived injustice, for instance.

I first learned of Merritting Attention after reading an article in *The Boston Herald* about a local inner-city fifth grade basketball team that had just won the national championship in Lexington, Kentucky. Immediately, I was proud of this scrappy group of kids from my "own" backyard. But as I read further, I found myself becoming angry. You see, despite this team's great achievement, they couldn't get an invitation to meet with the governor…even though the local Walpole, Massachusetts, Little League baseball team already had enjoyed such a meeting *before* they even went to Harrisburg, Pennsylvania, to play their first game in the Little League World Series.

This state of affairs struck me as being patently unjust, especially since, based on the newspaper photograph, I could see that the basketball team was made up primarily of African-American kids, and I knew the baseball team was not. I do want to point out that I know Massachusetts Governor Deval Patrick, and there is no doubt in my mind that he had absolutely no knowledge of this discrepancy. I am sure, instead, that this was just a case of someone close to the Walpole Little League team knowing someone who worked in the governor's office.

Still, this is an example of just how careful we must be as adults. For in this instance, a very nice and genuine favor specially done for one team had a terribly disillusioning effect on another great group of kids who definitely did not need another reason to feel "less than." Ultimately, my internal sense of regret over this injustice was the catalyst that prompted me to get involved.

Hoping that I could do something to encourage the members of this young basketball team, I did further research and discovered that the driving force behind their success was a program called Merritting Attention. The program was founded in 1998 by Larry Merritt, himself a former Boston high school football and basketball star, due to Larry's belief that young people, regardless of their ethnic or socioeconomic backgrounds, can be successful with the proper guidance, training, and opportunities.

Larry's philosophy exactly mirrors my own, and his mission—setting kids up for success by strengthening their sense of self-worth—is something I can understand personally. While I admittedly have a more privileged background than most Merritting Attention participants, I still know what it's like to grow up with low self-esteem. And for this reason, I feel that programs like Larry's that help to raise "our" children's self-worth—especially the self-worth of disadvantaged children—are crucial for our society.

In my mind, we are simply much less of a nation if we do not support such projects, because our inaction detracts from the potential of America's future generations. Thus, I didn't hesitate to get involved with Merritting Attention, and I'm still involved to this day, donating and raising money and sitting on the organization's board.

In the short time I've been involved, it's amazing how much Merritting Attention has grown. Larry has added girls' teams and expanded the age ranges to accommodate the many children who now want to join. Each year, Larry's kids do better both in the classroom and in the real world due to their required attendance at Merritting Attention's education and life skill classes. Plus, the number of state and national championships that these teams win each year is really astounding!

I have really come to admire and appreciate Larry and the work that he, his wife, Stephanie, and his coaches do. One of my favorite Merritting Attention events is the annual awards ceremony. It is very encouraging to see how classy, mature, and successful Larry's student athletes are. I also make a point (when I'm asked to speak that night) to encourage each of the children to really show appreciation to their parents, coaches, and especially to Larry and Stephanie for all that they do for them.

Looking back, I'm glad that I got so angry after reading that *Boston Herald* article: For if I hadn't, I never would have taken the time to pick up the phone and begin such a great relationship with Larry and his Merritting Attention. So be aware of situations and stories that initially push your buttons—you may just identify a way to give back that will change lives…including your own.

Women2Women: Sowing the Seeds of Peace

I'll warn you: The mission of the last organization I'd like to tell you about might sound a bit unrealistic. But as you'll see, that's what makes it truly extraordinary.

I was introduced to Women2Women (W2W) through its founder and my friend Rick Rendon. Today, Rick and I bring one hundred young women ranging in age from fifteen to nineteen years old to Boston for one week each August so that they can learn from some of the greatest women leaders in America. These young ladies come from the U.S., Israel, and as many as eighteen different Muslim countries. And therein lies the challenge. No doubt you're aware of the raw tensions that exist between Jews and Muslims around the world, especially in the Middle East, and you may be questioning how such a gathering is possible, much less beneficial.

Well, I'll be honest—over the years, W2W conferences have had their hiccups, including instructors who were initially unwilling to interact with one another because of longstanding cultural hostilities! But the bottom line is, the challenge undertaken in bringing traditional "enemies" together has paid off big time.

I am pleased to report that W2W successfully provides young women from such different backgrounds with opportunities to learn, network, and acquire the professional and leadership skills needed to make a real difference back in their own countries. In 2009, for the first time, we even expanded our guest list to the African continent, specifically inviting young ladies from South Africa and Kenya to participate.

No culture can live if it attempts to be exclusive.
—Mahatma Gandhi

During their week in Boston, the women focus on cultural leadership, government and public service, media technology, and literacy. And after the initial program has been completed each year, alumni attend annual reunions, as well as follow-up web events that keep them involved. For example, there are plans to hold a second reunion in Morocco during the summer of 2011. (The first reunion was held in Jordan in June of 2009.) W2W can thus continue to enable and encourage its graduates' work for democracy and peace within their own societies.

By keeping in touch with these exceptional young women through face-to-face and virtual contact, Rick and his team are seeing amazing results. Today we have alumni who have made documentaries, created magazines, and established other projects that depict the often very frustrating lives of women within their repressive and restrictive home countries. These efforts highlight the plights and roles of these women and, most importantly, try to initiate positive change within their societies.

I thoroughly enjoy being involved each year in the planning of this event, as well as doing whatever I can to make these week-long programs a tremendous success. Mostly, though, I just love getting to know these young women. With their help, I have learned that if you want to feel fifteen to nineteen years old again, all you need to do is spend lots of time with fifteen- to nineteen-year-old people. Thank you to all of my incredible new W2W friends!

Over the last several years, W2W has also taught me that with unique and important programs such as this one, you *must* keep pushing forward toward the outcome you're hoping for, and you *must* continue to have faith. It's okay if, at times, you take two steps forward and one step back, because eventually progress *will* be made. I'm convinced that initiatives like W2W are exactly what we need to be encouraging and backing if we want peace to come to the world's tumultuous regions one day.

People can only live fully by helping others to live. When you give life to friends you truly live. Cultures can only realize their further richness by honoring other traditions. And only by respecting natural life can humanity continue to exist.

—Daisaku Ikeda

My Hope for the Future

Without a doubt—and even without my always consciously realizing it—the way I see myself and how I fit into the world has changed quite a bit after I made giving a priority in my life. With all of these fulfilling experiences and more under my belt, and so many certainly yet to come, I hope over time to also be able to help others discover the beauty of giving.

I truly believe that the only reason that God gives people more money, time, and talents than they need for themselves is so that they can wisely give these gifts away to others who need them more. To me, that's plain old common sense. You can't take it with you—but you *can* make life here on Earth so much better for others.

Money is like love; it kills slowly and painfully the one who withholds it, and enlivens the other who turns it on his fellow man.

—Kahlil Gibran

And guess what? The truly astonishing thing is, as I've said before, that giving of your time and/or money isn't only beneficial to others—it's the greatest gift you can give to yourself in terms of your own personal health and happiness. It honestly is!

As you have seen, over the years I have invested in various projects that did not result in their desired outcomes. And it's very uncomfortable for me when, as is most often the case, the people behind these projects are so apologetic to me. To tell you the truth, I feel I have no reason at all to be upset with them so long as these people put forth their best efforts.

This is because for me, the actual *act* of giving—almost regardless of the outcome—really is its own reward. For it is while I am spending my time trying to help others that I honestly feel the greatest, the most alive, and the most connected to the world.

TIPS FROM TODD:
CHAPTER SIXTEEN

- **Pay it forward.** If you have been blessed with money, abilities, talents, or time, why hoard them? None of these things offer lasting security, and you can't take them with you, as the saying goes. Your only sure bet to get your "money's worth," so to speak, is to use your gifts prudently and purposefully every day. Through generosity and compassion, we truly can make this world a better place now.

- **Start slowly and give for the right reasons.** While philanthropy is eminently commendable and definitely worth getting excited about, make sure you take the time to truly research and learn about an organization before giving large amounts of your time or money to it. (In other words, don't over-commit yourself right out of the gate as I did!)

  Furthermore, give because you really want to help a specific cause—perhaps its mission or constituency resonates with you. It's important to constantly keep a finger on your own motivations. Your primary goal should be to help others, *not* to receive thanks, pats on the back, and "atta-boys" (or "atta-girls")! That sort of motivation leaves you vulnerable to being taken advantage of, and also forces you to give progressively larger amounts of your time and money in order to feed your own need for love, appreciation, and ego boosts.

  Once again, if you haven't learned to truly love yourself, you won't be in a healthy position to help other people.

- **Teach them to fish.** When you are offering aid to an individual or organization that will need to be sustained after you have moved on, don't forget the importance of *teaching* them to fish as opposed to *giving* them fish. By imparting the knowledge and skills that will be needed to survive and grow in the future, your gift will continue to give for some time to come.

  While I learned this lesson in the context of philanthropy, it can be played out in many other scenarios. For example, don't just put dinner on the table every night: Teach your kids how to cook! Don't just show up at the meeting with your recommendation: Teach the new hire in your department how to come to the same conclusion.

- **Other people are the greatest possible investment you can make.** When you give your money (whether it's $5 or $50,000) to improve the lives of others, you will reap the best possible dividends. More than padding your bank account or stimulating the economy, helping others changes the world in so many indelible ways. It infuses society with stronger values. It prepares future generations to excel. It gives the gifts of skill, self-respect, life, and happiness. And so much more!

- **Giving is its own reward.** If you are giving your time or money to help others based on a desired outcome, you're setting yourself up (at least partially) for failure. When you give with no strings attached, you let go of selfish motives, which has an incredibly freeing effect on you. By focusing your attention on the betterment of others, you are (somewhat paradoxically) investing in your own health and happiness.

- **Don't underestimate the value of time.** Not everyone can afford to donate large (or even small) sums of money on a regular basis—and that's okay! It's important to realize that giving of your time and talents is just as valuable. No matter what the size of your bank account is, you won't regret looking at your schedule and carving out a few hours a week to volunteer at a food pantry, walk dogs at an animal shelter, or tutor a child who is struggling in school.

CHAPTER SEVENTEEN

It's Time to Decide: A Final Call to Action

> "This life is yours. Take the power to choose what you want to do and do it well. Take the power to love what you want in life and love it honestly…Take the power to control your own life. No one else can do it for you. Take the power to make your life happy."
> —Susan Polis Schutz

I want to thank you from the bottom of my heart for giving me so much of your time reading my story. At the beginning of this book, I suggested that if I—a financially blessed, professionally successful man with a beautiful family and genuine relationships (i.e., assets that supposedly bring happiness)—could experience such a brutal breakdown, perhaps our society's idea of what constitutes "happiness" should be redefined.

Well, here's *my* definition of happiness today: **Happiness is the daily act of *choosing* to accept and love yourself as you are and for who you are.** (Assuming, of course, that you are honestly striving to live your best and most fulfilling life and that you are helping others in the process!)

Happiness is not created through money. You won't find it solely through achievement, accolades, honors, or pats on the back. Not even the unconditional love of others can bring about its presence in your life. That's because happiness isn't wholly dependent on outside factors. It has to exist within you apart from external circumstances.

I know as well as anyone that you can't always ward off depression or prevent anxiety. There's no such thing as a worry-free, mistake-free, or trouble-free life. Not even close.

However, I *have* learned that there is such a thing as choice:

Choice concerning what you focus your attention on.

Choice concerning how you react to various situations.

Choice concerning what you prioritize.

Choice concerning the type of people you surround yourself with.

Choice concerning how you treat your body, spirit, and mind.

Choice concerning how you view yourself and your circumstances.

All of these choices (and many more) have a crucial bearing on how happy, or unhappy, you will be.

The Wisdom of a Fisherman

Here's a story I love about a fisherman who truly was wise beyond his years. I think it really captures what we all need to remember throughout our own lives as we strive to make conscious choices based on what we really *do* desire— not what others tell us we *should* want.

A very wealthy, successful older man and his wife were vacationing on a beautiful tropical island. As this man sat in his beach cabana, he noticed a young islander rowing his small boat out into the waves each morning, and then returning with many fish within just an hour or two. This went on consistently day after day. Being curious, after about a week the older man approached the younger fisherman and asked him how he managed to return from the ocean with such an impressive catch day after day.

"Well, it's just a knack I've always had," the young man replied. "I can tell where the fish are going to be."

"Do you realize that with talent like that, you could make a fortune working for a large fishing company?" the older man observed. But to his surprise, the fisherman wasn't really interested.

"Why would I want to do that?" the fisherman asked. "I'm already happy with myself, my wife, my child, and my fishing boat. Every day, I go out on this beautiful ocean. Then I come back, sell as many fish as I need to, and go home. I cook the rest of the fish I have left on the grill. I relax, I play with my son, I visit my friends, and I make love to my beautiful wife. What more could I want?"

"Well, for starters you could make quite a bit of money," came the reply. "Actually, I'll even start you out. I'll set you up with several boats and workers to man them. I'll get you your own office here on the island, and we can travel together to grow the company. It'll be great!"

But still, the young man wasn't convinced. "What would be great about that? I would be working hard, probably much longer hours than I do now. I would be away from my wife. I wouldn't get to see my son grow up, and I wouldn't be able to swap stories with my friends. Doesn't sound like much of a 'great' life to me."

"Well, that's only temporary," the older man responded. "When you're older and as rich as I am, you'll be able to *buy* your own island where you can do all of these things that you love so much."

"No thanks," the young fisherman said, putting an end to the discussion. "I'm *already* on my favorite island doing all of the things that I love the most!"

The fisherman in this story could have made many different life choices. Also, he could have looked down on himself because he wasn't wealthy and because he lived a simple life. He could have chosen to beat himself up because he wasn't "going places." He could have chosen to believe that sacrificing many of his blessings and joys would be worth it for riches. He could have chosen to think that he "needed" material success to make him a worthwhile human being.

In other words, he could have chosen to put stock in many of our current world's damaging priorities. But he didn't. And because he made the choices that were best for him, he was truly a happy person.

Ultimately, we must all realize—**and this is very, very important**—that at any moment, even the richest and most successful person in the world can look at himself and feel just awful about his life. And conversely, the poorest person among us can choose to do just the opposite and feel tremendous about himself. It truly is up to each of us whether we feel good or bad about ourselves. And this decision will certainly have a huge bearing on our own abilities to be happy.

In this book, I've tried to give you the tools you need to begin making this vital shift in your self-perception. I hope that reading my story has inspired you to celebrate how great you really are! And I also hope that it has shown you that once you've learned a lesson from a mistake, you must just push that error aside and move on.

So—now it's time for you to make the critical choice. You must decide right now just how important it is for you, and thus your future lineage, to live happier lives. Remember, there's no substitute for learning how to love yourself.

It's time to look in the mirror and see the wonderful, gifted, one-of-a-kind individual who's really looking right back at you.

It's time to start giving yourself both more slack and more credit, as well as the mental empowerment you deserve.

It's time to stop basing your opinion of yourself and your own happiness on a disproportionately negative memory of who you were when you were younger, or on other people's opinion of you, or on performance reviews, or on the size of your paycheck.

Yes, it's time to put on a "new pair of glasses" with a new prescription—a much more "sunny" prescription, that is!

And here's a piece of truly encouraging news: If you choose to put on those new glasses and work toward a happier life for yourself, you don't have to go it alone. In Part Two of this book, I'd like to share with you my Twelve Weeks to Living a Happier Life, which I've developed from my own experiences. It is my hope that these weeks will give you the tools to take the first steps on your own journey to greater fulfillment, positivity, growth, and yes…happiness.

You've read my story…now it's time to begin a new chapter in your own! As you embark on this path, my ultimate hope is that you will come to understand that happiness is definitely a state of mind that occurs when you begin to take care of yourself—body, mind, and spirit—and, most importantly, when you learn to love yourself. And when you learn to love yourself, you will naturally be more loving to others. When you succeed in changing your own life, please do pass on the lessons you've learned and pay all the help you've received forward! Share what you know about the real nature of happiness and tell as many people as possible how they, too, can find it. Now that's a way to *truly* change the world for the better!

PART TWO

Twelve Weeks to Living a Happier Life

Finding Happiness: Twelve Weeks to Living a Happier Life

"No one can make you happy (or unhappy) but you!"
—Todd Patkin

As you have seen by reading many of the stories I've told in this book, one of my passions is helping people learn to live happier lives. And through my own experiences, I've come to the conclusion that if you *aren't* feeling happy and fulfilled, you need to take firmer command of your own life. You must no longer allow your negative moods and habits—the ones you were born with and/or developed in early childhood—to dictate your adult life.

It's only when you achieve this goal that you will begin to live a life filled with a great deal more excitement and joy…and much less stress, despair, and even depression. And guess what? The choice to be happy is almost entirely up to you.

*Insanity is doing the same thing over and over again and ex-
pecting different results.*

—Albert Einstein

Introduction to the Twelve Weeks

During the first few decades of my life, if you had told me that happiness was a choice, I would have told you that you were crazy. After all, if living a happier life was simply a matter of choice, we would all be doing it already, wouldn't we? I mean, no one *wants* to suffer, right? No one chooses to experience things like the pain of low self-esteem, anxiety, or depression.

I'm betting that you often feel—as I once did—that your emotions are totally out of your control. You probably feel at times that you are a victim of circumstances, and that the best you can do is to simply try to survive the day. Most likely, you also tend to focus on the bad stuff—worrying about things in the future that have not even happened yet, and quite frankly, probably won't. Also, I bet that you spend way too much of your time regretting many of the decisions you made and the things that happened in your past.

Well, as you know from reading this book, a lot has happened to me in my life. I've had some of the most amazing highs, but, boy, have I also had way, way too many terribly brutal lows, including a complete breakdown at the age of thirty-six. And ultimately, I've come to realize that my own happiness really is, almost completely, a choice that I myself make each and every day.

Let me be clear: Of course, you'll never wake up and have a perfect day with everything going just the way you would like it to. Rather, happiness is learning how to live your best life by figuring out a better way to react to what happens to you. It's the culmination of all of the little actions, choices, and habits that fill our days:

Whether to exercise or sit in front of the TV.

Whether to smile and be cheerful, or instead be more negative and partici-pate in water-cooler gripe fests.

Whether to proactively figure out a way to tackle your team's new project, or instead complain about the extra work.

Whether to invite your new neighbor over for dinner, or let her become acclimated to the neighborhood on her own.

Whether to accept that all things do pass and that we must often just go with the flow in life…or whether to stay worked up and in a frenzy.

The bottom line is, you'll never be able to understand or control every-thing that comes your way, and you'll never be able to eradicate the bad stuff.

But you CAN, no you MUST, choose how you respond to life. Each day, you can decide to focus on the people, things, and behaviors that enrich and fulfill you, and that inspire your positive mental, physical, and emotional growth. And doing that, I promise, will make all the difference in the world for you!

Here's another way to think about it: Have you ever considered the idea that your own happiness is like a muscle that you must keep strong? It's true! Just like your biceps or abs, your ability to be happy can get out of shape. And that's what happens to many of us. In fact, according to a 2007 Reuter's. com article[12], a study done by Italian researchers found that Americans are less happy these days than they were thirty years ago, despite our advances in technology, entertainment, medical science, etc.

And that, frankly, is a shame! Here's the problem as I see it: Quite simply, very few of us realize that we ourselves really *do* have all the power to make a difference in our own levels of happiness each day. And yes, of course, that's easier said than done—so I'd like to help you get started by sharing with you my twelve-week process to leading a happier life. In a nutshell, "Twelve Weeks to Living a Happier Life" will give you the tools you need to create your greatest life…one simple change at a time. Here's how it works:

Each week, you focus on a new task or lifestyle change, while continuing to keep up the habits you've begun in the previous weeks. Don't worry; every one of these steps is *doable*—none are overwhelming or difficult. We're going on the baby steps theory here. Basically, each weekly step will give you something to focus on. You'll learn why it's an important part of a happier lifestyle, and you'll receive suggestions on how to implement each change.

---

12   Babington, Deepa. "Americans less happy today than 30 years ago: study." *Reuters*. 15 June 2007. http://www.reuters.com/article/2007/06/15/us-happiness-usa-idUSL1550309820070615> (6 December 2010).

Take It at Your Own Pace

I've written this section on a step-a-week basis, but please feel free to modify that timeline as it suits *your* lifestyle. For instance, if you'd rather take two weeks to focus on each step, do so! If exercise (Week 1) is already a part of your schedule, skip ahead to Week 2. Just don't rush it. While this program can transform your life, lasting change doesn't happen overnight, and you will not master each step on day one! Remember, it's about progress, not perfection.

As you move forward, keep in mind that flexing your happiness muscle might take a bit of effort at first (and might leave you feeling sore afterward!). In other words, you'll have to be conscious, aware, and mindful as you take on each week's new task. You'll also have to be proactive in figuring out exactly how to fit each one into your life. And you can expect to slip up from time to time. (Of course, that's okay, and even expected—you're human!)

But here's the payoff: After twelve weeks, if you really "went for it," you will have formed new habits, each of which yields major changes in your attitude, your outlook, your mood, your relationships, and yes, your *happiness levels*!!!

> *First we make our habits; then our habits make us.*
> —Charles C. Noble

You may even find that by the end of our time together your goals change and that some of your "big" problems are minimized. Let's say, for example, that right now you hate your job and want to find a new one. You might discover by the end of this process that it's no longer true. Once you start being nicer to your coworkers as well as to your boss and/or employees, and once you stop beating yourself up for every little mistake that you make, you may realize that you didn't need to change jobs after all—you just needed to change the glasses through which you viewed your current one.

And better still, you're not the only one who will reap the rewards of your changes. Everyone with whom you come into contact—your spouse, your child's teacher, your coworkers, the grocery store cashier, and so forth—will benefit from your positivity. And most importantly of all, your children will see the habits you're forming and the choices you're making, and they'll learn from your example, too. (For extra motivation, remember that the opposite is also the case—if your children see you sitting on the couch, moaning about how bad your life is, that's unfortunately just the kind of people they will become, too.)

A Reminder for the Skeptics

If you're skeptical and need convincing that this process actually works, or if you become discouraged and need inspiration...just think back to the guy I described in Chapter 1. You know, the one who was so depressed, messed up, and unhappy that he couldn't even muster up the energy to decide whether to order coleslaw or potato salad with his lunch. These days, because of the following twelve steps, that guy is nowhere to be found. And I honestly couldn't be any happier.

As of this moment, it's time to stop allowing your negative moods and habits to dictate your life. It's time to take control of your thoughts, stress, anxiety, and maybe even despair. It's time to begin living a life filled with a whole lot more excitement, joy...and, yes (trust me!), happiness!

Focus on:
Exercising

I know, I know—*everyone* tells you to exercise. Admittedly, it's not unique advice, but it works. This is one small change you can make that yields really big, life-changing benefits. So even if you're feeling skeptical right now, I'm asking you, if you really want to have the best shot at finding this program helpful, to please trust me and give exercise a chance.

I've told you many times throughout this book just how therapeutic exercise has been for me. And because of that personal experience, I strongly believe that *exercise is the single most important thing you can do to improve your life right now.* My twelve-week program focuses on exercise first and foremost for this reason—and also because exercise is a fantastic energizer. It helps open you up to future change by invigorating your body and mind. It's kind of like tilling the soil of a field before planting new seeds in it.

Exercising will enable you to feel more powerful and less stressed as you take on each new weekly challenge! Specifically, exercise will begin to relax you, make you feel stronger, and improve your sleep. It's a natural anti-depressant that will improve your attitude and outlook, and as time passes, you may also gain the added bonus of being happier with your physical appearance as well.

Movement is a medicine for creating change in a person's physical, emotional, and mental states.

—Carol Welch

While it would be wonderful to commit to exercising even just a little bit every day, I understand that such a schedule change may not be possible. So this week, please agree to (at least) walk just twenty minutes every other day. That's it. I'm not asking you to completely reorder your life. When most people think of exercise, they envision gym memberships, running clubs, and spin classes. Those can come into play later *if* you so choose, but right now all you need is a pair of walking shoes.

You see, the key to instilling a habit in your life is to make it *doable*. (In fact, one of the biggest mistakes people make in regard to exercise is trying to do too much, too quickly—and thus their efforts are not sustainable.) Therefore, when I talk about exercise, I'm talking about inserting something simple into your existing routine. And what could be simpler than a twenty-minute walk every other day?

For example, you might walk around your neighborhood first thing in the morning (it's a great way to start the day!), or maybe take a few laps around your office building at lunch. You could even go to a track or use a treadmill. I've found that the earlier you take your walk the better, because if you wait till evening, "life" tends to get in the way. (Oh, and if you're so busy that you don't have twenty minutes to spare every other day, I'll even be happy with two ten-minute walks instead!)

Get Rid of the Excuses

The number one excuse that people use when they choose not to exercise is that they simply don't have the time. Honestly, this reasoning shows how backwards our thinking is today. If you don't take or make the time to take care of yourself, the stark fact is that you'll probably have less time to spend on this earth. Also, it doesn't take an expert to confirm that if you don't care for your physical and mental well-being, you're going to spend more time feeling sick and tired.

Think of taking care of yourself physically as an investment—because that's exactly what it is. Exercise is an investment in yourself, in your future, and in your family. Making this sort of investment means that you are taking yourself seriously, and it also sets the right healthy example for those you love.

Most fitness experts will tell you to walk briskly: fast enough to get your heart rate up a little, yet not so fast that it's tough to carry on a conversation. However, I strongly urge you to take it easy at first. In fact, when you're just starting Week 1, you may want to stroll. I promise, you'll know when (and if) you're ready to pick up the pace a bit, and you'll know when (and if) you're ready to increase the length and/or frequency of your walks.

Here's one final suggestion: Consider making these bite-sized chunks of exercise a priority for your whole family. When you're being active together, you'll grow closer to one another *and* you'll be more likely to stay on the exercise wagon. And most importantly of all, you'll be instilling incredibly beneficial health habits in your kids, who will then be likely to pass them on to *their* kids, and so on.

Ultimately, no matter when, where, or with whom you choose to be active, the point is: *Don't make exercising such a big deal that you stall at the starting line.* I promise you, you'll be surprised at what a big difference this first step makes if you keep at it and make exercising a consistent part of your life!

Focus on: *Taking Charge of Your Mind*

Last week we focused on getting your body up and moving on a regular basis. I hope you're already beginning to feel the difference that exercise can make in your life, because this week we're going to do the same thing for your *mind*…but in place of walking shoes, we'll use motivational books and tapes.

Yes, I know—motivational books and tapes sound a little hokey, maybe even touchy-feely. I'll allow you a few eye-rolls. But trust me when I say that the things I have learned from these resources have changed my life, and they can change yours as well. Let's return to the metaphor I used in Week 1. If physical exercise is like tilling the soil of a garden, cultivating your mind is like fertilizing it. So please, even if you have your doubts, stick with the program as we focus on filling your mind with "fertilizer."

Think about it this way: Why do you eat breakfast? To give your body the nutrients it needs so that you'll have energy to get through the day, of course. And let me tell you, your mind is no different. If you want your thoughts and attitudes to be positive, you must fill your brain with encouraging ideas, too. And just like exercising, I'm asking you for only twenty minutes a day. That's it: just twenty minutes any time of the day you choose.

Preferably, though, I'd like you to start your mornings with some sort of motivational material if at all possible. If you have an MP3 player, you could combine your listening with your morning walk. Or as I do, you might listen to a motivational CD in the car on your way to work, perhaps, or play a segment of a DVD while you're getting ready at home. If you're an early riser, you might even set aside fifteen to twenty minutes to read a section in a motivational book as you sip your coffee.

And you don't have to stop there if you don't want to: I find it helpful and relaxing to read a few pages of inspiration each night before bed, too. Yes, changing up your tried-and-true schedule might take a little getting used to, but you'll be glad you did.

If you've read my entire book, you know why I'm saying this. As you probably remember, one of the major turning points in my life occurred, of all places, in my car when I popped my first Tony Robbins tape into my cassette player. Tony was the first person to teach me (among other things) that I really did have a choice about how to lead my own life.

He taught me that I didn't have to stay stuck in my negative thinking and obsessive worries; instead, I could direct my mind to think more positively. Also, I learned, I could shape the direction of my life by changing the way I viewed the things that happened. Little did I know at that point just how true—and transformative—this message would be for me.

Mind Control…in a Good Way!

The human brain is an incredible thing, and changing the neural pathways and connections that shape your habits and actions isn't as simple as painting over a wall in your home. Controlling your mind instead of letting it control you is something that must be learned and then practiced over and over again. Activities such as meditation and yoga are also great ways to develop effective mind control for the purposes of relaxation and becoming more objective about what is going through your mind at any given moment.

There are two primary choices in life: to accept conditions as they exist, or accept the responsibility for changing them.
                                                   —Denis Waitley

Now it's your turn. You can continue paying attention to your own internal self-doubts and criticism if you want to...*or* you can begin to eliminate these negative voices and instead focus on all of the positive aspects of who you are, what you are doing, and what is great in your life.

And remember, kick-starting that process will take only twenty minutes (max!) of your day. I promise you that building "feed your mind" time (preferably in the morning) into your daily routine will put you into a more positive place for the rest of the day, and that you'll be amazed by the difference your new and improved attitude will make throughout your entire life.

Feed Your Mind! Todd's Suggested Reading and Listening List

As I've mentioned, over the years I've read and listened to a large amount of motivational material. If you're a newcomer to these types of books and tapes and are looking for a starting point, I've compiled a list of some of my favorites that you can choose from. My top picks are listed first, though all are well worth your time and attention.

Reading:
- *Your Best Life Now—7 Steps to Living at Your Full Potential* by Joel Osteen
- *Awaken the Giant Within* by Anthony Robbins
- *Leading an Inspired Life* by Jim Rohn
- *Defining Moments: Stories of Character, Courage, and Leadership* by Gordon Zacks
- *All You Can Do Is All You Can Do, But All You Can Do Is Enough!* by Art Williams
- *Success Is a Choice: Ten Steps to Over-Achieving in Business and Life* by Rick Pitino with Bill Reynolds
- *The Conquest of Happiness* by Bertrand Russell

- *In the Name of Sorrow and Hope* by Noa Ben Artzi-Pelossof
- *Marriott, The J. Willard Marriott Story* by Robert O'Brien
- *Tuesdays with Morrie: An Old Man, a Young Man, and Life's Greatest Lesson* by Mitch Albom
- *7 Strategies for Wealth & Happiness* by Jim Rohn
- *An American Life* by Ronald Reagan
- *Losing My Virginity* by Richard Branson
- *Big and Tall Chronicles: Misadventures of a Life Long Food Addict* by Gary Marino
- *Customer Satisfaction Is Worthless; Customer Loyalty Is Priceless* by Jeffrey Gitomer

Listening:
- *Personal Power II—The Driving Force* by Anthony Robbins
- *The Art of Exceptional Living* by Jim Rohn
- *The Psychology of Achievement* by Brian Tracy
- *A View from the Top* by Zig Ziglar
- *Lessons in Mastery* by Anthony Robbins
- *Think and Grow Rich* by Napoleon Hill
- *The Strangest Secret* by Earl Nightingale
- *The Weekend Event* by Jim Rohn
- *Thirsting for God: The Spiritual Lessons of Mother Teresa* by Dr. Lou Tartaglia
- *The Science of Personal Achievement: The 17 Universal Principles of Success* by Napoleon Hill
- *Goals* by Zig Ziglar
- *Leadership Mastery* by Dale Carnegie

I can't change the direction of the wind, but I can adjust my sails to always reach my destination.

—Jimmy Dean

Focus on: *Being Easier on Yourself*

Think back on the past week. Make a mental list of everything you feel you've done right and another list of everything you feel you've done wrong. Which list is longer?

I *hope* it's the "right" column, but I suspect it's the "wrong" one. You see, I've noticed that most of us in America (including myself for a large portion of my life) tend to focus a majority of our attention on the things we mess up, which then reinforces in our minds just how "subpar" we think we really are. We don't celebrate our successes nearly enough, but we sure do magnify our failures…and that sends us into a self-fulfilling prophecy cycle of ruminating on our mistakes and feeling inadequate.

To return to a metaphor I've used before, I feel that many of us are wearing eyeglasses with prescriptions in them that allow us to see only the negative things in our lives—for example, all that we could have done better and all of the things we feel we really messed up and handled poorly. And because we are all human—and thus fallible—there will *always* be plenty of these things in our lives to find and to feel bad about if we are searching for them.

Once we have identified our "mistakes," many of us then make ourselves feel even worse by scanning through all our memories in order to find similar screw-ups we may have made in the past. Now, we feel even more useless and dumb, causing us to naturally become concerned about the many more things we may possibly screw up tomorrow and the day after. With all of these negative thoughts running around in our minds, is it any wonder that we are such nervous wrecks and so unhappy?

A Happiness History Lesson

Why is self-acceptance virtually impossible for so many people? I believe the seeds of this problem are buried in the American mindset that has been ingrained in many of us for our entire lives—a mindset that is part of the very DNA of our immigrant heritage.

Think about it: Most of our ancestors came to America with very little money and spoke virtually no English. They had to work low-paying jobs almost 24/7 just to put food on their growing families' tables, all while acclimating to a new place, culture, and language. And if they wanted to get ahead and "make it" in this new land, they had to constantly examine what they were doing wrong and identify where they could improve in order to move up the ladder and earn more money. In their eyes, the worst thing they could do was to dwell on what they were doing right and give themselves a pat on the back for fear that this might encourage them to let up.

Here's the "funny" part: I believe that if you had asked most of these immigrants why they worked so hard, they would have said, "I'm doing it so that my children and their children and their children can live better lives. I want them to be able to enjoy their lives in this new land with their families and friends and not have to work as hard as I do." But what our ancestors failed to realize, and what we also fail to realize today, is that our children will almost always mimic us…even if our behavior is no longer necessary or no longer makes sense.

The truly tragic part of this story is that for every one thing most people do wrong in a week, they usually do a hundred things right. It's really sad that so many of us continue to wear these "negativity glasses" when we could so easily swap them for a pair of "positivity glasses" that would enable us to focus on those one hundred things we did well instead! And let me ask you, which do you think would make you feel happier each day: focusing on all you do badly, or focusing on the many, many more things that you do really well?

So this week, as you're continuing to exercise and feed your mind with motivational materials, I also want you to put on your "positivity glasses" and throw out your "negativity" ones. Work on being easier on yourself. To start with, think about how you'd react if your spouse, best friend, or child came to you extremely upset over a mistake she had just made. I bet you wouldn't say to her, "Yeah, you're right. You really are a good-for-nothing screw-up. Serves you right!" Instead, you'd probably tell her how great a person she is. You might even try to make her feel better by reminding her of all of her other past success stories.

Now, why don't you extend the same courtesy to yourself? If you want to be happy, you've got to learn to show the same love you do to your friends and family to yourself as well—which means giving yourself breaks when things don't go as perfectly as you'd like in *your* life, too.

Again, let me remind you that we are all human—which means that we are all fallible, and thus we are going to drop the ball every now and then. In fact, you'll probably drop it this week. But instead of using each mistake or bad decision you make as an opportunity to hammer yourself into the ground, I want you to try to learn whatever lesson you can from it…and then simply move on. (After all, you can't change what's past.) Depending on the circumstances, you might, as I often do now, even give yourself permission to have a laugh at your own humanity!

> *Self-love is not opposed to the love of other people. You cannot really love yourself and do yourself a favor without doing people a favor, and vice versa.*
>
> —Dr. Karl Menninger

At the same time, I want you to please start to keep an eye out for all of the good things you do, and not just the big stuff. If you give helpful advice to a coworker or lend your shovel to the neighbor, give yourself a pat on the back. If you cook a delicious dinner, bask in and remember your family's compliments.

If you offer an ingenious solution at a meeting, savor your boss's praise—and share the good news with your family that evening.

Basically, extend to yourself the same kindness, love, and sympathy that you would offer to others you care about. Until you give yourself permission to break free of the cycle of self-blame and negativity that causes you, like so many other Americans, to be stuck demanding perfection from yourself in every situation, you'll never have a chance to be a truly relaxed, content, and happy person.

Focus on: *Playing to Your Strengths*

Last week, you focused on celebrating your (many) successes rather than beating yourself up over your (relatively few) failures. This week you're going to take the "be easier on yourself" idea a bit farther by realizing that you should always try to play to your strengths.

How much time do you spend doing things you don't enjoy or aren't good at? If you're like most Americans, the answer is probably "a lot." You might even do these things forty-plus hours a week for a paycheck. In fact, it seems as though frustration, boredom, and discontentment are the bricks that are used to build the so-called "American Dream." And isn't life too short and precious to do things that make you miserable just so you can fit a certain mold?

To compound the problem, if we're not good at something, our natural tendency is to pour more time and effort into it in order to improve and succeed—thus taking time away from the things at which we *do* excel.

Here's how I see it: We all possess special abilities and unique talents. But many of us don't use them, or even recognize them in the first place. That needs to change if you want to be happy. (Plus, you'll make the biggest positive impact on others and the world if you're doing things you're good at as opposed to things that drain your energy, patience, and optimistic attitude.)

For example, I'm awful when it comes to doing projects around the house. I have very little mechanical understanding or skill, and I have no patience for these types of jobs. Changing a light bulb is about the extent of my handyman skills! For years, though, I'd try tackling these sorts of projects around the house whenever my wife asked me to. And then when I failed to put the pieces of a new desk together, for instance, I'd feel like less of a man. I'd fall into the mental self-flagellation we began trying to combat last week.

Well, guess what? I don't force myself to do these things anymore! I've finally accepted the fact that I will never be Mr. Home Improvement, and I don't waste my time or energy on that type of task. I know I'll just end up frustrated and down on myself! My time is much better spent utilizing my skills where they are best suited. I try to spend time with people and work on creative problem-solving projects. I pride myself on cheering the loudest at each of my son's basketball games, and I rarely feel better than when I am motivating or coaching someone through a tough time. So guess what? Those are the things I prioritize and seek out!

> *Success is achieved by developing our strengths, not by eliminating our weaknesses.*
> —Marilyn vos Savant

The lesson, I hope, is clear: If I am feeling proud of myself *more* often and down on myself *less* often, I am going to lead a happier life. This week, try to identify your strengths and weaknesses, and, as much as possible, spend more time doing things that you enjoy and are best at. Most likely, these will be one and the same.

Yes, I know—you can't instantly quit a job that you're not suited for, and you can't magically clear your schedule so that you'll have three free hours to work on a carpentry project. But you *can* start taking little steps in these directions. For example, begin looking at online job postings or for local classes in your field of interest. Instead of vegging out in front of the TV, go downstairs and dust off your table saw.

You must realize that one day you will be looking back on your life from a rocking chair, and I promise you, at that time you will regret much more than you might think, for example, not trying that new profession that you really wanted to or taking on the new hobby that seemed so cool back in your thirties, forties, fifties, or even sixties and seventies!

As always, this is about taking baby steps in a positive direction. So this week, spend just fifteen minutes of each day doing something that you consider to be one of your strengths. Whether you're by yourself in the garden or mentoring the new hires at work, you'll find that your sense of fulfillment and self-worth will begin to grow, and you will naturally feel happier, too!

Redefine Success to Focus on Your Strengths!

I think that many of us don't spend time on our strengths because our conception of what makes us "successful" has become terribly skewed. You see, our culture's mindset tells us that for our lives to be a success, we need to complete a "to-do" list that encourages us to earn more money, beat the competition, wear the most expensive clothes, climb to the next rung of the corporate ladder, etc. And if you don't check off those specific boxes? Well, you must not have led a very successful life.

Make no bones about it: That notion of success is "bull"! I firmly believe that if, at the end of your life, you have experienced, felt, and freely shared your talents and your love, you were a success. You can live in the same small house for your entire life and be just as successful as someone who moves into progressively bigger McMansions every five years. In fact, that McMansion owner might very well become the *most* confused and lost person as he tries to figure out why he is still empty and unfulfilled despite having reached all of his goals. He wouldn't have that problem if he'd lived in his strengths rather than in society's expectations.

The following story has resonated with me ever since I heard it, and perfectly sums up the problems with our world's notion of success:

The Buddha was talking with several of his disciples when one of them asked him, "What confuses you most about men?"

The Buddha replied, "I have observed many confusing actions and behaviors in the lives of men. But the thing that seems most senseless to me is this: Men spend nearly all of their time trying to make money when they still have their youth and health. And then, when they become old and less able to enjoy life, they often use all of that money trying to get back the time they gave up."

Make it a point to live in your strengths *now*...and at the end of your life you won't be trying to get back all of the years you lost. In fact, they'll have been time well spent.

If the American businessman is to be made happier, he must first change his religion. So long as he not only desires success, but is whole-heartedly persuaded that it is a man's duty to pursue success, and that a man who does not do so is a poor creature, so long his life will remain too concentrated and too anxious to be happy.
—Bertrand Russell

Focus on: *Eliminating Stressors*

Too much stress can honestly ruin your life! It prevents you from living in and enjoying the moment, and it can also cause negative long-term effects ranging from high blood pressure and insomnia to depression and anxiety. Thus, a crucial part of building a happier life for yourself is eliminating needless stress as much as possible.

That's what I want you to think about this week. First, ask yourself: *On a day-to-day or week-to-week basis, what things cause me the most stress?* And then ask yourself what you can do to alleviate this stress.

Eliminating stressors is definitely easier said than done. After all, you don't consciously try to pack your life full of worries and pressures. They just tend to develop as a result of the cumulative decisions you (and sometimes others) have made throughout your life. And some stressful circumstances—like the stock market's death spiral, say, or a family member's chronic illness—are 100 percent beyond your control.

So how do you eliminate stressors or at least minimize their impact? Well, sometimes there *are* specific changes you can make in your life—you just have to decide to finally make them. Other times it's a matter of changing the way you look at the thing that's causing you so much stress. I know from experience that a shift in perspective can make all the difference in your life.

> *Stress is not what happens to us. It's our response TO what happens. And RESPONSE is something we can choose.*
> —Maureen Killoran

Let me explain by reminding you of an experience I had in my mid-twenties. To recap what I told you in Chapter 9, at this time I was given the great privilege of overseeing my family's eighteen-store auto parts chain, but after a few months, the pressures were starting to overwhelm me. In fact, my father became so concerned about my mental health that he told me he'd have to take this job away from me if I couldn't learn to control my stress levels more effectively.

Back then, three things in particular caused my anxiety to skyrocket uncontrollably when they unexpectedly happened. As you might remember, they were: store managers quitting without giving me any notice at all, our store burglar alarms going off in the middle of the night, and employees—usually the store managers themselves—stealing from our company. So one evening, I decided that I couldn't continue to allow these situations to drive me to the edge of a nervous breakdown and/or to cost me my coveted management position.

Therefore, as I first told you in Chapter 9, I put into practice what I had learned from motivational expert Tony Robbins. First, I acknowledged that while I couldn't keep these lousy situations from happening, I *could* control my reactions to them. And so, I simply decided that for my pay, during each calendar year I should expect to have to deal with up to three of each of these stressful instances. However, if more than three instances of any one of these problems occurred during any twelve-month period, I gave myself justification to feel aggravated, upset, and to completely freak out.

Reframing how I thought about these problems by choosing to now see them as part of my job description rather than as emergencies that I shouldn't have had to deal with made a tremendous difference in my life. It certainly allowed me to manage each situation more calmly. And realizing that for the first time I had taken control of my life by managing my brain was a huge self-esteem boost, too.

On another note, I'm thankful that I learned to consciously control my reactions to adverse circumstances right before my son, Joshua, was born. For just as your children learn exercise and eating habits from you, they also tend to deal with problems and stress as you do. By training yourself to be less uptight and more even-keeled during difficult situations, you are improving your kids' futures in terms of their anxiety and overall emotional quality of life, as well as your own.

So—for your sake as well as your family's sake—this week's task is for you to identify the two or three things that cause you the most stress on a consistent basis. You may know instantly where the problem spots are—or you may have to do a bit of soul searching yourself…or even converse with family and friends to find them. Either way, make your list and decide what you're going to do about each stressor.

Maybe your house is never as clean as you'd like, and you are spending too much of your "free" time dusting, vacuuming, and scrubbing—which causes you to neglect your family and yourself, which in turn sets off a guilt-and-anxiety spiral. Or perhaps frantically trying to get the kids to school while making it to work on time yourself puts you in a bad mood and sets a stressful tone for the entire day. Or, like I was, you might be stretched to the breaking point by a recurring situation at work.

Once you've identified your most common stressful occurrences, brainstorm several possible solutions to them. Write each one down. (Many people find that writing things down really helps them to sharpen their thinking and focus on the best possible solutions.) Be as creative as you can be. In the case of the "messy house," possible solutions might be:

1) Hire a housekeeper. It may not be as expensive as you think. In fact, you could pay the housekeeper with the "guilt money" you've been spending on buying "stuff" for your children to make up for the time you don't spend with them.

2) Get family members to share the load. Why is all the housekeeping *your* job, anyway? You may need to have a frank discussion with your spouse and kids about dividing up the chores so you'll all have more time to spend together.

3) Re-think your need for super-cleanliness. Which is more important: getting the floor mopped three times a week or spending the time relaxing with your spouse or reading to your child? You may well decide you can overlook a little dirt!

If you are unable to eliminate a major stressor—as in the case of the stressful job you can't afford to quit—be prepared to view it now as a challenge. Decide beforehand how you will react differently today when specific stressful situations occur—visualize yourself handling these situations with poise instead of becoming outwardly or inwardly worked up. Having a game plan in place *before* the "beast" rears its ugly head really can reduce your negative reactions to stressors—big time.

> *When you find yourself stressed, ask yourself one question: Will this matter five years from now? If yes, then do something about the situation. If no, then let it go.*
>
> —Catherine Pulsifer

Here's one final piece of advice: If you're feeling stuck in terms of finding a new way to look at a stressful situation, I'd advise you to emphasize even more Week 1's and Week 2's tasks of exercising and feeding your mind with motivational material. If you are like me, after feeling more relaxed and powerful (due to exercising) and more motivated and less alone (thanks to the books and/or tapes), you may experience a shift in perspective that enables you to find the solutions to your challenges. If not, you'll at least make some headway in terms of getting better control of your thoughts.

As this week draws to a close, I bet you'll be pleasantly surprised by the difference that minimizing the impact of just a few chronic stressors makes to your life! Yes, these changes will take some thought, work, and maybe routine-rearranging, but it's worth it—because your sanity and happiness *definitely* are!

WEEK SIX

Focus on: *Living in the Present*

The question for this week is simple: Where do your thoughts and attention "live"?

When you're eating dinner or watering your garden or playing with your child, where is your mind? Are you savoring the taste and texture of each morsel of food…or noticing the way the drops of water look against the rose petals…or reveling in the sound of your child's laughter? Or are you stewing over an insensitive comment a coworker made earlier in the day or worrying about the big presentation that's due next week?

If you're obsessing over the past or agonizing about the future, you're missing out on life itself.

People are always asking about the good old days. I say, why don't you say the good now days?

—Robert M. Young

As I mentioned earlier in this book, I once saw a TV show in which a one-hundred-year-old woman was asked to identify one lesson from her life she would most like to pass on to future generations. She said that the most important lesson she had learned from looking back on her life was that she'd spent a large portion of it worrying about things that never actually happened. She regretted the time she had wasted in anxious thought, and advised others not to fall into the same trap.

I don't know about you, but I've made no secret of the fact that for a large portion of my life, this woman's "ailment" also afflicted me. I was a natural worrier—I tended to fixate on "what-ifs" and worst-case scenarios that never actually came to pass. I'm also guilty of the flip side—for a majority of my life I had a tendency to beat myself up over and over again for past mistakes. So between my obsessive concerns about the future and my ruminations on the past, there's no doubt in my mind that I have literally spent years not "in" the present moment.

In other words, I spent years *not* enjoying the many blessings that were all around me. I spent years exacerbating my anxiety and unhappiness by choosing to dwell on things I couldn't control. I spent years harming my self-esteem and not living up to my full potential. And if you're unhappy with your life, I bet you've been doing the same thing.

Thus, this week's task is to spend more time really *being* in the present. But first you need to do a bit of homework. Before you can effectively focus on the present, you'll need to start the process of letting go of the past and coming to terms with your anxiety about the future. (This may take longer than a week!) Also, you might find that writing your thoughts in a journal helps you to clarify where your particular mental sticking points are.

The Lesson of Lot's Wife

There's a story in the Bible that illustrates the concept of "looking back" in evocatively visual terms. When fleeing the burning city she had lived in her whole life, Lot's wife disobeyed God's order and looked back at what she had just left behind—and was turned into a pillar of salt. If you spend your time just looking back at the past, you will surely be frozen just as Lot's wife was, and you won't be able to appreciate the present.

In my experience, letting go of the past is the more difficult of the two tasks, because it usually involves forgiving others and/or yourself for past wrongs. Trust me, living with anger and resentment towards others for past disagreements is a recipe for misery, because these two emotions reverberate through your mind and body, stirring up toxic thoughts, physical stress, and even illness. And for what? *You* are the one walking around feeling miserable while the objects of your anger are often (now years later) totally oblivious to your feelings. Forgiveness is as much an act of self-love and self-preservation as it is an act of compassion for others. Consider forgiving others and yourself as an essential part of your happiness toolkit.

> *Resentment is like taking poison and expecting the other person to die.*
>
> —Anonymous

My advice regarding your future worries is a bit simpler. First, figure out how likely it is that every dreaded event you are worrying about will really come to pass. Most likely, you will have to admit that each is less than 25 percent likely to happen at all. And secondly, actually see in your mind every possible worst-case scenario playing out. Ninety-nine percent of the time, you will also see that even if your most feared outcomes happen, they will not kill you or be as devastating as you're making them out to be. There will always be some remedy within your reach, even if it isn't an easy one or a desirable one for you to swallow.

> *Never let the future disturb you. You will meet it, if you have to, with the same weapons of reason which today arm you against the present.*
>
> —Marcus Aurelius Antoninus

And now, because you have begun to take control of your past- and future-oriented thoughts, you can truly begin to appreciate the present moment. Make no mistake; this will take a lot of practice and mental discipline. You'll need to be aware of your thoughts, and at first you'll probably have to make a concerted effort to wrench your mind away from dwelling unhealthily on the past and on the future.

Don't get discouraged when you find yourself going back to these old mental habits, though. In fact, pat yourself on the back because you're *noticing* that you're doing something you don't want to do anymore. That's great! That's the first step in any important change. You can fix yourself only if you begin to become aware of mistakes you are still making that you no longer want to make.

Remember that learning not to dwell on minor setbacks is all part of the process. As is the case when one is quitting smoking or drinking, it's virtually impossible to stop worrying cold-turkey. As time goes by, though, you'll find yourself spending less and less time in unhealthy ruminations. And here's the ultimate payoff: When you're more fully present in the here and now, you'll begin living the adventurous, wonderful life you were meant to live!

Forever is composed of nows.

—Emily Dickinson

Focus on: *Spending More of Your Time with Positive People*

This week marks the beginning of the last half of "Twelve Weeks to Living a Happier Life." By now, you should be feeling better about yourself due to the exercise you've incorporated into your life and the motivational material you're reading and listening to. Hopefully, you're also beginning to be kinder to yourself both in how you think about yourself and in what you do. Plus, you're working to minimize your stress levels, as well as starting to live more fully in the present.

That's all wonderful. You're making great progress! But do you know what can undermine a lot of your positive work? Continuing to spend your time around negative people.

So, this week I want you to take a hard look at the people you regularly interact with and ask yourself, *Are these people helping or hurting my quest for happiness?*

Yes, this can be an intimidating task. So I don't want you to think, *Oh no, Todd's asking me to divorce my husband or cut my mother out of my life! I'd better scrap this program altogether.* If that's your gut reaction, I'd like to make two points: First, I would never ask you to do anything that drastic or awful. Second, it would be far better for you to postpone or even eliminate this step altogether than to abandon your happiness journey! So if it is more comfortable for you at this point, please feel free to hold off for now on Week 7 and simply join me again for Week 8!

That said, I feel it's my duty to tell you this: It's scientifically proven that we become more like the people with whom we spend the most time. Psychologists call this phenomenon of being influenced by the people to whom we're closest "social proof," and it happens because we instinctively look for validation and guidance from the people around us. Thus, if you begin spending as much of your time as possible with positive people, the physical and mental improvements you've made thus far will be more likely to "stick"—and you'll continually be inspired.

However, if most of your friends, family, and coworkers are negative, they will continue to keep you where you don't want to be. Like weights attached to your ankles, they will offset much of the positivity you are gaining from our twelve-week program. (Quite simply, it's easier to let others drag you down than it is for you to pull them up!) People who complain, criticize, or who are habitually condemnatory or cynical will inevitably pass their attitudes on to you. Thus, it's in your best interest to begin to "divorce" yourself from your negative friends and spend less time on the phone and in person with those negative relatives you *cannot* "divorce."

> *You are the average of the five people you spend the most time with.*
>
> —Jim Rohn

Now, I'm not telling you to completely cut off the negative individuals in your life with no warning whatsoever. You don't even have to do it this week. Over the course of the next seven days, I simply want you to notice all of the people with whom you spend your time and rate them on a scale of 1-10, with 1 being a completely negative influencer and 10 being a completely positive influencer.

Once your ratings are completed, you'll want to slowly start to spend more of your time with the high scorers and less time with the low scorers. (To be honest, as you begin to become more and more positive yourself, you will naturally find it more and more difficult to be around negative people anyway.) This might mean calling a positive friend and asking to meet up for coffee or a beer, or walking away from the water cooler when your coworkers begin to gripe and complain. It might also mean saying, "Mom, I'm trying to focus my attention on positive things, so I really don't want to rehash the argument you and your brother had over the holidays."

Over time, your goal is to make a significant shift in terms of the people with whom you surround yourself. I know it's hard to put distance between yourself and a person who has been a big part of your life. For many people, this step is a crossroads of sorts. It forces you to ask yourself, *How important is happiness to me, really?*

Keep Your Eyes Open for Crabs

If you do decide to consciously spend more time with the happier people in life, you need to know that you'll probably face opposition from friends and relatives who honestly mean you well, but who nevertheless are trying to hold you back. You see, as you become happier, you'll inevitably begin to act, plan, and dream on a larger scale. And it's a sure bet that those who love you will also say—out of love and concern for you—that they wish you would be "more normal" and "reasonable" in your plans and dreams because you might fail and get hurt.

These people are like crabs in a bucket. Yes, it's true: Whenever one crab in a bucket full of crabs tries to climb out, all of the other crabs instinctively latch onto him and pull him back down, thus sabotaging his bid for freedom. Don't let the "crabs" in your life pull you down. Surround yourself with supporters, not saboteurs. And when the latter get their claws around you, firmly but lovingly dislodge them and keep climbing.

Now that we've covered the basics, there's one specific person I want to mention in terms of surrounding yourself with positive people: the one who will have the greatest influence on whether or not you are able to attain and maintain happiness. This person is, of course, your spouse or significant other (if, that is, you choose to share your life with someone).

I know that, to some extent, love truly is blind—but nevertheless, it's in your best interest to make sure your eyes are open enough to honestly evaluate your "better half." Too many people allow sexual attraction and "fun" to lead them into relationships and marriages that are disastrous. Please, be smarter than that. You have a choice, just as I did, to decide what type of person you want to marry. If you are currently looking for Mr. or Ms. Right, go ahead and make a well-considered list of the personal and character traits you'd like to find, *with a happy person being tops, please!*

If you are already married to a person whose negativity is dragging you down, your best option is to convince him or her through words and example to commit to building a happier life alongside you. Otherwise, at some point in the future—after you've made every effort to "convert" your spouse—you may find yourself having to choose between your future happiness and your marriage.

For most people it's just too difficult to make such profound positive changes in your life if you are sharing a living space, time, finances, and plans with someone who remains entrenched in a negative mindset. That said, I would *always* strongly recommend that you try everything possible, including marriage counseling, to improve your situation before ending a marriage, especially if children are involved. We'll discuss this more next week.

The bottom line is, toxic relationships can grow in all areas of your life, and they won't eradicate themselves, either—you've got to take the initiative to identify them and weed them out of your life, just as you must purposefully spend more time with positive, happy people. Take the long view: This process might not be fun now, but it will help to create an environment in which your happiness will be able to grow and thrive less hindered for years to come!

Focus on:
Strengthening Close Relationships

If there is one thing I have learned during my forty-six years on this planet, it's that life is all about people. While it's true that you can't depend solely on any one person for fulfillment, your happiness and success hinge on your relationships with others. How could it be otherwise? Our lives are intertwined with the lives of others from the moment we get up in the morning to the moment we drift off to sleep at night.

Last week, you focused on identifying the people in your life who are positive influences and those who are negative influences. This week, we're going to focus on another group of people who may currently fall into either category: your closest friends and loved ones.

Without a doubt, the quality of your relationships with the people to whom you're nearest in heart can make or break the quality of your life. Loving, supportive relationships will majorly enhance your happiness levels. But fractious, unstable, or even distant relationships with your family members and historically close friends can leave you feeling unappreciated, angry, alone, and anxious. Unless someone in your immediate circle is truly, irredeemably toxic (a state of affairs we touched on last week), I believe that your closest relationships are always worth strengthening and improving.

Today we are faced with the preeminent fact that, if civilization is to survive, we must cultivate the science of human relationships.

—Franklin D. Roosevelt

This week, I would like you to consider the relationships you have with your family members and friends—keeping in mind that time continues to go by and that you can't get back a minute, day, or year that has already passed. If you are fortunate to have living parents or grandparents, ask yourself when you last spent meaningful time with them. Also, have you remained up-to-date with your siblings after going your separate ways as adults? Do you spend quality time with your own kids, or do you work too late and crash on the couch when you finally make it home? And what about your nieces and nephews? Furthermore, do you reach out to your friends on a regular basis, even if they don't contact you first? Or do you call them only when you need something?

Now, obviously, you can't strengthen ties with every one of these people in a week. But you can start! Beginning with the people you see most often (probably your immediate family and closest friends at work), tell them how much you appreciate and love them and why they are so special to you. If possible, also try to spend more time with them doing the things they like to do (perhaps playing a game of cards or doing a puzzle, or going out for ice cream or to the movies).

Then later, in subsequent months, start working outwards to the people you don't necessarily see every week. Make it your goal to reach out to all of the people who are truly meaningful to you within six months or a year, and tell them how important they are in your life. It costs you absolutely nothing to do this, and I promise this one new habit will have a surprisingly significant effect on your own happiness as well as theirs. Also, throughout this process, whether you're focused on your son or your mother or your best friend, try to address any unresolved grievances and apologize for things you may regret.

You'll notice that, so far, I haven't mentioned the most important person of all: your spouse or significant other. That's because I have something very specific to say about your chosen partner, whoever he or she may be: *You simply must make your marriage (or relationship) your number one priority each and every day!*

What a shame it is that so many people spend so, so much of their time maintaining their homes, their cars, their gardens, etc. but do almost nothing to keep their marriages in tip-top shape! And as a result, they and their partners grow bored and become distant from one another! Again, what a terrible tragedy. We all should have been told growing up that you *do* have to work on your marriage as well if you want it to stay exciting and great.

Marriage Maintenance

One of the most important things you can do to increase your happiness is to work toward a positive, healthy marriage. And you don't have to go it alone: Marriage counseling shouldn't just be a last-ditch "save our marriage!" resort. In fact, it's a tool that comes in handy for marriages of all shapes and sizes. I believe that all couples should be open to a few sessions of counseling if things become difficult or if they're facing a significant change or milestone as a couple. These "tune-ups" will get your relationship back on track if it's slipping, and will also keep it functioning at the highest level possible at all times. Sadly, it seems that our society is generally too proud or embarrassed to do something (namely, marriage counseling) that only makes decent marriages better and good marriages great once again. Please don't allow your marriage to sink because of your pride!

And there's a lot you can do all by yourself to rejuvenate your love simply by celebrating your spouse every day. Tell her how much she means to you, how much you love her, and how beautiful she is ten times a day. Or tell him how much you appreciate his parenting skills, how proud you are of him for getting that promotion, or how handsome he looks in his Sunday suit. I mean it! I have never heard anyone say that they hear such a compliment about themselves too many times.

Bring home flowers or a small gift "just because," not only on holidays or your spouse's birthday. Make an effort to speak gently and kindly. Do one of your partner's chores or pick up something special for dinner. Random acts of kindness are always powerful, and that's even truer inside a marriage. Trust me—I know!

Think not because you are now wed
That all your courtship's at an end.
                    —Antonio Hurtado de Mendoza

I am so incredibly blessed to have such a supportive and uplifting wife, and I can say with confidence that Yadira has been the single most positive influence in my life. I have no doubt that my mental and emotional health would be much worse—and that I would certainly be divorced—if I had married someone who was negative and self-centered, and who did not genuinely care more about "us" than she did about herself.

Now, I'd like to speak directly to individuals whose spouses fell into the "negative influence" category during last week's evaluation. As you'll recall, I stated that I believe every marriage is worth working on before the decision to walk away is made. And I think that in many instances, once you begin celebrating your spouse as I've just described, you might find that the whole dynamic changes. I sincerely hope this is true for you. Perhaps your spouse has been trapped in a cycle of negativity that has been fed by your own less-than-helpful attitude. And remember, people unconsciously begin to mirror the people they spend the most time with. This happens for the good as well as for the bad!

To conclude, once you begin to strengthen your close relationships, you'll find that your burdens aren't as heavy, and that you may have let go of guilt you might not have known you were carrying. You'll find that you're smiling more, and maybe even that your priorities in life have changed. As I told you at the beginning this week, everything—especially our happiness—really is all about our relationships with other people. The stronger and healthier those relationships are, the happier you are. It really is that simple.

Focus on: *Being Friendly*

Think back to the last time you were out running errands. Who, if anyone, did you speak to? What did you talk about? Did you acknowledge other shoppers, and did your interaction with the cashier go beyond the basics needed to conduct a transaction? If you use public transportation, did you make eye contact or speak with your fellow passengers and pedestrians? If you ate at a restaurant, did you sincerely thank the server for her attentiveness and maybe even compliment her nice smile?

Unless you're the exception to the rule, you were probably civil but pretty much kept to yourself. Based on my observations, that seems to be the direction our society is going. Although we're more and more "connected" by technology, as a rule we interact less and less with other people on a meaningful, face-to-face level. This applies to folks we see fairly regularly, like neighbors, as well as strangers. And it means many of us are essentially alone even in the middle of a crowd.

That leads me to this week's task: just plain being friendlier to everybody! Trust me, it's not that difficult. Even if you aren't outgoing and talkative by nature, you won't have to step very far out of your comfort zone. (A grin and a cheerful hello aren't that hard to muster, even for die-hard introverts!) And extending simple human kindness to people, in the form of a nice word and a smile, can make a big, big difference in their lives—and yours, too.

> *Too often we underestimate the power of a touch, a smile, a kind word, a listening ear, an honest compliment, or the smallest act of caring, all of which have the potential to turn a life around.*
>
> —Leo Buscaglia

Remember that we're all in this together, and that everyone on Earth is carrying some sort of heavy burden. It might be the ache of grief, the anxiety of trying to make ends meet, the stress of a demanding job, the worry that accompanies illness, or one of a million other things. You can't take those burdens away from other people, but you *can* be what I call a "lamp-lighter"—someone who makes others feel just a little bit lighter and happier along their journeys, even if only for five quick seconds.

A Life-Changing Conversation

Think about it: You never know what sort of impact your friendliness might have on another. I will never forget a television program I saw in which a young man was interviewed. He told of one day contemplating suicide as a high schooler. That afternoon, though, a fellow classmate just happened to stop him and spend a few minutes talking to him. And this one conversation was enough to prevent him from killing himself. Now, this young man is graduating from college and has a bright future ahead of him. And the real kicker? The student who had this conversation with the first young man (who was also interviewed on this show) to this day still has *no specific memory* of this talk even taking place…he was just being friendly. Truly, taking a few moments to reach out to another can mean the whole world to a fellow human being.

And guess what? These people to whom you're nicer aren't the only beneficiaries. I've found that when you treat other people with extra kindness, you feel so much better about yourself too...and you'll probably even be treated back with more friendliness as well. Who knows? You might even gain a new acquaintance or friend!

So, for the next seven days, I want you to reach out in some friendly way to all of the people you see on a regular basis (like your hairdresser and the butcher) and to the people you will probably see only once in your lifetime (like a cashier or bus driver). If you feel comfortable doing so, strike up a conversation with these individuals. If you don't, just smile. Actually, a habit I've recently begun combines conversations *and* smiles: I try to compliment the people I see on *their* great smiles (if they have one)...accompanied by a big grin of my own! And before you know it, those smiles are spreading.

> *What sunshine is to flowers, smiles are to humanity. These are but trifles, to be sure; but, scattered along life's pathway, the good they do is inconceivable.*
>
> —Joseph Addison

If you're not sure how to begin being friendlier to strangers without being intrusive, you may find it helpful to focus on living out the Golden Rule: "Do unto others as you would have them do unto you." For example, if you think a bank teller has been especially helpful, tell her so (and call her by name while you're at it!). You'd appreciate the gesture if your positions were reversed—it might even make your entire day.

Also, you might want to remember Thumper's advice in the classic movie *Bambi*: "If you can't say something nice, don't say nothin' at all." I know, I know—we're often tempted to take our frustration out on the nearest target when there's a delay in the checkout line or when a customer service rep's hands are tied by company policy...but if you think about it, you're really not accomplishing anything by snapping; you're only making someone's day worse.

The truth is, friendliness is a habit that you can wire into your brain (as is unfriendliness). To help amiability become "the rule" rather than "the exception," you might want to consider posting sticky notes with drawn-on smiley faces on your bathroom mirror or on the dashboard of your car to remind yourself of your objective. By the end of this week, your smiles and greetings might already be feeling "natural" to you.

And here's a word of advice for those of you who aren't naturally outgoing. I used to tell my store managers who were nervous about visiting their customers to think of someone who would certainly *not* be uncomfortable doing this—for example, their favorite comedian on television. Then, I'd tell them to pretend to *be* that person while visiting their customers. It sounds a little corny, I know…but I've seen it work time and time again.

I think you'll be surprised by how rewarding simple friendliness can be. You'll give people a reason to feel a little more lighthearted. You'll be more approachable, and others will be more likely to open up to you and help you out. You'll feel good about yourself for making a positive difference in the world. And all of that will make you happier too—I guarantee it!

Focus on: *Helping Others*

We've all heard the phrase "it's better to give than to receive" more times than we can count. That's because it's true! To put it simply, givers are happy people. And for that reason, this week's focus is going to be on helping others.

Before we get into the "how," though, let's look at the "why." Specifically, why is giving going to enhance your happiness? I can answer that question from experience, because, as you know, for years I have consciously tried to give as much as possible. Almost from the start, I noticed that giving and helping others just made me feel great about myself. That's because we humans are social beings, and we find our greatest fulfillment in helping others.

Hardwired to Help

Did you know that we are literally hardwired to want to help our fellow man (and woman)? It's true! There are areas of your brain called "mirror neuron circuits" that are specifically set up to feel empathy and compassion, and I don't think that's an accident. I truly believe that we are meant to share freely and help one another bear our burdens as we go through life.

Also, helping others really puts your own life into perspective. Here's how I see it: Everyone—no matter how rich, healthy, successful, etc. they are—can look to the right and see someone who has "more." But by the same token, everyone—no matter how poor, struggling, or unhappy they are—can look to the left and see someone much less fortunate than them, too.

Why torture yourself by looking to the right? Why beat yourself up because you think you're not doing as well as your neighbor? (And when did having more material wealth become the measure of happiness, anyway?) When you're focused on what you lack, you become self-absorbed and oblivious to your blessings. But when you choose to compare yourself to those to your left—the people who aren't as fortunate, and who you can tangibly help—you'll be able to more easily identify and put value on your own blessings. You'll also experience greater contentment and less of an impulse to strive for "more," because a focus on giving naturally squashes envious impulses!

> *When earning your daily bread, be sure you share a slice with those less fortunate.*
>
> —H. J. Brown

With that in mind, this week I want you to do at least one nice thing each day—and preferably, two or three!—that you wouldn't normally do to help another individual or organization in need. And before you get started, I want to point out that "giving" doesn't necessarily have to involve money. It's true that I've been financially blessed throughout my life, and I've used a lot of that money to help others. But the most meaningful gifts I've given haven't involved checks. Actually, it doesn't matter whether or not you have money to spare. You definitely have time, talents, skills, and compassion. The best gift you can give is yourself.

So this week, if you have a free hour or two, stock shelves at your local food pantry, go to the VA and visit a disabled veteran, or drive to the nearest home for the mentally challenged and ask about volunteering opportunities. If you can't fit something that time-consuming into your schedule on short notice, make plans for how you might do so in the future—and in the meantime start closer to home. You could always take a friend who's having a tough time out to dinner, do a chore for your spouse, or roll your neighbor's trash can up the driveway.

> *How wonderful it is that nobody need wait a single moment before starting to improve the world.*
>
> —Anne Frank

Lastly, I do want to mention giving financially. As I've said, you do *not* have to write a check to be a giver. But if you feel compelled to do so, look for an organization whose mission strikes a chord within you. And keep in mind that you don't have to bankrupt yourself to make a difference. Each dollar helps. Your family might even want to start a giving fund that consists of change found on the floor and in the washing machine, for example. That's definitely an initiative you can start this week—all you need is a jar and a sharp eye! And most importantly, this will begin teaching your children the joy of giving at a young age.

When you see yourself as a giver, you'll feel better and better about who you are as a person. Whether you're giving time, energy, money, or encouragement, being generous will build up your self-esteem, broaden your perspective, keep you anchored in reality, and connect you to your blessings—all components of a happy life.

> *In about the same degree as you are helpful, you will be happy.*
>
> —Karl Reiland

Focus on: *Your "Higher Power"*

There are two topics you're supposed to steer clear of in polite conversation: politics and religion. Well, I'm not going to bring politics into the twelve weeks to a happier life…but I can't in good conscience stay away from spirituality. In my view, believing in something bigger than yourself is essential to developing the kind of perspective you need to be happy. So this week, I'm going to ask you to work on deepening your relationship with your Higher Power.

Throughout this book, I have shared my lifelong connection to the Jewish faith, and as you know, I refer to my Higher Power as "God." Before I continue, though, I want to be clear that I'm not saying that everyone should espouse my beliefs. I'm not even saying that everyone should join an organized religion. And I definitely want to emphasize that having a relationship with a Higher Power doesn't necessarily mean that you must go to a church, temple, or mosque on a regular basis.

(Frankly, I believe you can feel as close to God in your garden or on a boat or just taking a peaceful walk in the woods as you can in a "holy" building—maybe even more so.)

God enters by a private door into every individual.
—Ralph Waldo Emerson

Being connected to a Higher Power means being aware of some other presence in your life. Whether you consider that Power to be God, Yahweh, Allah, Nature, the Universe, Buddha, Krishna, or another entity, being willing and able to see and feel His (or Her, if you prefer!) presence in your life will enable you to better enjoy happiness in several ways.

First, spirituality is the opposite of narcissism. A spiritual person recognizes that there is much more to life than feeding his or her own ego, and that all people are interconnected with each other and with nature. Because of this sense of unity, a spiritual person also feels compelled to use the gifts that have been given to him or her to make the world a better place. Thus, when you develop spirituality, you'll begin to move away from self-centeredness and you'll focus your energy and concerns on the greater community, not just on yourself. (Note how this ties back into giving, which we discussed last week!)

More Than Coincidence

I have included in this book several events that I attribute to God's hand working in my life. Foremost among these is Ariel Sharon's Israeli government's desperate need for money just forty-eight hours after I received an immense pay-out from the sale of my family's company. As you know, I felt very honored because I was able to help Israel at this crucial moment...but I was also incredibly humbled because I knew that the credit really went to God, not me. You may call my interpretation of this occurrence superstition, but I call it faith. And without faith, a person is much more apt to be self-absorbed and less likely to see how he or she is ideally (even divinely) placed to help others.

Secondly—as countless texts and testimonies have asserted over the centuries—faith in a Higher Power also helps you get through the tough times that will inevitably crop up in your life. In addition to having a source of divine support to whom you can pray, you will be able to interpret trials as ways by which your god is trying to build you up and strengthen you for his future purposes. In this way, your faith can provide you solace and give meaning to unfortunate events and life circumstances.

So this week, I'd like to ask you to do two things to strengthen your relationship with your Higher Power. First, make a conscious effort to clarify your thoughts about faith. Ask yourself what you do (or don't) believe, and why.

Don't hesitate to use holy books and commentaries to clarify your thoughts, if you feel moved to do so. I have personally spent a good deal of time learning about Judaism and its history, and the knowledge I've gained has helped me create a strong sense of identity that's rooted in a heritage I am proud of. On the other hand, you may find that if you simply sit quietly and reflect on the question, your heart will tell you what you need to know.

> *The finding of God is the coming to one's own self.*
> —Meher Baba

Secondly, I'd like you to make a conscious effort to connect with your Higher Power each day. Eventually this may or may not mean seeking out a place of worship if you're not part of one already—but for now it's sufficient to pray, meditate, write in an "attitude of gratitude" journal, or commit random acts of kindness. It doesn't matter what you do, as long as it's in line with your personal spiritual viewpoint and you approach it with pure intentions.

Eventually, I hope you'll begin to see your Higher Power as a source of inspiration, renewal, strength, guidance, and aid—as I do. While I sometimes haven't realized it until after the fact, God's presence in my life has always been evident. Were I not a spiritual person, I doubt I would ever have found my way to true happiness—or been able to write this book to share what I've learned with you!

> *Let God love you through others and let God love others through you.*
> —D. M. Street

Focus on: *Developing an Attitude of Gratitude*

During my own quest for a happier life, I have tried to determine what contented, joyous people have in common. It turns out that an attitude of gratitude is at the top of the list. Across the board, happy people are grateful people. Incidentally, they're also healthy people: Studies show that grateful folks are 25 percent healthier than their unappreciative peers.

I hope that giving back to others and becoming closer to your Higher Power have already begun the process of getting your gratitude to flow. During this final week, we're going to focus specifically on being grateful for everything we have.

I know, I know—living with an "attitude of gratitude" is a clichéd concept. The problem is, very few of us actually *follow* this piece of conventional wisdom. (Maybe we don't know how.) After all, we all have things we could complain about…but we also have so many things to be thankful for. Remember, as I told you in Week 10, you can choose to look to the right and get upset because of all the people who supposedly have more…or you can look to the left and realize just how fortunate you actually are.

I would maintain that thanks are the highest form of thought;
and that gratitude is happiness doubled by wonder.
—G.K. Chesterton

The Awesome Advantages of America

No, you may not have a limitless bank account. You might have to scrimp and save to make ends meet sometimes. And at some point in your life, you've probably had to deal with illness or loss. But think about it this way: If you're living here in America, you have access to excellent health care, and you can get a great education. Through hard work, you can build a comfortable life, if not more, for yourself and your family! For many people around the world, all of these things are impossible to attain.

The way I see it, we need to begin looking at all of the things we take for granted, and we need to thank both our Higher Powers and the people who came before us for giving us these blessings. Take your ancestors, for instance. At some point, they came to this country and probably worked seven days a week so that their children and grandchildren (perhaps you) wouldn't have to. Through hardship and sweat, they laid the foundation that your life is built on.

Consider also our nation's Founding Fathers. The "war heroes" we read about in our history books were real human beings, too, many of whom suffered and died so that we might live free and unthreatened in this, the greatest democracy ever to exist on earth. And what about our country's more recent veterans and current servicemembers? No matter what your politics are, these men and women deserve your gratitude for putting themselves in harm's way—and sometimes making the ultimate sacrifice—on our behalf.

I think it's time that we pay tribute to these people, and so many more, for the sacrifices they made to give us what are—make no mistake about it—great lives. (When you think about it that way, it's kind of silly to be jealous of your neighbor for having three cars versus just your two. In fact, your two cars ought to seem like a great privilege.) No, we can't tell our own ancestors or all of the previous American military personnel right up through today "thank you" since so many of them are already gone, but we can honor them by being aware of and appreciative of all they have done for us and given us, and we can make sure that we tell our children about them as well.

> *The Pilgrims made seven times more graves than huts. No Americans have been more impoverished than these who, nevertheless, set aside a day of thanksgiving.*
> —H.U. Westermayer

So this final week, please start looking at everything you have in your life: your health, your house, your family, the food you eat, the work you do, etc., and ask yourself how you got each one of these things. Chances are, you can't take full credit for any of these blessings—and that means you have some things to be grateful for.

Specifically, each day I'd like you to identify at least five unique things you're thankful to have in your life. Then, write down these "gratitude thoughts" in a journal. And if any of the things you're grateful for involve something someone did for you, tell that person "thank you" the next time you see him or her. In fact, I encourage you to start verbalizing your thanks whenever you feel it this week. It could be as simple as saying to a coworker, "Thanks for always smiling when you say hello. It really makes my day!"

> *God gave you a gift of 86,400 seconds today. Have you used one to say "thank you"?*
> —William A. Ward

When you realize how much you owe to others, you'll find that your selfishness and jealousy begin to dissipate. And as you become more and more grateful, any unhappiness about what you lack will naturally diminish as well.

Ultimately, the renewed perspective and sense of peace that consistent gratitude brings will foster more happiness in your life as you begin to see and acknowledge the excess God has given you. Once you start recording your blessings, you'll probably be amazed by how long the list is. And the humility that comes from knowing you owe so much to so many others will, in turn, spur you to give back more often to those less fortunate than yourself, too.

After the Twelve Weeks

Don't Be Afraid to Reach Out If Necessary

The fact is, not everything in life is under your control. No matter how much effort you put into them, the previous twelve weeks may not launch you into the happy life for which you are striving. And that's okay. As you know from reading my story, stress, anxiety, and depression can overwhelm even your best attempts to control them.

If you too have made every attempt to find happiness through following these steps (and perhaps others) and are still struggling, then you should seek professional help. Be especially vigilant if you are currently experiencing strong symptoms *and* have also had difficulty finding joy throughout your life, have experienced periods of marked depression, or have immediate family members who have suffered from depression. Under these circumstances, please seek help from a qualified mental health professional and take any recommended medications for anxiety and/or depression.

Remember that you often have little to no control over your brain's biochemistry. So please, *please* do not let your ego get in the way of doing what is best and necessary for yourself. If I had allowed my pride to prevent me from seeking the help I needed during my breakdown, believe me, I would not be half as happy as I am today…and I might still be unable to choose which side item—potato salad or coleslaw—to order with my lunch. I am not kidding!

Summing It Up

Ultimately, you're the one who makes the choice to improve your own life, the lives of your loved ones, and yes, even the lives of everyone you come in contact with each day. Be patient and trust the process. In fact, therein lies the real secret—to understand that there will *always* be difficulties as you move through life, no matter how much work you do on yourself. In other words, happiness is a *journey*, not a destination. Therefore, you must learn to not only overcome obstacles, but to better enjoy the process of surmounting them.

In all honesty, I too am still finding my way almost six full years after selling my own company. I'm still not exactly sure where I want to be in terms of my career right now. In fact, I recently began working three days per week again for Autopart International. I can't say that I am as excited every day to jump out of bed and get to the office as I was in my early years while I was running the company, and I sometimes miss the thrill of a good battle and the uncertainty of leading a challenging business.

However, am I happy? Absolutely! And it's because I have mastered my mind. I have learned out of sheer necessity a better way to view myself and my life…one that makes me feel so much better. And that, my friends, is the real key.

Instead of putting myself down and asking myself questions like, "What am I really accomplishing every day?" and "Why haven't I been able to find my perfect career path after five and a half years?" I say to myself, *Overall, I'm really doing pretty well considering all the changes that have taken place in my life. My relationships with my wife and my son are so much better because of the extra time I now spend with them, I am exercising consistently, and I am learning more and more every day about what will make me happy in terms of my work for the next forty years.*

And guess what? That's more than enough if you learn to view it that way!

About the Authors

Todd Patkin grew up in Needham, Massachusetts. After graduating from Tufts University, he joined the family business and spent the next eighteen years helping to grow it to new heights. After it was purchased by Advance Auto Parts in 2005, he was free to focus on his main passions: philanthropy and giving back to the community, spending time with family and friends, and helping more people learn how to be happy. Todd lives with his wife and love of his life, Yadira, their amazing son, Josh, and two great dogs, Tucker and Hunter.

Dr. Howard J. Rankin is the creator of www.scienceofyou.com and founder and president of the American Brain Association. He is a licensed clinical psychologist with a private psychotherapy practice, the Rankin Center for Neuroscience and Integrative Health, on Hilton Head Island, South Carolina. He has written five books and coauthored two more, including the bestselling *Inspired to Lose*. His video and workbook *The Five Secrets of Lifestyle Change* were released in early 2011.